Praise for

Agile Adoption Patterns

"In *Agile Patterns: A Roadmap to Organizational Success*, Amr Elssamadisy provides a clear and concise collection of patterns that will help you identify roadblocks in your organization's software development process and enable you to confidently make major improvements as you travel down the road to continuous and optimal process improvement."

—Bob Bogetti
Software Manager, Baxter Healthcare Corporation

"The subjects covered are comprehensive and easy to understand. Like the book says, there is no one size fits all for Agile. But the book offers the readers a buffet of practices and asks them to choose ones that apply to them. Even experienced Agile practitioners will find it useful, despite the author's preface. It's hubris to think you know it all and then get too comfortable. This book has reminded me about some key concepts that have fallen by the wayside in our own group. The concepts aren't always easy to convey, but Amr does a great job of making them accessible. The examples are well thought out, and the sequence of subjects seems very natural. I'd recommend it to anyone interested in Agile."

—David Chia
Lead Engineer, BabyCenter

"The hardest part about 'going agile' is figuring out how to tease apart all those inter-dependent agile practices into bite-sized pieces you can try one at a time and figuring out which bites to take first. Lots of books out there describe what an agile team looks like, but getting from where you are to that point can be frustrating! Amr's wealth of experience coaching teams toward agility shines through as he guides you toward an adoption plan custom-built to fit your context. Amr doesn't just explain Agile practices, he explains how to think about those practices in an agile way, so you can avoid common pitfalls and create an adoption plan that works for you. This is a book I've been waiting for someone to write for a long time and one I'll keep by my side when coaching new-to-Agile teams!"

—Ryan Cooper
Agile Coach/Developer

"Amr has clearly spent considerable time down there in the messy everyday reality of software projects and come out all the wiser for it. In this book he describes an intelligent approach to Agile adoption where the focus is always on the customer—delivering business value. Amr's style is clear and direct, offering practical, down to earth advice and ideas to the ordinary development team member. If like me, you've struggled adopting Agile practices in your organization, Amr's perspective on the problem will help you to think through your situation constructively and find a better way forward."

—Emily Bache
Software Developer

"The collection of patterns in Amr's book is a useful reference in itself, but what I particularly appreciate is the presentation in Chapter 5, which suggests that Agile practices should be seen as a system, gives a concrete model of how they relate together, and advises that to find the proper order for adopting practices, one should first look at what the business needs to get more value or solve its problems."

—Laurent Bossavit
Consultant, 2006 Gordon Pask Award Winner

"*Agile Adoption Patterns* fills a gap that most people don't even realize exists. Pr........
of theoretical completeness, but *to satisfy business goals*. Amr will show you hov
opment processes aligned with the business goals of your organization."

D1208538

"I loved the idea of the book. I only wish I had this book two years ago, when I was a member of a team that had a particularly hard time during adoption of agile methodologies. The book is a pragmatic (and agile!) guide to adoption of Agile practices. The book offers different adoption strategies for different project environments and helps you to choose individual practices in such an order as to maximize the overall business value."

—Dmitri Dolguikh
Agile Software Developer

"Amr has done a great job with his book on adoption patterns. This book will help you if you believe Agile software development is what your projects need, but you are unsure about where to start and how to overcome cultural and technical barriers. If you have trouble articulating the bottom-line benefits to your peers and senior management, Amr explains in a straightforward manner how the resulting improvements percolate up to the business level. Read this book especially if you are interested in introducing test-driven practices into your organization: it gives a comprehensive picture of available variations together with what they are good for (and not good for) as well as a roadmap for gradually progressing to advanced levels. The narratives Amr provides to motivate the patterns covered are easy to relate to: you'll quickly recognize whether a specific pattern is pertinent to your situation."

—Hakan Erdogmus
Editor-in-Chief, IEEE Software

"*Agile Adoption Patterns* is an excellent resource to help you find and tune the Agile practices that can make your project a great success."

—Dave Hendrickson
Architect

"Amr's fine book brings a unique, helpful approach to selecting which components of Agile you need to implement to fit your environment. Amr's work also details something many other books on Agile miss: a clearly defined business value for each of the component's vital ammunition when you're trying to pitch new concepts to your management and customers!"

—Jim Holmes
Microsoft MVP, Quick Solutions, Inc.

"This book outlines the steps and the structure for Agile adoption which I have not seen collected thoroughly in one material before. It helps find the path from why Agile all the way to measures of successful Agile adoption. I would recommend it for Agile adopters."

—Yasser Helmi
Senior Developer, ThoughtWorks, Inc.

"Amr is a true researcher on what it means to be Agile. I've worked, debated, laughed, and waved my arms during many discussions over the years with Amr. He harbors a burning desire to find the essence of what it means to be truly Agile, and then to find a way to make that information available to each and every person involved in software development. In this book you'll find some great things about the current state of successful software development and how you can do it better. I can't wait until I can get the final version of this book on my shelf so I can tear in to it!"

—Derek Lane
CTO/VP Development for Semantra, Inc.

"*Agile Adoption Patterns* does a very effective job of communicating what it truly takes to adopt Agile in an organization. He understands that there is no 'one size fits all' solution and therefore presents the reader with heuristic patterns (and smells) that can be matched up with their specific situation. And he doesn't just tell them how to do it, he insists on having the reader follow along, by answering questions and completing exercises, in order to select an adoption strategy that works for them."

—Don McGreal
Director of Learning Solutions, Improving Enterprises Inc.

"I know where it hurts— I just don't know how to fix it. That has been a complaint of mine for some time as I have worked to introduce lean thinking and agile practices to my development teams. With so many Agile practices to choose from, which ones should I focus on first, and which ones will be most effective at solving the real problems my teams are facing? *Agile Adoption Patterns* pulls together the best ideas of the Lean and Agile communities, giving you the entire landscape of available Agile practices, their relationship to each other, and their relative importance in contributing business value or eliminating undesirable "smells" from your teams. By breaking each Agile practice down into a standard pattern of adoption, this book provides you with a clean and simple roadmap for choosing which Agile practices to invest your time in. Not all Agile practices are created equal, so it is important to know which ones will truly solve your team's problems. Save yourself a lot of time and read this book. You'll be glad you did!"

—Perry Reid
IT Supervisor, E&P Systems—Custom Development Group, Chesapeake Energy

"*Agile Adoption Patterns* is a great reference for teams just learning Agile or established teams looking to take things to the next level. Amr covers a wide range of patterns to draw upon, from the often overlooked 'soft skills' of learning and communication to the core dev techniques around testing and pairing. There is clearly a lot of real-world experience and wisdom to draw from this book. Recommended."

—Rob Sanheim
Principal, Relevance, Inc.

"Transitioning to an Agile development environment in large organizations is tough and sometimes unre-warding, especially when there are so many people you have to 'convince' along the way. However, if you can begin to recognize patterns in people's reactions to Agile, you can start mapping them against your own transformation strategy. Amr's book helps us to overcome this quickly by focusing on the needs and goals of the organization. Engaging with the management team to help them create their own strategy and then demonstrating the practices that we have to implement to achieve their goals. Amr does this by clearly describing the benefits and the possible pitfalls of each step in our journey whilst allowing us to respond to the changing needs of the business by selecting the most appropriate adoption pattern from the clusters described in this book. Thanks Amr, the journey may still be a lone one, but there are fewer waves driving us off course."

—Sean Sheehan
Lean SW Transformation Manager

"Amr does a fantastic job helping the Agile beginner understand which ideas to apply first and how to get the selected practices assimilated into their own unique development environment. This book really digs into the issues around practical Agile implementation and provides detailed examples for real-world situations."

—Scott Weber
Senior Software Engineer

"Amr's book is a roadmap for anyone wanting to adopt agile practices while keeping their organizational structure, team culture, or customer in mind. This book guides the reader to identify their most urgent developmental bottleneck, suggests the best practices for improvement and explains the thinking behind the selection of the recommended practices. As opposed to instructing the reader on exactly what to do, this book will help the reader become a better thinker when it comes to Agile adoption."

—Niraj Khanna
Cofounder, GreenBar Consulting

AGILE ADOPTION PATTERNS

AGILE ADOPTION PATTERNS

A ROADMAP TO ORGANIZATIONAL SUCCESS

Amr Elssamadisy

✦✦ Addison-Wesley

Upper Saddle River, NJ • Boston • Indianapolis • San Francisco
New York • Toronto • Montreal • London • Munich • Paris • Madrid
Capetown • Sydney • Tokyo • Singapore • Mexico City

The publisher offers excellent discounts on this book when ordered in quantity for bulk purchases or special sales, which may include electronic versions and/or custom covers and content particular to your business, training goals, marketing focus, and branding interests. For more information, please contact:

U.S. Corporate and Government Sales
(800) 382-3419
corpsales@pearsontechgroup.com

For sales outside the United States please contact:

International Sales
international@pearsoned.com

THIS BOOK IS SAFARI ENABLED

The Safari® Enabled icon on the cover of your favorite technology book means the book is available through Safari Bookshelf. When you buy this book, you get free access to the online edition for 45 days.

Safari Bookshelf is an electronic reference library that lets you easily search thousands of technical books, find code samples, download chapters, and access technical information whenever and wherever you need it.

To gain 45-day Safari Enabled access to this book:

- Go to www.awprofessional.com/safarienabled.
- Complete the brief registration form.
- Enter the coupon code XPNZ-JWYL-ZBBW-RFLT-3MXJ.

If you have difficulty registering on Safari Bookshelf or accessing the online edition, please e-mail customer-service@safaribooksonline.com.

Visit us on the Web: www.awprofessional.com

Library of Congress Cataloging-in-Publication Data:

Elssamadisy, Amr, 1970-

   Agile adoption patterns : a roadmap to organizational success / Amr Elssamadisy. -- 1st ed.

       p. cm.

   Includes bibliographical references and index.

   ISBN 0-321-51452-1 (pbk. : alk. paper) 1. Computer software—Development. 2. Agile software development—Management. I. Title.

QA76.76.D47E42 2008

   005.1--dc22

                              2008015486

ISBN-13: 978-032-151452-3
ISBN-10: 0-321-51452-1

Text printed in the United States on recycled paper at RR Donnelly in Crawfordsville, Indiana.
First printing: July 2008

Editor-in-Chief
Karen Gettman

Executive Editor
Chris Guzikowski

Senior Development Editor
Chris Zahn

Managing Editor
Kristy Hart

Project Editor
Jovana San Nicolas-Shirley

Copy Editor
Karen A. Gill

Indexer
Erika Millen

Proofreader
Language Logistics, LLC

Publishing Coordinator
Raina Chrobak

Cover Designer
Alan Clements

Compositor
Gloria Schurick

To Khadeega. Welcome!

CONTENTS

Foreword   xxiii & xxvi

Preface   xxvii

Acknowledgments   xxxiii

About the Author   xxxvii

Part 1: Thoughts about Software Development   1

Chapter 1: Learning Is the Bottleneck   3
A Hypothetical Experiment   3
Examining Agile through "Learning Is the Bottleneck" Lenses   5
Cycles for Recognizing and Responding to Change   5
Cycle: Necessary but Not Sufficient   7
Why Is This Important? Theory to Practice   9
Keep Your Eye on the Bottleneck   9
Closing   11

Chapter 2: Personal Agility for Potent Agile Adoption   13
Why Adopt Agile Practices?   13
What Is a Successful Adoption?   14
Problem: Many Unsuccessful Agile Adoptions   14
Cause: It Depends   14
The Responsibility Process™ Model   15
I Want to Be More Responsible. How Can I Do It?   16
My Teammates Are Stuck in Blame. What Shall I Do?   17
Potent Agile   17
Successful Teams Have Responsible Members   17
Recognizing and Responding to Change Requires Responsibility   18
Successful Agile Development Begins with the Individual   18
Personal Agility   18
Theory to Practice   19

Part 2: Crafting an Agile Adoption Strategy   21

Chapter 3: Business Value   23
Reduce Time to Market   23
Increase Product Utility (Value to Market)   24
Increase Quality to Market   24

Increase Flexibility   24
Increase Visibility   25
Reduce Cost   25
Increase Product Lifetime   26
Business Values Are Organizational Goals   26
Theory to Practice: Determining Your Organization's Business Values   26

Chapter 4: Smells   **29**
Business Smells   30
Quality Delivered to Customer Is Unacceptable   *30*
Delivering New Features to Customer Takes Too Long   *30*
Features Are Not Used by Customer   *30*
Software Is Not Useful to Customer   *31*
Software Is Too Expensive to Build   *31*
Us Versus Them   *31*
Customer Asks for Everything Including the Kitchen Sink   *32*
Process Smells   32
Customer? What Customer?—Direct and Regular Customer
     Input Is Unrealistic   *32*
Management Is Surprised—Lack of Visibility   *33*
Bottlenecked Resources—Software Practitioners Are Members
     of Multiple Teams Concurrently   *33*
Churning Projects   *34*
Hundreds (Possibly Thousands) of Bugs in Bug Tracker   *34*
"Hardening" Phase Needed at End of Release Cycle   *34*
Integration Is Infrequent (Usually Because It Is Painful)   *35*
Pain as an Incentive   35
Theory to Practice: What Smells Can You Find?   36

Chapter 5: Adopting Agile Practices   **37**
The Practices   37
Patterns of Agile Practice to Business Value Mappings   38
Patterns of Agile Practice to Smell Mappings   *43*
Crafting Your Agile Adoption Strategy   49
Where Next?   50
Theory to Practice: Building Your Own Agile Practice
Adoption Strategy   51

Part 3: The Pattern Catalog   **53**

Chapter 6: The Patterns of Agile Practice Adoption   **55**
What Is a Pattern?   55
Using Patterns Effectively   57
Character Roles   58

Chapter 7: Goal   **61**
Business Value   61
Sketch   61
Context   62
Forces   62
Therefore   62
Adoption   63
But   63
Variations   63
References   64

Chapter 8: Cycle   **65**
Business Value   65
Sketch   65
Context   66
Forces   66
Therefore   66
Adoption   67
But   67
Variations   68
References   68

Part 3.1: Feedback Practices   **69**

Chapter 9: Iteration   **71**
Business Value   71
Sketch   72
Context   72
Forces   72
Therefore   73
Adoption   74
But   75
Variations   76
References   76

Chapter 10: Kickoff Meeting   **77**
Business Value   77
Sketch   77
Context   78
Forces   78
Therefore   78
Adoption   79
But   79
Variations   80
References   80

Chapter 11: Backlog   **81**
Business Value   81
Sketch   81
Context   82
Forces   82
Therefore   83
Adoption   84
But   85
Variations   86
References   86

Chapter 12: Planning Poker   **87**
Business Value   87
Sketch   87
Context   88
Forces   88
Therefore   88
Adoption   89
But   90
References   91

Chapter 13: Stand-Up Meeting   **93**
Business Value   93
Sketch   93
Context   93
Forces   94
Therefore   94
Adoption   95
But   96
Variations   97
References   98

Chapter 14: Done State   **99**
Business Value   99
Sketch   99
Context   100
Forces   100
Therefore   100
Adoption   101
But   101
Variations   102
References   102

Chapter 15: Demo   **103**
Business Value   103
Sketch   103
Context   104

Forces   104
Therefore   104
Adoption   105
But   105
Variations   106
References   107

Chapter 16: Retrospective   **109**
Business Value   109
Sketch   109
Context   110
Forces   110
Therefore   111
Adoption   112
But   112
Variations   113
References   113

Chapter 17: Release Often   **115**
Business Value   115
Sketch   116
Context   116
Forces   117
Therefore   117
Adoption   117
But   118
Variation   118
References   118

Chapter 18: Co-Located Team   **119**
Business Value   119
Sketch   119
Context   120
Forces   120
Therefore   121
Adoption   121
But   122
Variations   122
References   123

Chapter 19: Self-Organizing Team   **125**
Business Value   125
Sketch   125
Context   126
Forces   126
Therefore   127
Adoption   127

But   128
Variations   129
References   129

Chapter 20: Cross-Functional Team   **131**
Business Value   131
Sketch   132
Context   132
Forces   133
Therefore   133
Adoption   134
But   134
Variations   135
References   135

Chapter 21: Customer Part of Team   **137**
Business Value   137
Sketch   137
Context   138
Forces   138
Therefore   139
Adoption   139
But   140
Variations   142
References   142

Chapter 22: Evocative Document   **143**
Business Value   143
Sketch   143
Context   144
Forces   144
Therefore   145
Adoption   145
But   146
Variations   146
References   147

Chapter 23: User Story   **149**
Business Value   149
Sketch   149
Context   150
Forces   150
Therefore   150
Adoption   151
But   151
Variations   152
References   152

Chapter 24: Use Case   **153**
Business Value   153
Sketch   153
Context   154
Forces   154
Therefore   154
Adoption   155
But   155
Variations   156
References   156

Chapter 25: Information Radiator   **157**
Business Value   157
Sketch   157
Context   158
Forces   158
Therefore   158
Adoption   158
But   159
Variations   160
References   160

Part 3.2: Technical Practices   **161**

Chapter 26: Automated Developer Tests   **163**
Business Value   164
Sketch   164
Context   165
Forces   165
Therefore   166
Adoption   167
But   170
Variations   171
References   172

Chapter 27: Test-Last Development   **173**
Business Value   173
Sketch   173
Context   174
Forces   174
Therefore   175
Adoption   175
But   175
References   176

Chapter 28: Test-First Development   **177**
Business Value   177
Sketch   177

Context   178
Forces   178
Therefore   179
Adoption   180
But   181
Variations   181
References   182

Chapter 29: Refactoring   **183**
Business Value   183
Sketch   183
Context   184
Forces   184
Therefore   184
Adoption   185
But   186
Variations   186
References   187

Chapter 30: Continuous Integration   **189**
Business Value   189
Sketch   189
Context   190
Forces   190
Therefore   191
Adoption   191
But   194
Variations   195
References   196

Chapter 31: Simple Design   **197**
Business Value   197
Sketch   197
Context   198
Forces   198
Therefore   199
Adoption   200
But   200
Variations   201
References   201

Chapter 32: Functional Tests   **203**
Business Value   203
Sketch   203
Context   204
Forces   204
Therefore   206
   Item Inventory Management Tests   *206*
   Benefits of Automated Functional Tests   *208*

Adoption   210
But   211
   Implementation Smells   *211*
   Architecture Smells   *214*
Variations   215
References   217

Chapter 33: Collective Code Ownership   **219**
Business Value   219
Sketch   219
Context   220
Forces   220
Therefore   221
Adoption   221
But   222
Variations   222
References   222

Chapter 34: Pair Programming   **223**
Business Value   223
Sketch   223
Context   224
Forces   224
Therefore   224
Adoption   225
But   226
Variations   226
References   227

Part 3.3: Supporting Practices   **229**

Chapter 35: Coach   **231**
Business Value   231
Sketch   231
Context   232
Forces   232
Therefore   232
Adoption   232
But   233
Variations   234
References   234

Chapter 36: Engage the Community   **235**
Business Value   235
Sketch   235
Context   236
Forces   236
Therefore   236

Adoption   236
But   238
Variations   238
References   238

Chapter 37: Reading Circle   **239**
Business Value   239
Sketch   239
Context   240
Forces   240
Therefore   240
Adoption   241
But   242
Variations   242
References   243

Chapter 38: Workshop   **245**
Business Value   245
Sketch   245
Context   246
Forces   246
Therefore   246
Adoption   247
But   247
Variations   247
References   248

Chapter 39: Classroom Training   **249**
Business Value   249
Sketch   249
Context   250
Forces   250
Therefore   250
Adoption   250
But   252
Variations   252

Part 3.4: The Clusters   **255**

Chapter 40: Agile Iteration   **257**
Business Value   257
Sketch   258
Context   258
Forces   258
Therefore   259
Adoption   260
But   261

Variations   261
References   262

Chapter 41: Communication Cluster   **263**
Business Value   264
Sketch   264
Context   264
Forces   265
Therefore   265
Adoption   266
But   267
Variations   267
References   268

Chapter 42: Evolutionary Design   **269**
Business Value   269
Sketch   269
Context   271
Forces   271
Therefore   272
Adoption   273
But   274
Variations   275
References   275

Chapter 43: Test-Driven Development   **277**
Business Value   277
Sketch   277
Context   278
Forces   278
Therefore   279
Adoption   280
But   281
Variations   282
References   282

Chapter 44: Test-Driven Requirements   **285**
Business Value   285
Sketch   286
Context   286
Forces   287
Therefore   287
Adoption   288
But   289
Variations   290
References   290

Part 4: Case Studies   293

Chapter 45: BabyCenter   295
BabyCenter Agile Adoption Effort—Q1 2007   296
  Crafting an Agile Practice Adoption Strategy   *296*
  Conclusions   *301*
BabyCenter Agile Adoption Effort Revisited—Q1 2008   302

Chapter 46: Company X   305
Company X Agile Adoption Effort—Q1–Q2 2007   305
  Context for This Report   *306*
  Current Business Goals   *306*
  From the Trenches   *306*
  Suggested Practices for the Remainder of 2007   *312*
  Long Term   *316*
  Conclusion   *316*
Company X Agile Adoption Effort—Revisited   316
  Current State   *316*

Part 5: Appendices   321

Appendix A: Pattern to Business Value Mappings   323

Appendix B: Pattern-to-Smell Mappings   325

Appendix C: Getting the Most from Agile Practice Patterns   327

Appendix D: Further Reading   331

Bibliography   333

Index   339

FOREWORD

By Linda Rising*

I was on yet another flight recently—a plane so small that my seat was both on an aisle and a window! So it was easy for me to see my two neighbors across the aisle—both young girls who looked like sisters. They were alone and had obviously made this trip from Houston to Richmond before. They settled in as we started to taxi, and as the small plane popped up and became airborne, they reached in their carry-on bags and pulled out—could it be— yes, books! I was amazed at how amazed I was! Young folks reading! And they read the entire two-hour flight. It completely restored my sometimes-shaky faith in humanity. There is hope! One of the few good things about flying is the chance to have a little time to read and to notice that others are also reading—even youngsters.

There's something about patterns and books. They go together. I remember commenting about this in an early talk about patterns. Afterward, one of the participants came up and started looking through the stack of patterns books I had brought. He said, "Some of my happiest moments have been with books." Well said. Patterns people do like books. They buy books, and they read them. In fact, entire conferences are devoted to reading and talking about patterns, and many of the products of these conferences become books. But nowadays, you might feel there are so many books, and we have so little time. Agreed. My stack of books waiting for their plane trip is growing, and I find myself torn between attractive alternatives each time I assemble my own carry-on bag. So while I'm always happy to look at a book— especially a book about patterns—I always wonder if people will have the time to read it.

There are several reasons why I think Amr Elssamadisy's book will not face a life buried in someone's stack of books-to-be-read-sometime-on-some-flight-somewhere. It's not just because its a book of patterns. It's not just because it's a book about Agile development. I'm a believer in patterns. I'm also a believer in Agile development. Like many other believers, this faith in "a better way" is not enough to convince decision makers who are looking for costs

---

* Coauthor, *Fearless Change*, with Mary Lynn Manns

and benefits. Even though I earned a Ph.D. in computer science, working in the area of design metrics, and an M.S. in mathematics, I often find it hard to measure these costs and benefits satisfactorily. As the famous British writer Lewis Carroll cautions, "If you dont know where you're going, any road will get you there." [1]

Victor Basili had some recommendations in 1994 in his classic paper "The Goal, Question, Metric Approach" [2].

- Develop a set of corporate, division, and project business goals and associated measurement goals for productivity and quality.
- Generate questions (based on models) that define those goals as completely as possible in a quantifiable way.
- Specify the measures needed to be collected to answer those questions and track process and product conformance to the goals.
- Develop mechanisms for data collection.
- Collect, validate, and analyze the data in real time to provide feedback to projects for corrective action.
- Analyze the data in a postmortem fashion to assess conformance to the goals and to make recommendations for future improvements.

I guess what I'm trying to say is that this book is useful for practitioners who want to follow the advice in the Basili paper and apply this methodology not to metrics but in moving to Agile development. Yes, this book is written as a collection of patterns, but it doesn't get so wound up in being about patterns. Yes, it's about Agile, but it's not evangelizing Agile. The book is practical and readable, and the focus is on business value. The book makes the very wise observation that no one path to Agile (or any other worthwhile goal) is achieved in the same way by all seekers. There are no easy answers here. Amr takes the approach, often found in other Agile books that discuss code, by examining a list of "smells." This might be helpful, not only for pointing out applicable patterns but also for supporting your struggle to determine what your business truly values. This is a worthwhile exercise regardless of whether you are contemplating Agile practices or not.

Having said all that, I want to report that there are no silver bullets in this book. Sorry! Patterns revolve around a context that says when its appropriate to apply the solution. Authors of good patterns also include a signpost that warns the users of the consequences of applying the solution that, even if the context is appropriate, there are no guarantees that we will all live happily ever after. With patterns, as in life, the best advice needs to be considered carefully before rushing in. I'm happy to say that Amr adheres to these pattern guidelines. Even the book itself has a context. I always appreciate that when I'm browsing the pages. This author has done us all a favor by saying what audience he addresses. A quick look at the section "Is This Book for You?" will help you decide whether to buy the book or not.

I'm hoping that if you decide you are part of the target audience, you will buy the book, and, more than that, you will move it to the top of your book stack and read it. I believe that if you are able to do all this, you will find these patterns useful for moving your business to Agile. And that means I'll get to see you at the next Agile conference! Enjoy!

[1] Carroll, L., *Alice's Adventures in Wonderland*, originally published in 1865.

[2] Basili, V., Caldiera, G., and Rombach, H. D., "Goal Question Metric Paradigm," *Encyclopedia of Software Engineering*, pp. 528–532, John Wiley & Sons, Inc., 1994. www.cs.umd.edu/~basili/publications/technical/T87.pdf.

FOREWORD

By J.B. (Joe) Rainsberger*

Change campaigns are hard, and adopting an Agile approach to delivering software is no different. The processes are stressful for participants, for leaders, and for those who can only stand aside and watch. They're so hard, in fact, that I find it hopelessly optimistic to think that a single book could help people navigate through a successful Agile adoption—until now.

In the pages of this book, you will find concise, practical advice for all facets of adopting the Agile mindset. There is advice on which practices to adopt, how, and when. There is advice on how to foster the level of community involvement that effective software delivery demands. There is even specific advice on how to learn what you need. It is as comprehensive a manual as I have ever seen on the topic: specific enough for you to follow, but not so prescriptive that you forget to think for yourself. It is the closest I have ever seen to the One Book You Need to begin adopting an Agile approach to delivering software.

As someone who has written a "recipes" book, I am partial to the format that the author has employed here. I find that once I have gone past the manifesto or "why question" stage of exploring a new concept, I look for concrete practices to try, described concisely, with several thought-provoking points to consider as I begin my practice. That is what the author has provided here, and it couldn't suit me better. If you are serious about succeeding at delivering software, and you believe an Agile approach is a path to success, then start with *Agile Adoption Patterns: A Roadmap to Organizational Success*. Read it thoroughly, and examine its bibliography. There are considerable riches in these pages, even to mine for years. Get digging!

---

*　(http://www.diasparsoftware.com)
　　Your guide to software craftsmanship
　　JUnit Recipes: Practical Methods for Programmer Testing
　　2005 Gordon Pask Award for contributions to Agile Software Practice

Preface

In this book, you and I focus on adoption of Agile practices. I help you answer basic questions that are on your mind:

- Where do I start?
- What practice(s) are best for my particular environment?
- How can I adopt these practices incrementally?
- What pitfalls should I watch out for?

Is This Book for You?

Are you adopting one or more Agile practices or seriously thinking about trying out one or more practices on your team? Have you read any of the Agile methodology books on Extreme Programming, Scrum, or Test-Driven Development, and are you theoretically convinced about at least trying the practices?

Or perhaps you're coming off your first project and you've been asked to join another team to help them succeed as you did previously. Of course, every project is different. Are the same practices you used the last time going to be as effective on the next project? It depends! This book helps you get past "It depends!" to determine what practices should be adopted and give you some hints how they may need to be adapted.

Or maybe you are unlucky enough to have been part of a failing Agile project (or possibly are still on one). Read this book to get an idea why the practices you are using may not be applicable. Be agile about your Agile practices.

If any of these scenarios fit, this book is for you. It helps you look at the individual practices and their relationships and gives you a strategy that has been used successfully several times on multiple projects by multiple companies. It also provides you with warnings concerning how practices have gone wrong before and how you can recognize and respond to the problems that occur. This is not just one person's opinion or an untried method. All the patterns you will read about here come from *real-world* project experience.

Finally, let me say a few words about who this book isn't for:

- Advanced practitioners who already get Agile practices and are looking for new theories or practices. All the information in this book is collected from the experience of multiple projects, so chances are you've already heard about everything here.
- Beginners who want to start from zero. This book does not adequately describe the practices from ground zero. However, this book will be a good companion to other works that delve more deeply into full Agile practices.

THE PLAN

I give you even more questions that you should consider and answer on your journey toward adopting Agile practices. Does this sound too good to be true? It isn't really. Many of us who have been in the Agile community for several years have figured this out the hard way—by trial and error. This book shares those experiences. Here is an overview of what you will be able to accomplish by reading this book.

- Understand some of the basic drivers or principles and values that underlie all Agile practices and make them successful.
- Focus on business value to the customer. List important areas of value to many customers. An example of a business value would be Reduce Cost.
- Understand symptoms that occur when business value is not being delivered. I'll call these symptoms smells. An example of a smell related to the Reduce Cost business value is Customer Asks for Everything Including the Kitchen Sink.
- Tie these business values and smells to individual Agile practices.
- Use the information in the first four items to decide which practices to adopt to increase your business value and remove the smells present at your company. At this point, you will be able to come up with a coarse-grained adoption strategy for your environment.
- Provide a detailed description of each practice in pattern format and include adoption information for each practice.
- Call out practices that work well together as clusters. Relate these clusters to business values and smells. Describe the clusters and adoption strategies as done for the practices.

STRUCTURE AND CONTENT

This book is organized into several parts and subparts, so a quick overview of the structure and content of those parts is in order. I recommend that you read Chapters 1 through 8 straight through and do all the exercises where applicable. This will give you essential context concerning software development so that you and I are on the same page, take you step by step through the creation of an Agile adoption strategy tailored to your organization's context, and introduce you to the pattern format in which all the practices are presented in the pattern catalog.

After you have finished these eight chapters, use Part 3 of the book as a reference to implement the strategy you've created. Skip around or read straight through. Both will work; you can read the patterns presented independently. Each chapter will help you adopt a particular practice, warn you of pitfalls, and give you references for further reading.

Read the case studies to get a feel for how this approach has translated to other organizations, but beware—it gets messy in real-life situations. Finally, the appendices are chapters that were too useful not to include but didn't quite fit in with the flow of the book. They are short, so feel free to take a look at them at any time throughout your reading.

Part 1: Thoughts about Software Development

Part 1 covers some basic issues of software development and sets the context for the rest of the book. I examine reasons why software development is so difficult. I also look at why adoption of new practices—any practices, not just Agile practices—are difficult and depend on your personal involvement and commitment. Read the chapters in this section and keep the ideas in the back of your mind as you go through the rest of the book.

- Chapter 1, "Learning Is the Bottleneck"
- Chapter 2, "Personal Agility for Potent Agile Adoption"

Part 2: Crafting an Agile Adoption Strategy

Part 2 starts to get into the meat of the problem—picking and choosing Agile practices for your particular context. By the time you are done with these chapters and have completed the exercises, you will have an initial set of practices that your team should start to adopt. Be aware that for the purposes of creating an adoption strategy, I will refer to many practices that are described in the remainder of the book. So don't worry if you have a set of practices to adopt that you do not completely understand yet. Their descriptions are in the later sections.

- Chapter 3, "Business Value"
- Chapter 4, "Smells"
- Chapter 5, "Adopting Agile Practices"

Part 3: The Pattern Catalog

Part 3 is the pattern catalog. The pattern catalog details how to successfully adopt and adapt the practices that you've determined in Part 2 meet your organization's business goals. This section should be used as a reference to put your adoption plan to practice. Read Chapters 6, 7, and 8 and then use the rest on an as-needed basis to execute your adoption strategy. Note that the practices are organized into subparts as well.

- Chapter 6, "The Patterns of Agile Practice Adoption"
- Chapter 7, "Goal"
- Chapter 8, "Cycle"

Part 3.1 Feedback Practices

The feedback practices are predominantly concerned with working as a team and planning functions. They are practices that help you and your team "solve the right problem" by iteratively building your software system and consistently checking whether the system solves the needs of the customer.

- Chapter 9, "Iteration"
- Chapter 10, "Kickoff Meeting"
- Chapter 11, "Backlog"
- Chapter 12, "Planning Poker"
- Chapter 13, "Stand-Up Meeting"
- Chapter 14, "Done State"
- Chapter 15, "Demo"
- Chapter 16, "Retrospective"
- Chapter 17, "Release Often"
- Chapter 18, "Co-Located Team"
- Chapter 19, "Self-Organizing Team"
- Chapter 20, "Cross-Functional Team"
- Chapter 21, "Customer Part of Team"
- Chapter 22, "Evocative Document"
- Chapter 23, "User Story"
- Chapter 24, "Use Case"
- Chapter 25, "Information Radiator"

Part 3.2 Technical Practices

The technical practices are concerned with "solving the problem right" by creating and maintaining the code of your software system. They are the bit-head practices that your team will use to build and evolve the software system.

- Chapter 26, "Automated Developer Tests"
- Chapter 27, "Test-Last Development"
- Chapter 28, "Test-First Development"
- Chapter 29, "Refactoring"
- Chapter 30, "Continuous Integration"
- Chapter 31, "Simple Design"
- Chapter 32, "Functional Tests"
- Chapter 33, "Collective Code Ownership"
- Chapter 34, "Pair Programming"

Part 3.3 Supporting Practices

These are not Agile practices per se, but they are practices that you can use to support your team's adoption and introduce change into your organization.

- Chapter 35, "Coach"
- Chapter 36, "Engage the Community"
- Chapter 37, "Reading Circle"
- Chapter 38, "Workshop"
- Chapter 39, "Classroom Training"

Part 3.4 The Clusters

The clusters of practices are sets of Agile practice patterns that work especially well together. The first two clusters are focused on people, interactions, and teamwork. The practices that make up these clusters enable a team to recognize change as it happens and provide a working process for responding to those changes. The last three clusters are technical in nature and give the team the technical ability to respond to changes as they occur.

- Chapter 40, "Agile Iteration"
- Chapter 41, "Communication Cluster"
- Chapter 42, "Evolutionary Design"
- Chapter 43, "Test-Driven Development"
- Chapter 44, "Test-Driven Requirements"

Part 4: Case Studies

These are reports of two different adoption efforts. They get beyond the theory and show how two organizations are working through their Agile adoptions. One has been very successful, and the other is still struggling. Both are real companies, with real people and real politics. It gets messy. But, in the end, so will your adoption effort before you succeed.

- Chapter 45, "BabyCenter"
- Chapter 46, "Company X"

Appendices

The appendices contain material that does not quite fit in the main flow of the book but that could be useful to you.

- Appendix A, "Pattern to Business Value Mappings"
- Appendix B, "Pattern to Smell Mappings"
- Appendix C, "Getting the Most from Agile Practice Patterns"
- Appendix D, "Further Reading"

HOW TO READ THIS BOOK

Okay. So enough about what you are going to do. How do you do it? The first thing you have to do is come up with a set of Agile development practices for you and your team. You can do that by reading Part 1 and taking the time to do the exercises at the end of Chapters 3, 4, and 5. It is important that you spend the time to work through the exercises. After completing these chapters, you will have a list of prioritized practices to consider.

At that point, you can start with the third part of the book—the patterns. You will use the list of practices on your list to "dig deep" by reading each pattern and deciding if it is *really* applicable to your environment. When you find a practice that matches, you and your team will start adopting it incrementally using the guidance in that pattern. You'll also watch out for symptoms of that practice going bad by using the guidance in the "smells" documented in each pattern.

Finally, you'll continuously evaluate the effectiveness of the practices you've adopted and adapt them to get greater value from them for your business. Start right now by turning to the next chapter.

ACKNOWLEDGMENTS

Writing this book has been an adventure, an exercise in patience and humility, and a chance to work with many, many people to put these pages before you, the reader. As an avid reader, I rarely read Acknowledgements in the past, but after going through the exercise of writing two books, I now read them in detail. The Acknowledgements will let you know how much work went into writing the book and get a glimpse into the many minds that went into writing it. There is one name as the author, but—at least in my case and I suspect the majority of other books—the author is rarely the sole source of the work. So with that in mind, here are the other people who generously gave of their time, effort, and thoughts to make this work what it is.

First on the list is my wife Maha, who encouraged me, pushed me, pulled me, and generally got me to write. She spent hours of her time editing early versions of this book and many of the papers and articles I wrote in the years leading up to this book. She never let me quit and always kept the writing in the forefront of my mind.

Next on my list are Ashley Johnson, Dave West, and Ahmed Elshamy, with whom I spent two and a half days in Arizona in the spring of 2006 during the ChiliPLoP conference discussing patterns, Agile practices, and adoption. The four of us shared our experiences over the years and put them in pattern format. After that initial work, Ahmed helped me run a workshop at XP2006 and XP2007, where we presented our ideas and gathered more data for the patterns from over 40 practitioners around the world. Ashley spent countless hours discussing the ideas and refining the ideas in this book. Tim Snyder, my manager in the Valtech days, gave me the time, freedom, and opportunity to go to XP2006 and XP2007 conferences and build this body of knowledge. The same Tim Snyder, but this time my partner at Gemba Systems, has worked with me hand in hand in implementing these patterns with our clients.

Dave and I took the ChiliPLoP work and refined it to present at PLoP 2006, where it was reviewed yet again by another group. Special thanks to Ademar Aguiar for taking the time and effort to shepherd our work for PLoP. Linda Rising and Mary Lynn Manns have also read early versions of this work. Richard Gabriel led the workshop that reviewed this work. The reviewers were Donald Little, Rebecca Rikner, James F. Kile, Till Schümmer, Lise B. Hvatum, Joseph Bergin, and Guy Steele.

Jean Whitmore coauthored a paper with me earlier this year that was the basis for the Functional Tests pattern and Test-Driven Requirements cluster. Special thanks to Jason Yip for shepherding this pattern and helping us refine the work for presentation at PLoP. The group that reviewed this pattern included Ralph Johnson, Jason Yip, Hesham Saadawi, Dirk Riehle, and Paddy Fagan.

This book was written in two rounds. The first round culminated in the publishing of a minibook by InfoQ in March 2007, *Patterns of Agile Practice Adoption: The Technical Practices*. The second round was an expansion, refinement, and revision.

Filippo Borselli, John Taylor, Ron Jeffries, Floyd Marinescue, Deborah Hartmann, and Kurt Christenson took the time to read drafts of the minibook and give their feedback to make this a much better work than it was originally. Floyd Marinescue and Deborah Hartmann from InfoQ gave me the opportunity to write the minibook and make it available to the public. That work allowed me to get much more feedback from others in the community when I started with the second round of writing.

That second round of this book had its start at PLoP 2006, where I met Christopher Guzikowski of Addison-Wesley (AW). He had read the paper that Jean Whitmore and I wrote about Test-Driven Requirements as a pattern and was intrigued about writing about my desire to write about Agile adoption in pattern format. Chris G. took the minibook and presented it to the editorial committee as the draft of the book you have in your hands (which indeed it was).

I've had a whole team at AW help move this work forward. Chris Guzikowski got the ball rolling. Without him advocating the work as a positive contribution to the community, it wouldn't have gotten off the ground. Next on the AW team was Raina Chrobak, who shepherded my work once it was accepted as a project. She coordinated all the work as we moved step by step in this long process. (The minibook was an ad hoc work, and the quality difference shows.) Raina kept me sane and assured me there was a light at the end of the tunnel. She also helped me keep on schedule to get this work out by summer 2008—before the Agile 08 conference. Thanks, Raina!

After finishing the complete first draft, Christopher Zahn patiently worked with me over several months doing the first round of editing. Chris Z. spent hours going through each chapter correcting my mistakes and very politely telling me where things just didn't make sense. I never knew so much was involved in writing a book...

Halfway through the work with Chris Z., a technical committee of experienced Agile practitioners started reading through the book. These gentlemen are Jim Holmes, Celso Gonzalez, Rob Sanheim, Dave Hendricksen, Michael Ward, and Robert Bogetti. Their comments were *really* brutal. Thanks, guys! They caught even more of my mistakes, argued with my reasoning, told me when I was just plain wrong, and shared their own experiences. The work is much better for it. Thank you for taking the time and effort to give me a hard time.

From a review standpoint, there is a group of people outside of AW who has reviewed my work. These people did the same job as the technical committee as a favor to me. Thanks to Emily Bache, Dr. Hakan Erdogmus, Ken DeLong, and Sean Sheehan.

Thanks to the production team also, Karen Gill and Jovana San Nicolas-Shirley, who caught the remaining language errors and made a collection of Word documents into a book.

Thanks to the entire AW team!

The patterns collected in this book are the result of my own experiences and those of many others. This work would not have been possible without the participation of the people who were willing to spend their time, share their knowledge, and struggle to find the commonalities in the ChiliPLoP 2006/ ChiliPLoP 2007 workshops, XP2006/XP2007 workshops, and XPDay Montreal 2006 Open Space session (in alphabetical order):

Noura Abbas, Soile Aho, Görge Albrecht, Walter Ambu, Giovanni Asproni, Emine G. Aydal, Emily Bache, Geoff Bache, Wojtek Biela, Meir Ben-Ami, Roberto Bettazzoni, Gilad Bornstein, Filippo Borselli, Ole Dalgaard, Ian Davies, Vasco Duarte, Magnus Erikson, Emmanuel Gaillot, Al Goerner, Gabor Gunyho, Jyrki Hamalainen, Janne Hietam[um]aki, Mina Hillebrand, Tuomos Jarvensivu, Ashley Johnson, Kan Karkkainen, Tuomas Karkkainen, Maaret Koskenkorva, Krisztina Kovacs, Juha Laitinen, Andreas Larsson, Mikko Levonmaa, Artem Marchinko, Youri Metchev, Absar Mirza, Aivar Naaber, Paul Nagy, Stefan Niccolai, Keijo Niinimaa, Loua Nordgvist, Virva Nurmua, Marko Oikarinen, Jukka Ollakka, Paolo Perrotta, Dimitri Petchatnikov, Ron Pijpers, Aussi Piirainen, Ilja Preus, Timo Pulkkinen, Niko Ryytty, Abdel Aziz Saleh, Aki Salmi, Meelis Salvvee, Timo Taskinen, Olavi Tiimus, Ingmar van Dijk, Jussi Vesala, and Daniel Wellner.

Also, thanks to the development group at BabyCenter, especially Ken Delong and David Chia for sharing their experiences, and the development group at Company X—hang in there. You'll make it!

Finally, a huge thank you to Linda Rising. I first met Linda at Agile 2005 in an open space when I was looking for a nonanecdotal way to share my experiences and those of others in adopting Agile development practices. Linda's work on patterns of organizational change was the first spark for this work. She also helped me get the initial forms of this work to the PLoP community and helped me steer through some choppy waters as I struggled to learn from others and still keep the core of this work true to my vision. She also took the time to read the book and write the Foreword. I'm pretty sure that without her, this book wouldn't be here.

So if your curiosity has led you to read these acknowledgements, you now know that this book in your hands is the result of many minds and hands. Thank you to everyone for helping me bring this book to completion, and here's hoping that development teams out there can use the information in this book to build better software!

—*Amr Elssamadisy*
Amherst Massachusetts
April 9, 2008

ABOUT THE AUTHOR

Amr Elssamadisy (www.elssamadisy.com) is a software development practitioner who works with his clients to build better, more valuable software. He and his colleagues at Gemba Systems help both small and large development teams learn new technologies, adopt and adapt appropriate Agile development practices, and focus their efforts to maximize the value they bring to their organizations.

Amr's technical background and experience in C/C++, Java/J2EE, and .NET allows him to appreciate the problems of development teams and offer them support.

At the same time, he realizes that most problems—even in software—are people problems that are not solved by tools and technology. Therefore, Amr and his colleagues at Gemba Systems focus on issues such as personal agility, team building, communication, feedback, and all the other soft skills that distinguish excellent teams.

Amr is also the author of *Patterns of Agile Practice Adoption: The Technical Cluster*. He is an editor for the AgileQ at *InfoQ*, a contributor to the *Agile Journal*, and a frequent presenter at software development conferences.

Part 1

Thoughts about Software Development

Software Development is Hard—with a capital "H." We, in the Agile community, believe we have found a significantly better way of building software. We also know that we have not found *the* answer, just a better one.

The chapters in this section delve into two important issues in software development that are there no matter what software practices you use. They are as follows: 1) learning is a large part of software development, and 2) highly productive teams are made up of individuals who take initiative and responsibility to solve problems as they emerge.

These two issues are doubly important when discussing a topic like Agile adoption because they form the backbone of all successful adoptions. Without frequent learning, your team will never be able to recognize and respond to changes that occur. Without individuals taking initiative and responsibility, your practices will fall flat. Read these chapters and keep their lessons in mind as you work through this book.

Chapter 1

LEARNING IS THE BOTTLENECK

Professional trainers and coaches have seen it again and again. It's a pattern that too many Agile teams get hung up on—getting stuck in the just-average "norming" stage, rather than progressing into the exciting, high-performing stage of team growth.[1] Consider that there may be one common element of all software development projects which, when maximized, could help make productivity soar. In fact, many of the most successful teams (both Agile and traditional) are already leveraging the seemingly simple but too-often forgotten "secret sauce" of software development: frequently making time to reflect and learn. Learn about what? Everything: each other, the technology, the domain, the customer, and more. A team that learns quickly succeeds. Read on for more about the invisible learning bottleneck that stunts team performance.

A HYPOTHETICAL EXPERIMENT

What can we do to make software development better? What are the typical bottlenecks in software development? Is there any one commonality?

The days where anyone could run a definitive experiment utilizing an actual, real-life software project are long gone, if they ever existed at all. Among other problems, to run a true experiment, you need to be able to build the same project twice. That is, unfortunately, prohibitively expensive in today's business environment. Therefore, it is currently unrealistic to construct experiments to figure out exactly what the common weak points are.

At the same time, we all have experience developing software as practitioners. So here is a hypothetical situation that I have presented to many of my students:

---

1. The Forming-Storming-Norming-Performing model of team development was first proposed by Bruce Tuckman. http://en.wikipedia.org/wiki/Forming-storming-norming-performing.

3

Suppose I was your client, and I asked you and your team to build a software system for me. Your team proceeds to build the software system. It takes you a full year—12 months—to deliver working, tested software.

I then thank the team and take the software and throw it out. After that, I ask you and your team to rebuild the system. You have the same team, requirements, tools, and software. Basically, nothing has changed. It is the same environment.

How long will it take you and your team to build the system this time?

When I present this hypothetical situation to my students—many of them with 20+ years of experience in building software—they typically respond with anywhere between 20 percent to 70 percent of the time. That is, rebuilding a system that originally takes one year to build takes only 2.5 to 8.5 months to build. It is a huge difference! Do you know any one thing that can affect software development that much? I don't.

So, what is the problem? What was different? The team has *learned*. The members learned about each other as a team and gelled over the year. They learned about the true requirements—not just those written down. They also learned to use the toolset, experienced the idiosyncrasies that come up during all software development, and worked through all the unknowns until they built and delivered a successful software solution. Learning is *the* bottleneck of software engineering.[2]

The learning that occurs makes up a significant percentage of the time spent on the work. That's the main reason that Agile practices work so well—they are all about recognizing and responding to change. All Agile practices, from Test-First Development and Continuous Integration to Iterations and Retrospectives, consist of cycles that help the team learn fast. By cycling in every possible practice, Agile teams accelerate learning, addressing the bottleneck of software engineering. Call it "scientific method," "continuous improvement," or "test everything."

---

2. This hypothetical story and the "learning is the bottleneck" idea comes from Ashley Johnson at Gemba Systems.

EXAMINING AGILE THROUGH "LEARNING IS THE BOTTLENECK" LENSES

Agile software development works. That is an established fact. Hundreds of successful war stories have been documented over the past eight years.[3] One of the interesting things to note about Agile development is that most of the practices are not new—in fact, they are very old. Agile has simply distilled many of the most successful software development practices and brought them together. In fact, the Agile manifesto was not creating something new, but finding commonality among a number of lightweight methods that had already been successful throughout the 1990s (two different accounts by Jim Highsmith[4] and Robert "Uncle Bob" Martin[5] are available). Reflecting on many of the most effective practices reveals some interesting commonalities...

CYCLES FOR RECOGNIZING AND RESPONDING TO CHANGE

So how do we learn? One obvious way we learn is from our mistakes (if we are paying attention; many do not). How do we learn faster? By making more (smaller) mistakes faster—"fail fast." Immediate application of what we've learned is a key to cement learning and make it "stick." By immediately applying what we've learned in the previous cycle, we compound the effect of learning (like compound interest!).

A common cycle we find again and again looks like what is shown in Figure 1-1.

1. Set a goal.
2. Perform an action to achieve that goal.
3. Compare the outcomes of the action to the original goal.
4. Change the action accordingly and go back to step 2.

Learning happens in step 3 and is applied in step 4.

---

3. For those interested in reading these success stories, the proceedings from XP 2000–XP 2007, XP Universe 2001–2004, and Agile 2005–2007 are three of the largest Agile conferences around the world and contain many case studies and experience reports.

4. For one history of commonality among the early lightweight methods, see Jim Highsmith. www.agilemanifesto.org/history.html

5. For another history of commonality among the early lightweight methods, see Robert Martin. http://blog.objectmentor.com/articles/2007/07/10/the-founding-of-the-agile-alliance

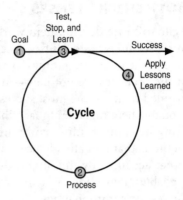

Figure 1–1   The learning cycle

This simple cycle is the basis for many of the practices in Agile development:

- **Test-First Development.** 1) Write a failing test, 2) write code to make the test pass, 3) run the test—does it pass? 4) if the test still fails, go to (2).
- **Daily Cycle.** 1) Set the daily tasks for the team and report these at the daily stand-up meeting, 2) perform the tasks, 3) report back the next day on past progress and obstacles, and 4) apply what's been learned to the plan for the next day.
- **Test-Driven Requirements** (TDR). 1) Define the requirements as tests, 2) develop the software, 3) run the tests; if they pass, you are done; if they don't, then 4) find out why and go back to (2).
- **Iteration.** 1) Define a "done state," 2) commit to a set of requirements that form that iterations backlog, 3) work throughout the iteration to build the backlog, 4) close the iteration by testing each item against the "done state," and mark them done or put them on the backlog again for later consideration.
- **Demo.** Usually performed at the end of the iteration, the demo gives the customer a chance to test whether the requirements envisioned when implemented really solve the problem at hand. The cycle goes like this: 1) (implicitly) determine the business needs/values addressed by the requirements, 2) define the requirements, 3) build the requirements during iteration, 4) evaluate the implemented requirements against the business needs.
- **Retrospectives.** 1) Decide on a way the team will work, 2) work that way for an iteration, 3) reflect on how well the practices worked, and

4) come up with actions and with owners and dates that are intended to create a more effective process and implement them.

- **Release.** 1) Create a vision for the release and set the business goals that the release is to meet, 2) create a release backlog, 3) perform several iterations to build the release, 4) deploy it to customers, and collect feedback for the next release.

- **Scrum of Scrums.** In dealing with multiple projects at once, each project has its own set of cycles running independently while synching up via regular meetings—Scrums of Scrums—where representatives from each project report to the rest, providing an opportunity for recognizing and responding to change at an enterprise level.

- **Management Tests.** 1) Work with a product owner or with business stakeholders to define, at a high level, how they will measure the success of a project or release, 2) keep these "tests" visible as the team works to deliver on these expectations, 3) incorporate an evaluation of management tests into retrospectives, 4) have the team and product owner work together to align each iteration with these tests.

Furthermore, these cycles feed into each other—constantly—as learning occurs that invalidates a higher cycle. The test-driven development loop is nested within the test-driven requirements—that is, for each requirement, several test-driven development cycles occur to fulfill that one requirement. Therefore, for example, a broken test may mean bad code, but it also may mean that, for the requirement to be built, another previous requirement may need to be invalidated. So learning in the test-driven development loop brings about requirements learning. Similarly, iterations are nested within releases. Therefore, an iteration that fails to meet one or more of its goals because of a technical limitation that could not have been foreseen also increases the effort needed to complete a significant portion of the system. The team then regroups, considers the release backlog, and does some reprioritization and scope modifications to accommodate the new information.

CYCLE: NECESSARY BUT NOT SUFFICIENT

The cycle is one of two basic requirements for recognizing and responding to change—it provides the opportunity. The second requirement is communication. Communication magnifies the learning by involving everyone. The emphasis on "information radiators" in Agile development approaches reflects this effort to communicate.

Information needs to be communicated to the rest of the team and beyond. Without communication, issues may go unrecognized. And without communication, those who see issues but can't spot solutions may never get the input of others with different skill sets who can see the solutions. In a team environment, it is not always obvious who is best suited to solve a given problem. By telling everyone, you invite suggestions from any interested party, not just the team "experts." Sometimes novices or outsiders are able to "think outside the box" and surprise us!

Communication accelerates and accentuates learning, and a formal pause for reflection can ensure that this communication does not fall on ears deafened by cries of "hurry, hurry!" This pause could be as formal as a retrospective or as informal as a shared meal at the end of the iteration—as long as learning and improvement are on the agenda. And, although communication should happen in a planned manner at the beginning (communicating goals) and end (test results) of each cycle, we also benefit dramatically from informal, "osmotic"[6] communication as each cycle unfolds.

Like cycles, a significant number of Agile practices directly focus on communication, both formal and osmotic:

- **Self-Organizing Team**. A team works together to respond to changes. They collectively do what needs to be done to build the software.
- **Co-Located Team**. The team members sit down together and regularly have group conversations, they overhear others, and individuals are aware of what is happening by osmosis.
- **Cross-Functional Team**. A team with multiple disciplines works together to solve a problem from end to end. By working together, the members share their individual areas of expertise.
- **Pair Programming**. Two people working together to solve one task is a deep form of sharing experience and expertise.
- **Information Radiators**. These are big visible charts whose sole purpose is to communicate important data to anyone passing by.
- **Evocative Documents**. Agile teams build documents together to have conversations. Those documents then evoke the entire discussion and context when read later. These are much more valuable than traditional throw-over-the-wall documents, which are representational in nature—that is, there is a (false) belief that the documents actually are the thing they describe.
- **Stand-Up Meeting**. Agile teams synchronize daily by communicating tasks completed, roadblocks met, and tasks planned for completion in the next day.

---

6. "Osmotic" communication on Agile teams: www.agilemodeling.com/essays/communication.htm.

Communication, when added to a cycle, allows the entire team to learn faster and respond as a team. After all, software development is a team effort. If learning is the bottleneck for the team, the entire team needs to learn as much and as fast as possible.

If Agile team members are using the practices well, they learn about everything—not just technology—quickly: design (TDD, pair programming, cross-functional team), requirements (demo and TDR), the product (iterations, releases), and the people (retrospective, stand-up meeting).

WHY IS THIS IMPORTANT? THEORY TO PRACTICE

All this information is well and good. After all, learning seems to be an important part of software development. In fact, it is probably even more important than we currently give it credit for. But so what? How can this focus on learning help my team or yours produce better software?

Despite all the examples of "learning" practices cited earlier, Agile teams are not immune to the learning bottleneck. Urgency sometimes presses us to take the short-term win by cutting out the learning step ("oh, we'll do that later"). Agile teams that fail to learn may display any or all of the following symptoms:

- Fatigue (not working at a truly sustainable pace), leading to morale problems
- Repeated inability to "get to done" in a single iteration
- Consistently under delivering on promises (some promised features or stories are not even started)
- So many defects consistently coming back from deployed software that development plans are derailed
- Devaluing or eliminating retrospectives ("because we never actually solve the problems we identify")

KEEP YOUR EYE ON THE BOTTLENECK

Consider Figure 1-2. Each step has a speed indicated in parentheses below the step name. Inventory builds up between two steps when they are of mismatched speed; therefore, because step A is faster than step B, an excess of product A waits to be processed by B. Throughput of the overall system will always be limited by that bottleneck. The idea is that if you want to increase the overall throughput of the system, you need to focus almost exclusively on improving the performance of the bottleneck. Efforts spent elsewhere are wasteful and could even be counterproductive. That means, for the simple sequential process in Figure 1-2, the only way we can make an improvement is to fix step D. If we address anything else, we will not improve.

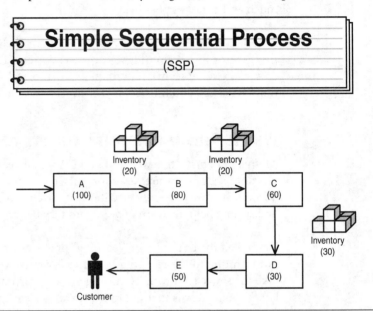

Figure 1–2   A simple sequential process

As Figure 1-2 illustrates, if learning really *is* the bottleneck of software development, this should elevate it to our number-one priority in making things better. It means that any efforts we spend on anything other than learning will not improve our productivity. It means that anything that *does* improve our productivity has somehow improved our learning.

Now, when were reflecting on our process, contemplating ways to deliver more value, we should remember that we are usually delivering several sorts of value to the businesses we serve: working software, certainly, but also maintainable and changeable software, and a responsive team to continue that work. Priorities for the first two should be solicited from the business, but the third is simply an expectation of professionalism and is usually within the control of the development organization. This last form of value, team agility, is actually an asset of the organization that can outlive individual projects, creating the opportunity for greater profit or speed on subsequent projects.

Agile teams should be relatively stable organisms that live for six months or more together, to grow into effective teamwork. Building such a team requires a strategic view, which must be considered with the immediate needs of the business in each iteration. If this balance is not maintained, a time will quickly come when the team fails the business due to unresolved booby traps in their process that work against predictable velocity and quality.

To avoid creation of a fragile and inconsistent team, when we reflect on process, we should be asking two questions:

- How will this affect our velocity in the next iteration?
- How will this affect our learning (which in turn affects our velocity and responsiveness in all following iterations and projects)?

So instead of simply asking, "Will pair programming slow us down?" we should also ask, "Will pair programming slow our rate of learning, or will it speed it up?" Instead of asking, "Should we really have demos every two weeks, although our stakeholders are only available on a monthly basis?" we should ask, "How will reducing demo frequency to once a month affect our learning?" Instead of asking, "Which tools should I install to support Agile?" we should ask, "Does tool ABC increase our learning, or does it slow it down by reducing our communication bandwidth?"[7]

When we understand that learning enhances the corporate asset called "the team," we have a vocabulary to explain the benefits of our learning practices to stakeholders. "Yes, pair programming looks expensive at first glance—let me explain how it offsets risks and outweighs the apparent cost in the long haul..." Don't forget—with Agile's short cycles, "the long haul" may be as little as three to six weeks!

CLOSING

I had one purpose in writing this chapter. It was not to analyze the theory and mechanics of learning, which can—and, in fact, has—filled many, many volumes. Neither was it to categorize or evaluate different Agile practices; those mentioned are simply examples—reminders that we already have many ways to learn, if we choose to.

---

7. Better yet, wait until a need is discovered to track information (to learn from it) and then find a tool that provides it with the least amount of work on your part. See "Appropriate Agile Metrics: Using Metrics and Diagnostics to Deliver Business Value," Deborah Hartmann and Robin Dymond, 2006. www.berteigconsulting.com/archives/2005/01/agile_work_reso.php

My writing objective was to bring learning to the forefront of your mind and actions because it is the key to the success of Agile practices. Don't just keep learning in the back of your mind—bring it to the forefront. This chapter stands as a reminder that the Agile approach already offers many learning practices and mechanisms. Are all of them being used to their best advantage, to serve your team and your business?

See the world through "learning is the bottleneck" glasses. It can significantly reduce the chance of cargo culting[8] Agile practices and focus your efforts for maximum effectiveness.

---

8. During World War II, a number of airbases were built on remote tropical islands inhabited by preindustrial societies. During the war, soldiers built airfields and control towers and engaged in various activities that resulted in large airplanes full of cargo landing and discharging their contents. The native inhabitants shared this cargo. After the war, the soldiers departed, and no more cargo was available to the natives. So they adopted, as best they could, the superficial form of airstrips, control towers, and ritual behaviors intended to induce the return of planes full of cargo. A cargo cult is any group that adopts form instead of substance and believes that doing so will bring about a desired result.

Chapter 2

PERSONAL AGILITY FOR POTENT AGILE ADOPTION

By Amr Elssamadisy and Ashley Johnson[1]

As Agile becomes better known, many troubled teams are deciding to adopt Agile practices to help fix their problems. Most clients seeking our help with their Agile adoption want to start by pursuing process and tools. The more dysfunctional their teams, the less tolerance they have for focusing on individuals and their interactions.

The most effective teams—those that show a tremendous improvement in productivity and value to their organizations—have individual team members who take ownership, act responsibly, and are disciplined in recognizing and responding to change at a personal level. These individuals adopt Agile practices because they have made a conscious decision to do so. They do what it takes to make things work.

This chapter suggests that a team that has individual members that freely commit to the way they work and then take personal responsibility are able to adopt Agile practices that significantly improve their productivity and increase the value they give the organization.

WHY ADOPT AGILE PRACTICES?

Why do teams adopt Agile software development practices? The answer varies depending on the situation. They may have adopted Agile methods to reduce bug count, improve time to market, or reduce the overall cost of development. Or, maybe there was a vague "something is seriously wrong" feeling in the way they were producing software, and they or someone in

---

1. This article was originally published in the summer 2007 issue of the *Agile Journal* www.agilejournal.com/articles/articles/personal-agility-for-potent-agile-adoption.html.

their organization read about this newfangled technique called Agile that is supposed to help. Or, increasingly, as Agile becomes mainstream, someone in management thinks it is a good idea and has mandated that the department or organization adopt Agile. Management was trying to help and not hinder software development in some way. All these reasons have a common thread of wanting to make software development better and ultimately deliver more value to the organization.

What Is a Successful Adoption?

We adopt Agile development practices to build better software and deliver more value to the organization. Is this adoption always successful? Well, that would depend on the definition of "successful," wouldnt it? If successful means "we are practicing one or more Agile development practices," chances are, most adoptions are successful. But that is not a very satisfying (or useful) definition. We really should go back to the original goals that we used to justify adopting a new software methodology. That is, have we decreased our defect rate? Have we reduced our time to market? Have we become more productive? Are we more productive at creating better software that is providing increased value to our organization? That should be the measure of successful Agile adoption, and it will be the definition of success used here.

Problem: Many Unsuccessful Agile Adoptions

Unfortunately, fewer and fewer Agile adoption efforts are successful by our definition. In the early days of the Agile development community, frequent reports of up to five times more productivity gains were reported. These teams made progress in leaps and bounds and delivered software that truly helped their organizations move forward. Why aren't all teams seeing this improvement?

Cause: It Depends

So why aren't many teams seeing productivity improvements upon adopting Agile practices? Why are they inefficient or unsuccessful? Is there some secret? Is there yet another practice that only the successful know? Well, unfortunately, the answer is no. The causes are as varied as the teams. There is no one solution to our problems. But there is a commonality that we find in all successful teams; their members take ownership for tasks and do what needs to be done to make them work.

THE RESPONSIBILITY PROCESS™ MODEL

Now well switch gears for a bit and come back later to tie the different ideas together.

Figure 2-1 represents an invaluable model in helping individuals *become* agile rather than simply going through the motions of *acting* agile.[2] It explains the mental process that we, as human beings, go through when we avoid responsibility and destroy the ownership behavior that is essential to self-organizing teams.

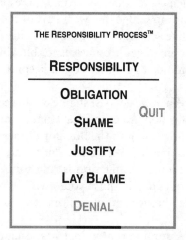

THE RESPONSIBILITY PROCESS™

RESPONSIBILITY

OBLIGATION

SHAME   QUIT

JUSTIFY

LAY BLAME

DENIAL

Responsibility Process™ and the Responsibility Process™ graphic are trademarks of Christopher Avery and Bill McCarley. For more information, please visit www.ChristopherAvery.com.

Figure 2–1 The Responsibility Process™ model

Imagine that youre leaving home for a critical meeting. You're not late yet, but you have no time to lose. You grab your laptop bag, reach for your keys, and…they aren't there! What's the first thing that crosses your mind? "Who moved my keys?" Or, "Honey, did you take my keys?" Regardless of the exact words, most of us instinctively look for someone else to blame when something goes wrong. This behavior is a strategy that we use unconsciously to avoid taking responsibility for our situation. (In the diagram, you are on the next to bottom behavior—laying blame.)

---

2. See the research of Christopher Avery and Bill McCarley. According to them, this instinctive response crosses age, gender, and race.

Now imagine that you arrived five minutes later for a meeting. As you walk in the door, what do you say? "Sorry I'm late. I lost my keys." Or perhaps, "Sorry I'm late. Traffic was bad." Why not stop at "Sorry I'm late." Why continue with an explanation? According to Avery's research, the next instinctive response we have once we escape blame is to justify. It's not my problem—the universe is at fault.

When we get past blame and justification, the next natural response is shame. When coming from blame or justification, we externalized the problem—we believed we had no responsibility for it. When we get to shame, we acknowledge that were part of the problem—but instead of taking constructive action, we beat ourselves up. Regardless of the words out of our mouth, were flogging ourselves for blowing it again. This is not a resourceful state of mind; it's another detour keeping us from responsibility.

When we get past shame, we have one more way to avoid responsibility—obligation. An example: "Honey, I'm sorry I won't be home for dinner tonight. I have to join the boss for dinner with a client." No, you don't *have* to go to dinner with the boss. You're choosing to. You own your life. You make your choices. Obligation is rule-following behavior—using explicit or implicit rules to relinquish your ownership of your life. This doesn't mean you should go home for dinner. It means you should be conscious of your choice.

Assuming that we get past each of these potholes, we find ourselves at responsibility. This is a state of mind where we take ownership for our situation. If things aren't as we prefer, we take action to change them. This state is the starting point for personal agility.

I Want to Be More Responsible. How Can I Do It?

So you've decided you want to model responsible behavior. Now what? There are three keys to adopting this process in your life. First, you must have an intention to act from a position of responsibility. Avery and McCarley's research suggests that the natural response is not responsibility; the intention alone isn't enough. You have to learn new behaviors/responses. Therefore, the second step is to become aware of when you are coming from any of the nonresponsible states. For example, if you hear yourself saying, "I have to…" you are probably in the obligation state. Third, when you find yourself in one of the nonresponsible situations, you must confront yourself on this issue. It is as simple and as difficult as this. [3]

---

3. To readmore about the Responsibility Process model and its effect on teams, we refer you to Teamwork is an Individual Skill by Christopher Avery.

My Teammates Are Stuck in Blame. What Shall I Do?

One interesting aspect of the Responsibility Process™ model is that it can only be self-applied—period. If your teammate (or worse, your spouse) is stuck in blame, he does have a problem. However, if you point it out to your teammate, he now has two problems—and *you* are the most immediate of those problems.

If you want others around you to be responsible, you can do two things: 1) model responsible behavior and 2) share the model with them, but not in moments of conflict. The rest is really out of your control; change comes from within.

POTENT AGILE

Now let us come back to Agile development. How does the Responsibility Process™ model fit in with Agile development? Specifically, can it help our Agile adoptions be successful? If so, how?

Successful Teams Have Responsible Members

One of the principles in the Agile Manifesto is the following:

> *The best architectures, requirements, and designs emerge from self-organizing teams.*

Consider teams you've worked with, from dismal to hyperproductive. Would you agree that massively productive teams have members that embody responsible behavior, that take ownership and drive to the goal? Would you agree that mediocre teams consistently display one or more of the responsibility killers listed earlier? (This, by the way, is completely independent of Agile practices and methods.)

The most successful teams that we've worked with have had members who have done what was needed to get done to meet their goals. The team members understood the team goals and what success meant to them and their customer. They realized that success means accepting failures and learning from them, so they were comfortable with sharing failures and asking for help. The team members were individually aware of their true progress and were willing to step out of their comfort zone to help others. The team members demonstrated an ownership mentality toward the shared team goals.

Recognizing and Responding to Change Requires Responsibility

Here's another of the principles in the Agile Manifesto:

> *At regular intervals, the team reflects on how to become more effective, then tunes and adjusts its behavior accordingly.*

Consider teams you've worked on that successfully adopted one or more development practices. Did those practices just fall in place, or were they tuned for your particular environment? Who tuned them? Was the tuning "mandated," or was it taken up by one or more individuals of the team? If you decided to write tests first as a team, didn't that require discipline from each team member to do so effectively?

Recognizing changes as they happen is at the core of successful Agile development. Responding to change is often difficult and painful. Successful changes require the individuals on the team to step up, propose solutions, act on those solutions, and frequently admit that those solutions were not effective and need to be changed. Teams who are successful at tuning and adjusting behavior do so at the individual level. Team members are responsible. They take ownership and act accordingly.

Successful Agile Development Begins with the Individual

Self-directed teams aligned to a clear goal are the essence of agile behavior and the engine behind the stunning results that some teams claim for Agile. We believe that individual responsibility, as defined by Avery, is a prerequisite to such agile interactions. That is, responsibility, as defined by the Responsibility Process™ model, is necessary (but not sufficient) for successful Agile software development.

PERSONAL AGILITY

The Responsibility Process™ model is one tool that we've found useful in helping teams achieve success—but it is only one of many. It doesn't have much to do with software development per se. It is a life skill that can be used virtually anywhere. It is not our model, nor are any of the other tools in the personal agility toolset—they come predominantly from the psychology, business, and management worlds. The works of Peter Senge, Franklin Covey, and others help you attain personal skills that make the tools more effective. None of them are useful until you take 100 percent responsibility for yourself.

All these tools focus on the individual. And this, if we go back to the Agile Manifesto's first line, is the core of Agile development:

Individuals and Interactions over Process and Tools

The values and principles in the Agile Manifesto were not "made up;" they were reverse-engineered from several years of successful development using lightweight practices and methods to deliver working software that met the user's needs. The Agile Manifesto can be seen as a set of observations and principles that have been found to be a common thread in writing successful software.

Personal agility brings back the focus on individuals. Individual responsibility is the bedrock of personal agility. Without team members being responsible, there is little chance for Agile development practices (or any practices) to have a significant positive effect upon a team.

Observe teams at your organization. Which ones are the most successful? Do their team members act from responsibility? We expect you will be able to validate what we have presented here with your own teams.

THEORY TO PRACTICE

As you work your way through this book and create an Agile adoption strategy and then choose practices for you or your team to adopt, keep the Responsibility Process™ model and Personal Agility in the back of your head. Ultimately, your team/organization/enterprise can only adopt practices at a personal level. You can, however, help create an environment within your sphere of influence to help others. You also can lead by example. In the end, you and your team will have to make a decision for yourselves, individually, of which practices to adopt.

Part 2

Crafting an Agile Adoption Strategy

So you are interested in Agile development. Why? Chances are, you want to improve your software development process. Why is that? Many will answer "to build better software." But why do you want to build better software? In the Agile community, our focus is on the customer. We want our software to deliver more value to our customers.

In this part, I will focus on the idea of delivering more value to customers. Not all customers value the same things. What does your customer value? Chapter 3, "Business Value," introduces several common business values that customers find important. After reading that chapter and doing its exercises, you will have a solid understanding of what your customer values. This knowledge will help you choose the practices to adopt to deliver the most value to your customer.

The focus of this book is on adoption. Not everyone will adopt new development practices to improve the current status. If you are like me and only look for new solutions when there is a problem, then Chapter 4, "Smells," is for you. Read this chapter to get an idea of what things smell like when a software development process goes wrong. Do the exercises at the end of this chapter in preparation for creating an adoption strategy that will alleviate your team's pains.

The final chapter in Part 1, Chapter 5, titled "Adopting Agile Practices," shows you how to use business value and smells to successfully adopt a set of Agile practices that will address issues that your customers value. At the end of this chapter, the exercises will lead you to create an initial, prioritized list of practices to adopt that are tailored for your environment.

Chapter 3

BUSINESS VALUE

Delivering value to the customer is the main driver for all Agile development practices. How many of us know concretely what specific values are most important to our customer's business? How many of us know what business value[1] is delivered by the software development practice we use? In this and the following chapter, I will show you how you can answer these questions and use those answers to decide what practices you should adopt.

In this chapter, you and I will examine different areas of business value as they relate to Agile practices. The remainder of the chapter covers the most common business values and their descriptions. Read them to get an overview of what customers find valuable.

The exercises at the end of this chapter are a necessity. If you really want to adopt the correct Agile practices, do the exercises. They will lead you to discover what business values your customers find important. Share these findings with your colleagues—being aware of business value is a necessity for every team member.

REDUCE TIME TO MARKET

Reducing time to market of developing software brings more value to customers because they can begin to use the product earlier. A company producing the software can start to earn money earlier if it is a commercial product. This is straightforward.

---

1. Here, business value means software that delivers value to your business. This does not mean that this is only good for corporate applications. Scientific programs have a "business" of that particular science.

Furthermore, consider this: Would your customers find any value in partially delivered functionality (for example, two out of a possible five use cases)? Often your customers will be able to get some early use out of a subset of functionality that you can deliver early rather than rolling out everything in a single release. So not only is the overall reduction in time to market valuable, but frequent, incremental releases can increase business value and utility.

INCREASE PRODUCT UTILITY (VALUE TO MARKET)

Software development involves taking abstract requirements and building a system to satisfy those requirements. Going from the abstract concepts to running software is a type of invention—the development team comes up with a solution to meet the business need. However, there are multiple possible solutions that can conceivably meet the business needs. Which one is best? Practices that help make this decision correctly create business value.

So how do you determine which is a better solution than the other? Ultimately, it is the most useful software to the customers. Does it help them do their jobs better? Practices that help the customers determine what the better solution is and communicate that to the team correctly will deliver business value as well.

Finally, increasing product utility is related to reducing time to market. Products that get to market faster have the potential of getting market feedback earlier. So there is an opportunity for the team to increase the product's usefulness to the customer by frequently incorporating concrete feedback.

INCREASE QUALITY TO MARKET

Quality to market has to do with issues such as defects, usability, and scalability. These are probably the most visible issues to your software development team. Practices that help improve these issues increase the business value delivered.

INCREASE FLEXIBILITY

How easy is it to respond to changes in business direction? This is the business value behind the buzzword Agile. It is an increasingly important issue in today's markets. So, for example, if tax regulations change in one state where your financial software is being used, you need to be able to modify your software to comply.

This value is not always directly visible to the customer. The lack of this factor appears in other business values like slow time to market or low quality to market. So why do I describe this as a separate value? The notion of flexibility—of being agile—is one that more and more businesses are aware of directly. Customers want to know about your ability to respond to changes they request.

INCREASE VISIBILITY

This is the customer's ability to see the true state of the project as it progresses. This is important because it allows the customer to steer the software project and manage risks and expectations.

Lack of visibility results in the customer's surprise and disappointment when a project doesn't meet its deadline or doesn't deliver the functionality sought. This, in turn, engenders lack of trust, blame, and CYA[2] cultures.

On the other hand, software practices that increase visibility will allow customers to get the most benefit throughout the project development cycle and engender trust and cooperation with customers.

REDUCE COST

Faster, better, cheaper. That's what we all must do to survive. We've already covered faster (time to market) and better (quality and value to market). This business value is about building the system for less (cheaper).

Some of the costs associated with software development include man-hours to build the system, maintenance of the system over time, and hardware as well as software platform costs. Practices that reduce any or all of these costs without sacrificing quality reduce the overall cost of the system.

Another way to reduce cost is to write less code. The 80/20 rule says that roughly 20 percent of the product is used 80 percent of the time. Practices that help a team build only what is needed in a prioritized manner greatly reduce the cost of the product and provide business value to the customer.

---

2. For readers not familiar with this acronym, it is used to indicate a state where someone is focused on avoiding personal blame instead of providing value to his team.

INCREASE PRODUCT LIFETIME

Longer product lifetime directly affects the product's return on investment (ROI). Every year that your product is productively in the market, it makes money for your company. As maintenance cost goes to zero, the investment made in the product approaches being passive. Unfortunately, software tends to age poorly. Maintenance becomes more difficult, and it acquires inertia. Companies that support multiple aging versions of a product spend great effort keeping those products alive, and then they finally have to discontinue support because of the cost.

For many product companies, this is an important business value to address. Many of the Agile development practices will improve the maintainability and flexibility of the code base that, in turn, increases the ability of the development team to keep the product alive. These practices that directly and indirectly increase product lifetime have business value to the customer.

BUSINESS VALUES ARE ORGANIZATIONAL GOALS

Business values are not necessarily confined to those listed here; these are common ones found in many, but not all, organizations. For example, if your organization is in academia, you will probably have some goals listed here and others that are not. The important thing is to *know* your organization's goals and communicate those goals to the team. Those goals are the ultimate drivers and tests for your Agile adoption strategy.

THEORY TO PRACTICE: DETERMINING YOUR ORGANIZATION'S BUSINESS VALUES

Answer the following questions to get a realistic understanding of what business values are important to your customers and organization. It will be to your advantage to get others in your organization to independently go through the answers and compare them later. Once gathered, share with others—there is a good chance they are not aware of this information.

- Which business value factors are most important to your clients? Rank them.
- Invite your business customers to rank the importance of the business value factors. How do their rankings compare to yours? What might you do differently based on the businesss rankings?

- What other business value factors are key in your business? After answering this yourself, ask your business customers. (Some examples are "personal growth" and "supporting open-source development.")
- Given your awareness of business value, are you focused on issues that increase business value? Are members of your team aware of where business value really lies? If not, then by all means, spread the word!
- Given the information you discovered earlier about business value factors in your organization, how can you adjust your practices to deliver greater value to your customers?
- For each business value, come up with at least one way you can take a measurement of progress made. That is, if you are to implement a practice to improve a particular business value, you need to take a periodic reading to verify that the practice is working. This does not have to be quantitative. It may be qualitative in nature. Just make it as simple as possible. For example, if you want to take a measurement to reduce cost, a simple (and rough) reading would be the number of hours put in for a major release.

Chapter 4

SMELLS

The Agile community has adopted the word smell as an indicator of something that has gone wrong. Smells are indicators that business value is not being delivered where it should be. They are a useful concept when deciding what issues need to be addressed and in what order. It is more natural for many to recognize and respond to painful issues (smells) than to put in the effort to improve working processes.

The relationship between smells and business value is not necessarily a one-to-one relationship. Every smell is a symptom of one more business value that can be improved. Conversely, every major business value that can be improved will cause one or more smells to be present.

In this chapter, I introduce two types of smells. Business smells are smells that can be perceived by the customer. Process smells, on the other hand, are only visible to the development team and not to the customer. Even though they are not visible to the customer, process smells have a direct effect on the business value delivered.

The remainder of this chapter contains a listing and description of several business smells and process smells. These are your indicators that something is not right with the development process. They are good starting points in determining what practices should be adopted—namely, those that will be effective in removing the smells. Read through the smells in this chapter and see if you recognize any of them within your organization. I won't cover the solutions to these smells in this chapter; don't worry, the rest of the book addresses which particular Agile practices address these problems.

As always, please take the time to do the exercises at the end of the chapter to tie the ideas in this chapter into your organization's environment.

BUSINESS SMELLS

Business smells are the flip side of the business value coin. They are the pains that a customer experiences when the software does not meet the need. The following sections cover several common smells and their descriptions. The descriptions are written from the development organization's perspective.

Quality Delivered to Customer Is Unacceptable

Our customers are not happy with the quality of our product. In fact, we have a hard time getting them to upgrade to our latest versions. They have, unfortunately, learned by experience that upgrading to the latest version means having to deal with several bugs we didn't catch. We are losing customers and getting a bad reputation in the market. We have to be able to deliver better-quality code. It is beginning to affect our bottom line.[1]

Delivering New Features to Customer Takes Too Long

We are having trouble adding new features that our customers request. It takes too long to add a new feature, fully test it, and then deploy it to our customers. Competitors have added new features faster than we can keep up— we are losing the race. Our release cycle is long because of many issues that just can't be changed.

- Features rely on expert resources that are bottlenecked.
- The testing cycle takes significant time.
- Features required were unforeseen and are hard to add given the existing architecture.

Features Are Not Used by Customer

Our studies show us that many of the new features we add are not used by our customers and are ignored. This has happened because of several compound reasons.

- Customers didn't know what they really needed at the requirement phase; therefore, we built the system upon the wrong assumptions.
- Our organization's marketing department sometimes proxies for customers. Requirements from marketing are just a forecast, and the forecast isn't always on track.

---

1. Net income is equal to the income that a firm has after subtracting costs and expenses from the total revenue. Net income is informally called the bottom line because it is typically found on the last line of a company's income statement.

- Some features are used much less frequently than we anticipated. We believe this indicates that our priorities are not in line with the customer's priorities.
- Developers have been known to add features that they were sure would be useful but were not.
- Requirements changed.

Software Is Not Useful to Customer

Our software has not really helped our customer do their work in a more efficient manner. In fact, we are flooded with usability complaints. Key functional areas are incomplete. This is not our fault—we built what we were told to build in the requirements. To be fair, it is not our client's fault either. She told us what the problem was. Neither of us knew how to solve the problem completely when we set the requirements in the beginning. We only learned later, but then it was too late—we were already committed to the requirements we had set earlier.

We now have a system that we've spent time and effort building and for which our clients have paid. The end users are frustrated and see our software as a burden rather than a useful tool.

Software Is Too Expensive to Build

The software process is expensive. The costs for building a successful project involve a large number of highly paid professionals over several months (sometimes several years). The value returned on each of these projects does not always validate the investment we put into building them. We are losing much of our business to developers overseas, where the cost is significantly cheaper (but this comes with its own set of serious problems).

Us Versus Them

Those customers don't know what they want! Those developers never give us what we need when we need it. The testers are not team players—they just don't understand how crucial it is to deliver on time. Marketing always promises things that we cannot possibly deliver. Do any of these sentiments sound familiar?

Software development involves an incredibly diverse set of people. If they are blaming each other, problems are exacerbated. Each subteam—the developers, the customers, the testers, and so on—will optimize for its team and not the business value(s) that the organization needs. This wreaks havoc with the organization's goals and achievements. Us Versus Them at any level indicates that there are communication barriers and that business value is not on the radar. The most successful teams, Agile or traditional, have a "whole team" mentality.

Customer Asks for Everything Including the Kitchen Sink

The relationship between customers and software development organizations is not always based on trust. In fact, the typical situation today is that the requirements are done upfront, and there is an official sign-off as a contract. Any new requirement changes must be put through an extensive change-management process that puts an extremely high barrier on change requirements. The end product may satisfy the requirements "by the letter of the law" but may not meet the customer's *real* needs.

Customers understand this. Therefore, they ask for everything they can possibly think of because they know they have one chance of getting it right. This smell indicates that we are not giving the customers exactly what they need and not giving them the opportunity to learn, refine, and really find out what they need and want. In the end, all participants pay dearly. Business smells such as Software Is Too Expensive to Build and Features Are Not Used by Customer result because there is not enough feedback for the proper system to be built.

PROCESS SMELLS

Process smells are symptoms of internal software process problems. They are invisible to the customer. They are indirectly related to business value because software process problems negatively affect the business value delivered to the customer.

Process smells are generally easier to diagnose than business smells. But because they are not directly related to business value, they should not be the main drivers of adoption. If you find one of these smells, relate it back to its business value(s) to ensure that you address the smells with the most important business values for your organization.

Customer? What Customer?—Direct and Regular Customer Input Is Unrealistic

Scenario 1: We are a product company. We do not have real customers available to us. Our marketing team is our pseudo-customer. They are separate and have their own work to do. They cannot (as in *will not*) spare the time to be part of the development team. So they work with managers who in turn work with their underlings who work with us, the development team, to build the correct functionality.

Scenario 2: Our customers are the business members of the company; we are their support. They do not have time to work with us. Every so often, they spend a little time with us, and we take notes. We have their contact information and are free to contact them by e-mail and have regular meetings. This is good enough. Our customers are busy people, and it is our job to build the software.

In both of these scenarios, there is little customer input. This is a process smell that leads to the business smells: Features Are Not Used by Customer, Software Is Not Useful to Customer, and Software Is a Burden to Use. That is, to solve the right problem, frequent customer input and feedback are required.

Management Is Surprised—Lack of Visibility

Management has little visibility into the *real* progress of a project's development. Development teams are optimistic. Despite the fact that several pieces have had problems, they are sure they will be able to pull things together at the last minute with heroic efforts. Unfortunately, the details of what might go wrong are not only unknown to management—the development team members themselves aren't quite sure. *Integration* is coming up in a few months' time. The development team knows it will be painful but not exactly how painful.

Of course, when the actual deadline rolls around and the team can no longer deny that the deadline will be missed, it is too late for management to respond effectively. This happens all too often, and management has learned to buffer any promises made by project teams; a lack of trust evolves.

Bottlenecked Resources—Software Practitioners Are Members of Multiple Teams Concurrently

To produce the highest quality software, all members of a development team are encouraged to specialize their skill sets. The side effect of this is that these skills are almost always needed in more than one place at a time. A few key practitioners become bottlenecks in the progress of more than one project. It is also difficult to move members of the development teams to other projects.

This results in members of the organization being assigned to multiple development teams concurrently. That's the nature of the beast when you are in a large organization and there are multiple projects to complete—isn't it?

Significant research shows that multitasking is significantly less efficient than single-tasking. Working on multiple projects concurrently is a much less productive use of time. If time to market and ability to respond quickly to changes are important, you must remove these bottlenecks.

Churning Projects

Projects miss their deadlines multiple times. One deadline is missed, then another, then another. Major design decisions did not foresee issues that later surfaced. The project churns as several attempts are made to deliver useful, high-quality software to the business. Sometimes these projects are discontinued but only after a significant investment. Other times, the project churns away until, finally, a working system is built.

Hundreds (Possibly Thousands) of Bugs in Bug Tracker

When a bug is found, it is entered into our bug-tracking tool and then prioritized. We resolve all showstopper bugs and most high-priority bugs before release. Anything of lower priority goes to bug purgatory and stays forever. Sometimes in a new release, a portion of the medium-level bugs are addressed—but many times they are stale by that point.

A large set of bugs in a bug tracker indicates wasted work. The effort is made to find, locate, and identify these bugs—but no business value is delivered until that bug is solved, integrated, and released to the customer. A large number of bugs in the bug tracking system is a direct indicator of a significant investment in work that is never released to the customer and thus has zero value.

"Hardening" Phase Needed at End of Release Cycle

Before releasing code, there needs to be a period where no "new feature" check-ins are made to the code base. The code base must be frozen, branched, and closely tested. Only high-level bugs can be fixed, and each one must be approved before doing so. After a sufficient time, typically anywhere between one to three iterations, the code is released.

This is a good practice, right? Why is it in the "Smells" chapter? If iterations are done properly—that is, at the end of each iteration, a working, integrated, tested system is demonstrated—there should be no need for the hardening phase. The hardening phase indicates that our iterations are not true iterations but are merely time blocks of work. Hardening iterations indicate that the previous iterations let defects go unfound and unaddressed.

Integration Is Infrequent (Usually Because It Is Painful)

Integration is done a few iterations before releasing because it is a difficult and time-consuming task. Specialized teams work on the different parts of the application. Documentation and design documents are created up-front to ensure that the parts fit together at release time. Of course, they are rarely (if ever) integrated smoothly.

This seems to be the natural way of building applications for most development teams. Although it would be nice to integrate and test the fully working system, it is just not possible. Many of the parts that the teams work on will not integrate until the very end. The actual build and link time takes such a large effort that it is felt it would be too time-consuming to do regularly. What can be gained by integrating more frequently? Why is this a smell? The lack of integration results in a significant amount of untested code. Integration is key to the feedback cycle. Without full integration, a significant number of errors, miscommunications, and misconceptions remain undiscovered until the end of the release cycle. This inhibits the team's ability to evolve the system as a coherent whole and accurately determine project progress.

PAIN AS AN INCENTIVE

Smells are a good way to diagnose what is wrong with the current way things are done. They are often the driving reason for process improvement initiatives. The fact that you have this book in your hands means that you probably are aware of one or more of these smells in your organization and are looking at Agile practices to address them. This is a valid, and the most common, reason to look for another way of doing things. Smells are not, however, organizational goals the way business values are, so be careful of focusing on the wrong thing.

THEORY TO PRACTICE: WHAT SMELLS CAN YOU FIND?

Answer the following questions to discover, understand, and rank the different smells in your organization.

1. Find as many business smells as you can in your organization. A good place to start would be with your customers, customer support staff, and marketing staff. They know what is wrong. Rank these smells according to their importance and the amount of pain they cause.

2. Relate those smells to business values. Are they the same business values you identified in the previous chapter as ones that are important to your customer?

3. Find and rank as many process smells as you can. Relate them to business values.

4. Is your smell ranking different from your business value ranking? For example, is the most painful smell related to the most important business value? What does this indicate?

5. Based on your environment, would it be more useful to address value or smells? Why?

6. Rerank your smells with the information you have just gathered. Is it different from your original rankings? If so, what changed?

Chapter 5

ADOPTING AGILE PRACTICES

So far you have read about business value and smells. You have also done the exercises at the end of each chapter and come up with a prioritized list of business values and a prioritized list of smells that need fixing. If you have not done so yet, please stop now and go back and do so. Armed with an understanding of your customers' priorities and the main pains your company is experiencing, you are ready to determine what practices you should consider adopting to alleviate those pains and get the most value for your efforts.

In this chapter, I will give you direction on how to go about successfully choosing which practices to consider adopting. I'll also ask you to benchmark your work—even if you just do it subjectively—so you can be "agile" about your adoption. This is, however, only advice on how to come up with your own priorities and your own list of practices to adopt. If you are looking for a prescription—do practice A, then B, but not C—you won't find it here. (And if you do find it elsewhere, my advice to you is not to trust it.)

THE PRACTICES

The bulk of this book contains patterns of Agile practice adoption—that is, Agile practices written up in pattern format with a focus on adoption. In this chapter, your goal is to choose the practices that fit your organization's context. That comes down to relying on the work you've done in the previous chapter in prioritizing your business values and smells and using it to choose which practices to adopt to improve your business values and reduce your smells.

PATTERNS OF AGILE PRACTICE TO BUSINESS VALUE MAPPINGS

Let's start with the meat of the chapter. Figures 5-1 through 5-7 provide diagrams for each business value and the practices that improve that business value. These mappings, like all the patterns in this book, are built by aggregating experiences from several Agile adoption efforts. Each of these practices corresponds to a pattern that is documented later in this book. Don't worry if you don't know exactly what some of these practices are at this point in time.

Lets examine Figure 5-1 to understand how to read these business value charts. Arrows between practices indicate dependencies; therefore, Refactoring depends on Automated Developer Tests. Also vertical ordering is important; the higher up a practice is, the more effective it is for the business value. Therefore, Iterations are more effective than Automated Developer Tests, and Test-First Development is more effective than Test-Last Development with respect to decreasing the time to market. Use these diagrams to determine what practices to consider adopting. Take the suggestions accompanying each diagram as just that—suggestions. All the practices in each diagram positively affect that business value, and you may discover upon reading the details of the suggested practices that they do not apply in your particular context.

Time to Market

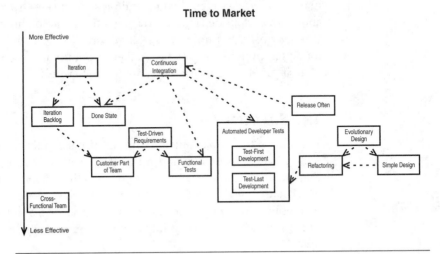

Figure 5–1   Time to Market practices

Small steps and failing fast are the most effective methods to get things out quickly. Weed out defects early because the earlier you find them, the less they will cost, and you won't be building on a crumbling foundation. That is why Iteration and Continuous Integration lead the practices that most positively affect time to market. They are both, however, dependent on other practices. Consider starting with automated tests and the Iteration trio—Iteration, Done State, and Iteration Backlog—when you want to improve time to market.

Figure 5-2 gives the practices that increase product utility. By far, the most effective practice is Customers Part of Team. Go there first. Then consider functional tests if you are already doing automated developer tests or an iteration ending with a demo.

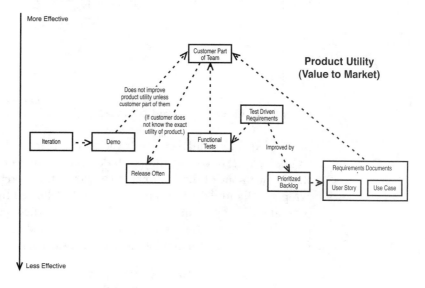

Figure 5–2   Product Utility practices

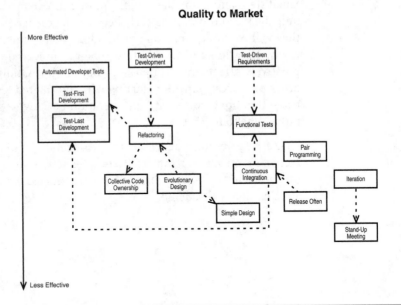

Figure 5–3   Quality to Market practices

Although quality to market test-driven development and test-driven require-ments are king, of course, they both depend on other practices. So consider starting with one of the Automated Developer tests (preferably test-first de-velopment) and Pair Programming, closely followed by Refactoring. Pair programming helps you come up to speed with these particularly difficult practices. Once you are comfortable with automated developer tests, aim for full-fledged test-driven development and consider functional tests.

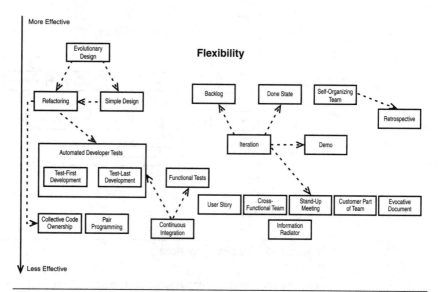

Figure 5–4   Flexibility practices

There are two general types of flexibility in software development: team flexibility and technical flexibility. Team flexibility is the team's ability to recognize and respond to changes that happen. For a team to respond to changes by changing the software, there needs to be technical flexibility. Therefore, you need both team flexibility and technical flexibility. Start with Automated Developer Tests, a self-organizing team, and the trio of Iteration, Done State, and Backlog. The testing gets you on your way to technical flexibility, and the remaining practices enable your team's flexibility.

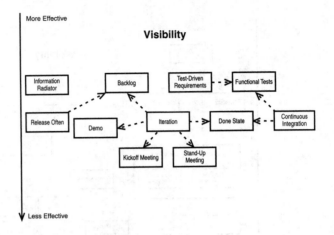

Figure 5-5 Visibility practices

The backlog and information radiators are your first easy steps toward increased visibility. Depending on your need for increasing visibility, you can take an easy route and consider iterations with a done state and a demo or a more difficult but effective route with functional tests and test-driven requirements.

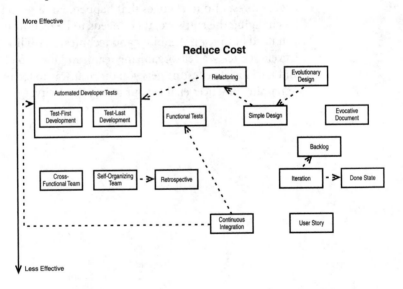

Figure 5-6 Reduce Cost practices

You can reduce cost in two ways: make the code easier to maintain and write less code—that is, code for the most important features first. Automated tests, followed by refactoring, simple design, and evolutionary design, are your path toward reducing the cost of maintenance. A backlog, iteration, and done state reduce the amount of code written.

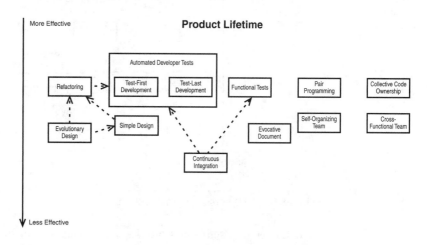

Figure 5–7   Product Lifetime practices

Product lifetime is inversely proportional to the cost of software maintenance. There are two ways that we know how to reduce maintenance costs: 1) build a safety net of tests that allow changes to the software system and reduce the cost of change and 2) spread the knowledge of the design of the software system. Automated developer tests are your key to (1), while pair programming and collective code ownership are good starts for (2).

Patterns of Agile Practice to Smell Mappings

There are two types of smells: business smells and process smells. The business smells are inverses of business values, and their patterns of Agile practice mappings are identical:

- Quality Delivered to Customer Is Unacceptable: Quality to Market
- Delivering New Features to Customer Takes Too Long: Time to Market
- Features Are Not Used by Customer: Product Utility
- Software Is Not Useful to Customer: Product Utility
- Software Is Too Expensive: Reduce Cost

The remaining smells have their own mappings to patterns of Agile practices (see Figures 5-8 through 5-15).

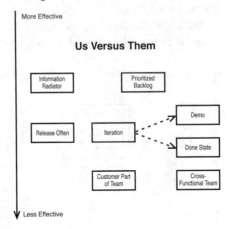

Figure 5–8   Us Versus Them practices

The Us Versus Them smell can best be alleviated by having frequent conversations about the true nature of the project. Start with increasing visibility by creating information radiators that show the key points in your development. Create a prioritized backlog by involving the whole development team—including the customers. Use these practices to increase visibility and build trust. When you are ready, take it further and build more trust by delivering often by adopting the iteration, demo, and done state trio.

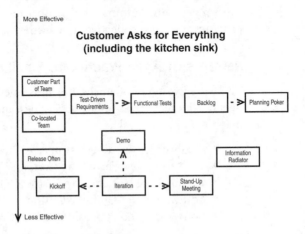

Figure 5–9   Customer Asks for Everything practices

Understand that when the customer asks for everything, it is a symptom of lack of trust from the customer that the features will be delivered promptly and a legacy of change-management barriers in traditional development. The best way to address this issue is to bring the customers in as part of the development team. Have them build the Backlog with the teams input and be responsible for its prioritization.

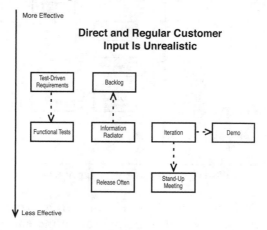

Figure 5–10   Direct and Regular Customer Input Is Unrealistic practices

If direct input from the customer is not possible, mitigate this problem by reducing the number of communication errors. You can do this by building functional tests and slowly working toward test-driven requirements, where the customer's requirements document becomes an executable specification. This particular practice will take a long time to adopt correctly, so start early and be patient. In the meantime, create a backlog and start delivering work incrementally, with iterations ending with a demo.

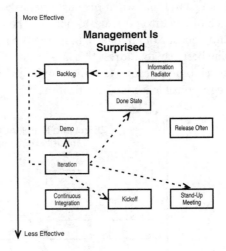

Figure 5–11   Management Is Surprised—Lack of Visibility practices

To keep management from being surprised, you need to do two things: 1) build your application incrementally from end to end and 2) communicate your true progress. Address 1) by defining a done state that is as close to deployment as possible and then working in iterations. Communicate your true progress by working through information radiators showing your true progress and using a demo at the end of every iteration.

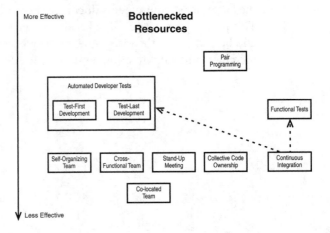

Figure 5–12   Bottlenecked Resources—*Software Practitioners Are Members of Multiple Teams Concurrently* practices

Bottlenecked resources happen because of specialization. Pair programming is your single most effective method to share knowledge and spread the specialization. This, in turn, allows more than one person to address issues that were previously the domain of a single expert. Automated developer tests help this in another way—they allow people to work in code they do not know well and rely on a safety net of tests to tell them if they have broken any previously working code. This should be your second step toward alleviating resource bottlenecks.

Projects churn when there is no clear prioritization. Prioritize requirements by creating and maintaining a backlog. To make sure that the backlog is an accurate reflection of customer needs, make your customers part of your team and put together a cross-functional team that can build those requirements end to end. This will give you and your customers a better understanding of requirements, their priorities, and a feedback loop to make course corrections quickly.

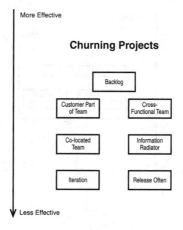

Figure 5–13 Churning Projects practices

Hundreds of bugs need to be reduced. Start with automated developer tests supported by pair programming to reduce the number of bugs you are introducing and start building a safety net of tests. Then work with iterations with a done state to find as many bugs as possible. Don't put off painful issues such as integration. Fix things early.

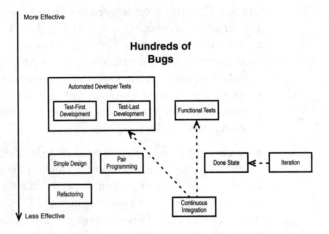

Figure 5–14   Hundreds (Possibly Thousands) of Bugs *in Bug Tracker* practices

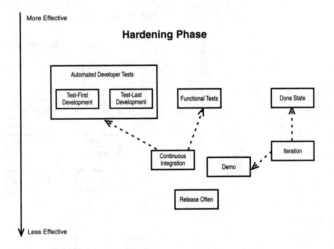

Figure 5–15   Hardening Phase *Needed at End of Release Cycle* practices

If you have a hardening phase, you've let a significant number of defects accumulate. Stop doing what you've been doing and add tests as you develop code via automated developer tests. Choose a good done state—one that takes you as close to deployment in every iteration as possible—to weed out those difficult-to-find bugs early.

CRAFTING YOUR AGILE ADOPTION STRATEGY

You can use the information you have gathered so far about business value and smells to determine which practices you should consider adopting.

- **Choose practices based solely on business value delivered.** In this scenario, you are not suffering from any severe pains. You just want to improve your software development process by increasing the business value that your team delivers. Use the Business Value to Practice mapping in Figures 5-1 through 5-7 to choose practices that most strongly affect your organization's business values.
- **Choose practices to alleviate smells that have been prioritized by business value.** This technique focuses on alleviating pains that you have while keeping business value in mind. Smells are prioritized according to your customers business values. Then, from the prioritized smell list, you choose the appropriate practices to adopt with the help of the Smell to Practice mappings shown in Figures 5-8 through 5-15.
- **Choose practices to address the most visible smells.** This is common, although I wouldn't recommend it. It's plain and simple "fire-fighting"—trying to get rid of the biggest pain regardless of the business value it delivers. This is all too common when the technical team determines the priority without customer input. (I've often been guilty of this.)

The information found in the figures at the beginning of this chapter is prioritized by effectiveness. Therefore, the first practice in the figure is the most effective practice for increasing the business value or alleviating the smell. Get your feet wet with the first practice, and after you've successfully adopted that, come back and take another look at the remaining practices and clusters related to your business value or smell.

No matter how you prioritize your list of practices to adopt, you should adopt those practices as iteratively as possible. Armed with the list of practices, here is how you can successfully adopt the Agile practices on your list.

1. Start with an evaluation of the status quo. Take readings (even if they are subjective) of the current business value(s) you want to improve and the smell(s) you want to alleviate.
2. Set goals that you want to reach. How much do you want to increase the business value? How much do you want to reduce the smell? What is the time frame? Take a guess initially and modify it as you know more through experience.
3. Pull the first practice or cluster off the list you created.

4. Read the pattern that is related to that cluster or practice. Decide if it is applicable or not by matching the context and forces to your working environment (more details on what patterns are and their different sections in Part 3: The Pattern Catalog). If the practice is not applicable in your environment, go back and pick the next one off the business value/smells table.

5. Once you have determined that the pattern is applicable in your environment, read the pattern thoroughly. Follow the advice in the "Adoption" section in the pattern to get started.

6. Periodically evaluate whether the business value you are addressing is improving or that the smell you are addressing is being resolved. If it is not, adapt your practice for your environment using hints from the "Variations" and "But" sections in the pattern. (You might want to take a quick read of Chapter 6, "The Patterns of Agile Practice Adoption," at this point to get an understanding of what an Agile adoption pattern looks like.)

7. Go back to step 1 and re-evaluate your business value or smell. If it needs more improvement (that is, you still have not met your goal set in 2), consider adding another practice or an entire cluster to resolve the issue. If it has met your goals, move on to the next one.

So where is the test-driven part of this approach? Your tests are your goal values that you set in step 2. In step 6, you check your readings after adopting a practice. This is a test of how effectively the practice(s) you adopted has already met the goal set earlier. This loop—set a goal, adopt a practice, and then validate the practice against the expected goal—is a test-driven adoption strategy.[1]

WHERE NEXT?

With the completion of this chapter, you are ready to create your own Agile adoption strategy that focuses on the business values and smells of your organization. This is not a one-shot deal—remember to be agile about your adoption. Measure your progress against your goals and revisit them regularly. Modify your strategy as you learn more about each practice and your own environment. It is natural to make a few wrong turns, but fail fast and quickly recover.

---

1. In management practices, this is commonly referred to as the PDCA cycle (Plan, Do, Check, Act), originally developed by Walter Shewhart at Bell Laboratories in the 1930s and promoted effectively in 1950s by the quality management guru W. Edward Deming.

For the remainder of this book, we dig into the details of each practice. There is a pattern for each practice mentioned in the mappings that describes the practice, what problems it solves, how others have successfully adopted and adapted practices in various environments, and what missteps they have taken upon adoption so you can watch out for them.

THEORY TO PRACTICE: BUILDING YOUR OWN AGILE PRACTICE ADOPTION STRATEGY

Answer the following questions to build an adoption strategy. (Use the answers from the Chapter 3 and 4 exercises here.) Also read Chapters 45 and 46 for real-world examples of how this might be done.)

1. What are your goals for adopting Agile practices? Do you want to alleviate smells or add business value? Be specific. If you have more than one goal, prioritize them.
2. Take readings of the current business value(s) and smell(s) you want to address. Don't worry if they are subjective or fuzzy. Know, to the best of your ability, where your organization is today with respect to business values and smells.
3. Choose an adoption strategy. Choose practices using that strategy to adopt.
4. Read the next chapter, which introduces the patterns. Then start following the steps outlined in this chapter to adopt your first practice. Don't forget to periodically take readings of your business value/smell to make sure the practice is effective.
5. Congratulations and good luck! Youve started on your path to Agile practice adoption!

THE PATTERN CATALOG

Part 3 is a catalog of patterns. Each pattern describes an Agile practice and how to successfully adopt that practice. This part of the book serves as reference material and should be used accordingly to support your Agile adoption strategy.

Chapter 6

THE PATTERNS OF AGILE PRACTICE ADOPTION

Before we delve into the details of the patterns and how to adopt and adapt them to meet your goals, some introductory material is in order.

WHAT IS A PATTERN?

A **pattern** describes a particular problem and its solution context. Specifically in this book, a pattern describes a (set of) problematic situation(s) on a development team that can be fixed by applying an Agile practice. Patterns are to be trusted because each one has been used several times on real development teams and projects. Patterns are not one-off solutions or good ideas that might or might not work. Patterns are discovered, not created.

The pattern format used in this book is as follows:

- **Name.** The name of the pattern.
- **Description.** A brief overview of the practice or cluster.
- **Dependency Diagram.** A diagram showing interpractice dependencies (for practices) and groupings (for clusters).
- **Business Value.** A sorted description of the business values that this practice or cluster improves.
- **Sketch.** A fictional story that describes this pattern being used on a software development project in context.
- **Context.** The preconditions and environment where this pattern is useful. The context is a collection of invariants—issues that do not change by applying the pattern.
- **Forces.** Used to elaborate context and give specific issues that are problems (partially) resolved by this pattern. In fact, correct application of the pattern should remove many of the forces.

- **Therefore.** The pattern description. The pattern resolves the forces within context.
- **Adoption.** Steps, ordering, guides to adopting this pattern.
- **But.** Negative consequences that can occur from applying this pattern.
- **Variations.** Different ways that this pattern has been implemented successfully other than that described in the "Therefore" section.
- **References.** Where to read more.

Use the "Name," "Description," and "Dependency Diagram" sections to get a quick overview of the pattern. You may find yourself browsing the pattern descriptions and dependency diagrams to get a feel for what the different practices are and how they are related to each other. Read the "Sketch" section to get a big-picture example of how you can use this pattern in practice.

If you find yourself considering the applicability of a pattern to your environment, "Context" is the section for you. This section contains any preconditions that must be met and environments where this pattern is useful. If your environment does not match the context, the pattern may not be effective.

The "Forces" section documents the issues and problems that drive the type of solution that this pattern represents. Similar to the "Context" section, the "Forces" section helps you make a decision about whether to adopt this pattern. If you find some of the forces present in your project, that is a good indication that this pattern will have a positive effect and will help you resolve these problems.

The next section, "Therefore," is the solution. It is a description of the practice itself. Use this information to understand the practice and its details. But remember that this book is not meant as a tutorial. If you have no idea what the practice is, you may need to go to other sources to get a more in-depth discussion of it.

The next three sections are going to be useful in your actual adoption of the practice. The "Adoption" section gives you an incremental strategy to successfully start using this pattern. The "But" section lets you know what may go wrong as you go about adopting a pattern. And the "Variations" section gives you nonstandard ways in which others have successfully used this pattern. Use these three sections as step-by-step instructions to help you get to the point where you are practicing the pattern as described in the "Therefore" section.

Where applicable, the "References" section gives you pointers to material where others have documented this practice. Instead of having these references in the bibliography in a jumble for the entire book, each pattern has its own pointers on where to go to read more.

Using Patterns Effectively

You can read a pattern in several ways. Here are some ways that the patterns can be used, depending on the situation.

- I am already practicing the pattern, and it has no problems. I just want to see how others have used the same pattern.
  - Look up the pattern by name.
  - Read the "Context" to see if you are using the pattern in the same environment that others have.
  - Read the "Therefore" and "Variations" sections and match them to the way you are using the practice.
- I am practicing a pattern, but it doesn't seem to be very useful. Am I incorrectly using the pattern, or is the pattern just not useful in my environment?
  - Look up the pattern by name.
  - Read the "Context" section. If your environment doesn't match the context, consider modifying the practice or dropping it all together.
  - Read the "Forces" section. Are you trying to solve the same type of problems? If not, consider that the practice might be working but that you need another practice to solve the problems you have in mind.
  - Check out the "But" section. You will find how others have gone wrong and read some advice on correcting the problems to get the full benefits from the practice.
- I have problems on my team that I want to solve by adopting Agile practices.
  - Go back to Chapter 4, "Smells," and try to match your problems to smells.
  - Read the practice(s) that addresses that smell.
  - For each practice:
    - Read the context to make sure it applies to your environment.
    - Read the rest of the pattern.
    - If you decide to adopt the practice, follow the advice in the "Adoption" section.
    - Periodically check for any of the smells documented in the "But" section.

- I couldn't find the problems I want to solve in Chapter 4. Does that mean that none of the practices can help?
    - No. Read the "Forces" section of the individual patterns and see if you can find similar problems to the ones you want to address. You will probably find a match.
- We are adopting a particular practice. Are we there yet? Have we successfully used the pattern to its fullest?
    - Find the practice pattern by name.
    - Check the "Forces" section. Are any of the problems in the "Forces" section still problems on your team?
    - Check the "But" section. Are any of the smells in that section present? If so, address them.
    - If none of the problems occur, you have gone beyond what is documented in this book. You probably have enough experience and intuition to tailor the patterns on your own. Congratulations!

Finally, please treat these patterns with a modicum of disrespect. The pattern format is an excellent format to help you tailor your own solution. Every one of these patterns is based on multiple projects using the practices. They are proven in the field several times over. Nevertheless, there is no silver bullet. These patterns will be wrong in some instances. Use these patterns as guidance, but when reality contradicts theory, choose reality.

CHARACTER ROLES

Each of the patterns in this book has a sketch that describes a fictional—but typical—use. The characters in these sketches have specific backgrounds, attitudes, and expertise. They join the development team at one time or another throughout a couple of release cycles. Here is a brief overview of who these people are.

- Amy Architect is a technical architect. She is an experienced technical person who made her way up the ranks of the development side. Before joining the team, she typically spent time in the beginning phases of projects setting the architecture and then leaving the team to build out the system according to her guidelines.
- Aparna Analyst is an analyst. She has domain expertise in the retail business for which software is being built. Her experience is a mix of technical and business; she originally started in the retail business and worked to help their IT group build some software. After that, she

wrote requirements as use cases for several years until joining this team.

- Ashley Analyst is also an analyst. He has gained expertise in the retailing domain, but his original expertise is technical. He has experience coding and writing use cases.
- Bob BuildMaster is a developer on the team with an expertise and inclination for low-level support code. He has taken it upon himself to make sure the build environments are in order and the continuous integration machine is in tip-top shape.
- Cathy Customer is playing the customer role on the team. She is from the business group that is paying for and ultimately using the software being built. Whereas Aparna and Ashley are proxy customers, Cathy is the real thing. She has less analytical experience than either Aparna or Ashley, but she knows the ins and outs of the business better, and she is familiar with her department's requirements and environment.
- Caleb Consultant is an outsider brought in to mentor the team as an Agile coach.
- Cindy Coder is a developer on the team.
- Dave Developer is another developer on the team.
- Scott ScrumMaster is the ScrumMaster of the team. His background is in project management and the PMI, which is a well-known project management certification. He has thoroughly enjoyed working with this talented team and does all he can to support their work.
- Tim Tester is a member of the QA team who is straight out of college. He is a talented ad-hoc tester and is quickly becoming familiar with some of the automation tools available to his department.
- Tina Tester is also a member of the QA team. She is an experienced and methodical tester who, over the years, has gained a strong knowledge of the retail domain.
- Uthman Upfront Design is a developer who, previous to joining the team, was making his way up the ladder and had been doing more design than coding recently. He is a good developer with better-than-average design skills.
- Will Waterfall is an experienced developer. He believes in designing first, then coding, and then testing.
- Xena XP was the team lead in the company's pilot XP project. She is an extremely talented and passionate developer. She was a major driver of adoption of test-first development and led by example.

Chapter 7

GOAL

The Goal practice needs to be enacted from the beginning of the project. A goal is a specific target that must be met. Setting a goal before starting any activity is crucial to evaluating the effectiveness of the practices executed to reach that goal.

BUSINESS VALUE

Goals are key to determining the success or failure of the teams progress. Like retrospectives, goals play a part in all business values. For example, a goal of reducing time to market to six months gives a team a success criterion for their efforts. This, in turn, gives the team members the power to recognize ineffectual practices and enables them to modify such practices accordingly.

SKETCH

After some time on Xena's XP team, the members, during one of the retrospectives, reflected on some of the major successes they had. Near the top of the list were quick, achievable, measurable goals at every part of the development cycle.

Initially, the iteration backlog was used by the team to make regular, measurable progress. It was hard in the beginning for the team members to set such small goals, but as time went by and they became more experienced, it became natural. They started seeing goals at every level of development. Functional tests were used as detailed goals for each feature, developer tests were used as micro-goals throughout the day, the iteration and release backlogs were used as goals for customer value delivered. The hitting or missing of these goals was always available via information radiators to track progress and determine issues to focus on in retrospectives. At this point, the team was implementing the Goal pattern.

CONTEXT

You are on a development team, and you are about to start a cycle. You are using the cycle to fail fast and learn to improve the practice or product produced by the cycle.

FORCES

It is too easy for team members to start one or more practices and believe they have done all they need to do to improve their development. You know there is no silver bullet.

- What works well for one team may not work as well for another.
- Practices frequently must be adapted to individual teams and environments for effectiveness.
- Improving a business value is not necessarily valuable to your organization unless it is a value your members want or need to improve.
- People learn by making mistakes but only when they realize a mistake was made.

THEREFORE

Before embarking on any cycle, determine the desired results. What will make it a success? When will it be considered a failure? Be explicit. The desired results are your goals.

Make your goals specific, measurable, achievable, relevant, and timely (S.M.A.R.T.). Specificity helps you and your team understand the desired results in no uncertain terms and helps you focus. Measurability enables you to track your progress and determine when you are done. The measures you use have to be neither complex nor quantitative. For your sanity, your goal must be achievable; otherwise, you are setting yourself up for failure. Goals should be relevant within your context and environment; if not, you can attain the goal but have no positive effect upon what really counts. Finally, your goal should be timely—delivered when it is needed.

Test-first development is a type of goal setting—where the goals are the tests to be passed. Test-driven requirements is the same thing at the scope of an iteration. In fact, a majority of Agile practices have a common structure: set a goal, perform practices to meet that goal, inspect the result to see how well that goal was met, and then act accordingly.

ADOPTION

Goal is an abstract pattern; the adoption techniques vary with the specific goals to be attained. The common challenge in all of these is to make the goal as concrete as possible and easily evaluated (ideally the evaluations will be automated) to allow effective and easy comparisons.

- Get individual commitment from those who will be responsible for achieving the goal.
- Make your goals S.M.A.R.T.
- Make goals fit into one cycle and mark them as either "done" or "not done." Don't allow percentage completions.
- Break up large goals into smaller ones that are also S.M.A.R.T.

BUT

There are some common problems that potentially show up with any goal.

- The goal is not specified in enough detail; therefore, a realistic evaluation of success/failure cannot be performed.
- The goal is hard to measure, so measurement is not done when time is an issue (which it frequently is). Choose goals that are easy to measure. If that is not possible, perform the difficult calculations and make them available to the team via an information radiator.
- Progress toward your goals is not measured frequently. This robs you of an opportunity to correct course and reach the goals more efficiently.
- A goal is chosen to fix something that is not under your control or is not achievable. Don't choose that goal or make it achievable by bringing in the people who can affect that goal.
- Too many goals are chosen at once, and few, if any, goals are met. This is ineffectual and demoralizing. Only bite off what you and your team can chew.

VARIATIONS

All inspect and adapt cycles have goals set at the beginning that are used for evaluating the success of the cycle and feedback.

- **Test-first development.** The goal is the test written in the beginning of a cycle.

- **Test-driven requirements.** The goal is the functional test written at the beginning of an Iteration.
- **Continuous integration.** The goal of continuous integration is to have a fully compiling, running, and tested system at all times.
- **Backlog.** The goals are the individual requirements.
- **Retrospective.** At the end of each retrospective, a set of actions to be performed are agreed upon and committed to. These actions are frequently driven by goals to be met to improve the way the team works together.

REFERENCES

Covey, S., *The Seven Habits of Highly Effective People*, NY: Free Press, 2004.

Derby, E. and Larson, D., *Agile Retrospectives: Making Good Teams Great*, North Carolina: Pragmatic Bookshelf, 2006.

Chapter 8

CYCLE

The Cycle pattern is the basis of all iterative development techniques, and it is a major tool in the Agile development toolbox. A cycle is a period that starts with a goal and ends with an evaluation of the progress made toward achieving that goal. The evaluation results are fed into the next cycle to better achieve its goals.

BUSINESS VALUE

Cycles affect any and all business values depending on the goals they address. They accelerate learning by allowing you and your team to periodically see progress made and respond appropriately. For example, continuous integration is a type of cycle that helps increase time to market, visibility, and quality.

SKETCH

Six months into their release, the team stopped focusing on the practices explicitly because they had become second nature. The team members also started getting creative in their retrospectives to keep moving in the right direction.

In one instance, they revisited their understanding of the organization's overall strategy and their understanding of the specific business goals of their project. Because product utility was one of the main business values, the team members decided to get regular feedback from real users of their systems via cycles. They hired a Human Computer Interaction (HCI) expert to join their team and worked with him to gather information and run experiments using the current software on a per-iteration basis.

CONTEXT

You are building a system with uncertainty in at least one aspect of software development. This includes but is not limited to

- Working with a new team
- Developing software where the requirements are not 100 percent clear or may change
- Using new software
- Using new hardware
- Using new tools
- Working with unfamiliar development practices

FORCES

Software development is a cooperative game of communication and invention [Cockburn]. Coordination and communication are extremely prone to errors, and invention is an intense learning exercise.

- People learn by trial and error, if they have time to reflect on their errors.
- Learning is the bottleneck of software development; therefore, accelerating learning is one of the best ways to increase productivity.
- Visibility of progress is extremely important for correct planning.
- Regular and small achievements are good for morale and help a team maintain its energy and commitment.
- Regular rhythm helps a team synchronize its work.
- Regular rhythm gives a team confidence that constant progress is being made.

THEREFORE

Start all your work with a goal and then incrementally and iteratively work toward achieving that goal. Work in short cycles to achieve that goal. You and your team will learn quickly by examining the results of the cycle and comparing them to the goal. Your progress—or lack thereof—will be immediately obvious to you, and you will be able to do better the next time around the cycle. This constant feedback is empowering because you constantly know your true progress, and the small successes along the way when goals are met will keep you and your team energized. The regular rhythm formed by the cycle will help you synchronize your work and move in step with each other.

ADOPTION

Start small and don't be discouraged if at first you can't seem to meet your goals at the end of the cycles. This failure is natural. Just hang in there, and it will get better!

- Start each cycle with one or more specific, measurable, achievable, relevant, and timely (S.M.A.R.T.) goals.
- Keep your cycles short and break up your goals to fit into smaller periods.
- Specifically call out successes and failures and communicate them to the team. This visibility will allow all in a self-organizing team to keep things on track.
- Complete goals within a cycle and track them as either "done" or "not done." Don't use percentage completions. If the goals are too large, break them up. Percentage completion dilutes focus, and you can easily fall into the "90 percent done 90 percent of the time" syndrome.
- Pair your cycles with information radiators when appropriate. Err on the side of visibility. Encapsulation is good only for software objects.

BUT

Each cycle has its own missteps; however, each cycle has common errors.

- The cycle is too long. This means you have a longer time to make mistakes without knowing about them. One telltale sign of a long cycle is extremely inaccurate estimates. We are not good fortune-tellers. Keep the cycle short for more accurate planning.
- Goals don't fit in small cycles; therefore, cycles are expanded to fit the goal. Don't do this because you have just increased your time until feedback and reduced the amount of information you get to make course-corrections for. Instead, split the large goal into smaller ones that will fit in the allotted time.
- Cycles frequently expose errors and inconsistencies that were previously ignored or unseen. They are then mistakenly seen as the cause of the problems and not just the messenger. The messenger is shot; that is, cycles are discontinued because things are just too painful. Don't do this! You'll be better off fixing the real problem.
- The cycle has erratic rhythms. Whether it shows up in practices such as Test-First Development, Continuous Integration, or Iterations, if the cycle time keeps changing, it is hard to get into a regular rhythm of work, and synchronization becomes difficult. This is a warning sign that your goals are either not S.M.A.R.T or are too large.

VARIATIONS

A significant portion of software development practices in Agile are cycles:

- Requirements (Test-Driven Requirements)
- Coding stories (Continuous Integration)
- Coding tasks (Test-First Development)
- Development in general (Iteration with Retrospective, Release with Retrospective)
- Working together, Pair Programming as a form of code reviews
- Evolutionary design

All of these and more are cycles that make up the Cycle pattern.

REFERENCES

Cockburn, A., *Agile Software Development: The Cooperative Game (Second Edition)*, Boston: Addison-Wesley, 2007.

FEEDBACK PRACTICES

Chapter 9

ITERATION

The relationship of Iteration to other practices is illustrated in Figure 9-1. Iteration is a constant time box where the development team builds a part of the system completely as defined by the Done State. This allows the team to learn by taking a concept from requirements to as-close-as-possible to deployment and provides true visibility into project progress.

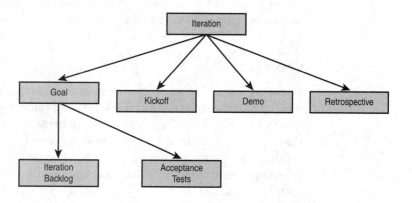

Figure 9–1   The Iteration practice needs a goal to be set during Kickoff and a Demo and Retrospective to wrap things up. Work in each Iteration is taken to a well-defined Done State.

BUSINESS VALUE

Iterations improve product utility by giving regular feedback to customers. They increase visibility because they are touch points for reviews, and they provide constant, concrete feedback on the progress of the work. Iterations improve a team's flexibility by enabling members to change their minds based on feedback from previous work. There is little "work in progress" between Iterations. Finally, time to market is reduced because every time-boxed iteration is a potential release, and taking the software to the Done State regularly reveals defects early in the process for cheaper and faster removal.

SKETCH

Will Waterfall and Amy the Architect were wary of iterations and iterative development as defined by Scott the ScrumMaster and Xena the eXtreme Programmer. Will wanted to control the scope to be able to promise his customer a delivery date with certain features up-front. Amy, on the other hand, didn't trust Xena and her cohorts to change the design every few weeks; it sounded much more like hacking than effective design.

Will and Amy were surprised when they saw Scott and Xena's team deliver iteration after iteration successfully. When Amy participated in a design review of the project, she was pleasantly surprised by the simplicity and quality of the design that Xena's team had put together (although Amy doubted it would scale). Will noted that Scott's customers were happy with the delivery, although they didn't get exactly what they asked for to start off with. The delivery was surprising—and a bit mysterious.

CONTEXT

The team is working on development of a project according to a plan that was put together in the initial weeks of the project's startup. Features and functions are estimated and executed independently, each within its own timeframe. Integration of the different subsystems is scheduled a few months before release to the customer and (from previous experiences) is expected to be painful. Developers sometimes take a piece of functionality and work for months to finalize it with infrequent (or no) feedback from the customer until the function is completed. Of course, by that time, too much effort has been put in for the customer to say, "Umm…now that I've seen this, I realize it is not what I want." A rigorous change management process is in place to keep this from happening. Deliveries are frequently delayed to get the promised features working. Some promised features work as specified but are of much less value to the user than previously expected. There is the possibility of low morale because everyone knows the project will slip its date…again!

FORCES

These are some common aspects of software development.

- Requirements and true needs of the customer sometimes diverge.
  - Feedback between customers and developers is infrequent.

- Customers may not know exactly what they want until they see a working piece of software.
- Environments change, forcing change in requirements mid-release.
- Integration is infrequent, costly, and often extremely painful as a product nears release.
- A "hardening" phase is frequently scheduled before a major release date to ensure that the product quality is acceptable. This phase includes no new feature additions and is focused on bug fixes only.
- Function completions are out of synch, so integration is usually pushed to the end of the release cycle.
- Functionality is complex, and developers have a tendency to "go off track" and come back to the customer with an incorrect solution.

THEREFORE

Break up your development cycles to fixed-size blocks of time, between one and six weeks, where the development staff works on producing useful business functionality. You give yourself and your customer a chance to evaluate the solution. Take the work done as near to deployment as possible to find and correct as many defects as possible. Defects found later are much more expensive to fix. The time block is short enough that if a miscommunication happens between the customer and developer, a course correction can be made without sacrificing too much investment. This also reduces the amount of "work in progress" because everything is fully complete, which provides a more accurate picture of the true progress of the project and reduces the amount of partially done work that will be discarded if requirements change.

Work done in this period, called an iteration, needs to be accepted by the customer, tested, and integrated into the current version of the system. The level of completion that your team achieves is determined by your definition of Done State. An iteration in Agile is different from a traditional iteration because time drives the amount of work done. There should be no partially done tasks. They are either done or not done.

A sprint, as defined by the Scrum process, is another name for an iteration as defined here.

ADOPTION

An iteration should be started with a kickoff meeting. These meetings must unambiguously define the goals of the iteration, usually called a backlog. This means specific acceptance criteria must be set before the iteration begins.

Iterations should end with a ceremony and review to contemplate the successes and failures and to improve the next iteration. These practices are called Demo and Retrospective, respectively.

An iteration should have a length of anywhere between one and six weeks. The rule of thumb for choosing iteration length is to make it as short as possible while still being able to produce useful functionality (from the customer's perspective). This means that planning, development, testing, and integration should all be done within this timeframe. As a rule of thumb, new teams should choose a length between two and four weeks as a starting point and err on making the iteration too long. As the team gains experience, they will contract the iteration length to get faster feedback.

Iterations should be closed to the introduction of new functionality. That is, once an iteration has started, it must be allowed to continue to completion without disruption. That means there can be no changing of scope or requirements.

A Trial Run (as defined in *Fearless Change* by Mary Manns and Linda Rising) should be used for at least three iterations. Because of the learning curve, expect that teams must slow down before they can speed up. If the team members are not used to testing and integrating frequently, this will be a painful period as they figure out how to do so effectively within the time box of the iteration.

The team members should define what their success priorities are before they start. That is, which of the forces do they want to alleviate or resolve by introducing iterations? This allows the proper evaluation of the Trial Run and avoids religious debates when it comes to the final analysis.

To summarize, the practice of Iteration cannot be correctly performed without nonambiguously setting the goal, performing some type of kickoff for the iteration, and wrapping it up with a demo and a retrospective.

BUT

Problems frequently occur on teams that are implementing iterations for the first time.

- Often, expectations of the efficacy of iterations and success priorities are not set. The pain first encountered in moving to iterations causes teams to slide back to noniterative development or cyclic development without a working and integrated system.
- People forget that iterations are closed to functionality changes. They need to be reminded that new functionality must be scheduled for the next iteration.
- Teams sometimes become too aggressive in decreasing the time of their iteration. Iterations end up being not long enough to produce useful functionality to the user.
- Many factors can cause an iteration not to deliver to the expected velocity. All of these things can lead to development teams padding estimates. This padding serves no purpose other than to artificially increase a team's velocity. Retrospectives and stand-up meetings can shed light on the real issues that block and eliminate the need for estimate padding.
- The code written within an iteration is not ready. There may be leftover errors or poorly designed code. By iterating in this manner, the code base quickly develops inertia, and each iteration becomes more difficult than the last. Many times, "hardening iterations" are added to a release schedule to clean up everything that the team missed. This process of not addressing issues early is not scalable in the long run. Practices such as Test-Driven Development should be put in place to enable the design to evolve instead of stagnate.
- A demo is seen as a waste of time and is dropped. This omission greatly reduces the customer's visibility of the software and his satisfaction. Equally important, it removes one of the key opportunities for feedback and improvement.
- Retrospectives are not performed because they are seen as having limited value and being too "touchy-feely." This exclusion greatly reduces the development team's ability to tailor the iteration to its needs. It also enables lingering smells to fester.
- Iterations are run without a customer present. There is no feedback to or from the customer, which is a degenerate form of iteration that may help "build the problem right" but miss "building the right problem."

- Iterations are often started with all developers working in parallel. This is often a recipe for failure because, at the end, there may be 80 percent of the requirements completed 80 percent, which is a 20 percent completion rate. This also does not give enough time for acceptance testing if it is not yet automated. A better alternative is to work on only a few requirements at a time, finish them, and allow testing to begin, and then move on to the next requirement. That way, if estimates are off, you will have 60 percent of the requirements completely done.
- Iterations are mistaken for incremental development, where requirements are built in small pieces but not synchronized to a time box. This misses the opportunity to build a team rhythm that allows for better visibility to management and more accurate planning. It also does not force smaller pieces of work to be done, which, in turn, means defects from integration and system testing stay longer in the system until being discovered and fixed.

VARIATIONS

Iterations are not new, but in the Agile community they are more strictly defined. An iteration must produce working, integrated, and tested code.

These are some common groupings and clusters of practices that form successful Agile iterations:

- Automated Acceptance Tests, Kickoff Meeting, Demo, Retrospective
- Iteration Backlog, Stand-Up Meeting, Demo, Retrospective
- Iteration Backlog, Automated Acceptance Testing, Kickoff Meeting, Demo, Retrospective

REFERENCES

Beck, K. and Andres, C., *Extreme Programming Explained: Embrace Change (Second Edition)*, Boston: Addison-Wesley, 2005.

Larman, C., *Agile and Iterative Development: A Manager's Guide*, Boston: Addison-Wesley, 2004.

Schwaber, K., and Beedle, M., *Agile Software Development with SCRUM*, Upper Saddle River, New Jersey: Prentice Hall, 2001.

Chapter 10

KICKOFF MEETING

A kickoff meeting is used to synchronize the team's efforts and to plan and commit to work to be done for an iteration. The goals for an iteration are determined in the kickoff meeting. The relationship between the Kickoff Meeting practice and the Planning Poker practice is shown in Figure 10-1.

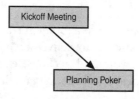

Figure 10–1   A Kickoff Meeting uses Planning Poker for estimation.

BUSINESS VALUE

Kickoff meetings improve the visibility of a software development effort because all team members are present to discuss and commit to the work to be done for the next iteration. These meetings are key to successful iterations; therefore, they have a secondary effect on all the business values directly affected by an iteration.

SKETCH

A regular meeting for the entire team? What a waste of time! Developers, analysts, testers, managers, and customers in the same room on a regular basis—how could this ever be productive? Cindy Coder thought that the new move to Agile Development was going to get rid of wasteful practices—and this kickoff meeting for the iterations seemed like a waste of time.

Cindy was surprised by the focus of the first iteration kickoff meeting. The analysts and customers had been preparing beforehand and had a prioritized list of requirements, which they called user stories. The developers worked with them to break up and estimate the user stories—and *they* got to say how long things take without any ifs, ands, or buts! Testers got involved to make sure that the acceptance criterion for each user story was detailed enough to nonambiguously know when the story would be done. By the end of the day, the entire team had a single goal for the iteration, and the work had been split up among developers with supporting testers and analysts. Cindy had to admit, it wasn't a total waste of time.

As iterations came and went, the team became much more efficient at running the kickoff meetings, and they were scaled back to half a day instead of a full day. The team was in a rhythm and felt good about setting and meeting specific goals for every iteration.

CONTEXT

You are part of a development team that has decided to implement iterations. Each iteration is to deliver a working, integrated, and fully tested system. Therefore, you need to choose enough requirements to build and make sure they are of appropriate size and difficulty.

FORCES

- An iteration requires a set of requirements determined in the beginning to be developed. These requirements need to be understood enough to estimate.
- If the team uses a backlog, this also needs to be finalized at the start of the iteration.
- One of the best ways for developers and testers to understand the requirements is by having direct conversations with the customers and analysts.
- Communication through documents and "throwing it over the wall" is error-prone and time-consuming if you need to get to the done state every iteration.
- Face-to-face conversations regarding requirements, design, and estimation are productive and allow the participants to clarify misunderstandings quickly.

THEREFORE

To enable a successful iteration, a set of prioritized requirements must be understood, estimated, and scheduled for completion within the iteration. The expertise to perform this task well is found in all the members of the team because all of them are committing to doing part of the work to reach the done state. That means developers need to estimate coding time; testers, customers, and analysts need to estimate time for proper acceptance testing; database experts need to estimate required database work; and so on.

Workshops are an excellent method to use when a diverse set of people need to work together toward a goal. The workshop at the beginning of an iteration to produce a backlog is called the kickoff meeting.

ADOPTION

Because a kickoff meeting is a workshop, all the adoption advice in Chapter 38, "Workshop," applies. To keep the length of the meeting time reasonable, a few things should be done.

- The customers and analysts should elaborate requirements before the meeting. They should come into the kickoff meeting prepared to describe the requirements to the other members of the team.
- Use a way to quickly estimate the effort required for the work to be done. The most well-known method for doing this is planning poker, which relies on our strengths in relative estimation.

BUT

The kickoff meeting is a long meeting including the whole team. If it does not meet its goal—to produce a set of requirements to be built in the iteration—it can easily be an expensive waste of time.

- Developers have a tendency to overdiscuss requirements and go into time-consuming design discussions to make estimates. This can make these meetings extremely lengthy and painful and end up without a useful backlog at the end. Consider using the Planning Poker practice to come up with estimates and only go into design discussions when the team diverges in its estimate.
- Frequent missing of the goals set indicates that the estimation is error-prone. Teams have a tendency, at this point, to increase the length and rigor of the meetings, but that is a painful and costly exercise. Consider making iterations shorter, which will make the requirements necessarily smaller. It will also make the time required to meet the requirements easier to estimate.

- For large teams, the meeting can be excruciating. Consider breaking up into independent groups during the day to perform the necessary estimation and commitment to work. For example, a team with 25 developers, 5 analysts, and 10 testers can break up into 5 groups. Notice that each group still has the necessary diversity of skills. Don't group these teams by layer, but group them as cross-functional teams so that each requirement is built end to end.
- Use a retrospective to address any pains.

VARIATIONS

Scrums kickoff meeting is called a sprint meeting, and in eXtreme Programming, it is called the planning game. Both are workshops run by a self-organizing team to produce a list of requirements that will be built during the upcoming iteration.

REFERENCES

Beck, K. and Andres, C., *Extreme Programming Explained: Embrace Change (Second Edition)*, Boston: Addison-Wesley, 2005.

Schwaber, K., and Beedle, M., *Agile Software Development with SCRUM*, Upper Saddle River, New Jersey: Prentice Hall, 2001.

Chapter 11

BACKLOG

Backlogs are prioritized lists of requirements used to schedule work to be done for iterations and releases. They enable variable scoping of requirements to meet deadlines and still deliver the most valuable features. Figure 11-1 shows the relationship of the Backlog practice to other practices.

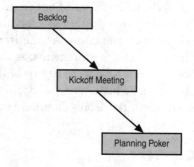

Figure 11–1 The Backlog is created in a Kickoff Meeting, and the items on the Backlog are estimated using Planning Poker.

BUSINESS VALUE

Backlogs are goals for iterations and releases. They improve product utility and increase visibility by enabling high-quality feedback regularly as the goals are met and reviewed. In a sense, they also decrease time to market because the prioritized list enables negotiation of scope and early release with the most valuable functionality.

SKETCH

Aparna Analyst and Cathy Customer joined Scott ScrumMaster's team, expecting to have a few months to work out the detailed requirements and initial specifications to hand off to the technical team. They did not realize that things were going to be so ad hoc! They were given only two weeks to come up with an initial list of requirements. This was quite a surprise, but they were calmed when Ashley Analyst (no relation to Aparna and had previously worked with Scott) sat down with them to explain the idea.

They would work to come up with an initial list of the requirements in broad terms. These sketchy requirements would then be prioritized by Cathy according to perceived business value delivered to her organization. This main list is the **product backlog**. To prepare for each iteration, Cathy and Aparna will flesh out enough of these requirements so that the rest of the development team can use them to build out the software system in that time frame. This set of requirements was agreed to by the entire team and became the **iteration backlog**—that is, the list of fleshed-out requirements to be built in one iteration.

At first, Aparna and Cathy felt that this was going to take too much of their time with little return. But iteration after iteration, they became huge fans of this technique. They did not waste their time fleshing out a huge set of requirements that they felt was too fuzzy; they only did so on an as-needed basis for each iteration. As the iterations moved on, Cathy was able to reprioritize the requirements, as she understood the problem and solution better through frequent demos of the working software system. Aparna was able to make better analysis decisions as she learned, along with the entire team, about the details that could not have been foreseen.

CONTEXT

You are on a development team that has decided to adopt some Agile development practices, including Iteration. You have decided to go away from the old technique of up-front requirements and a detailed specification document as a handoff from analysts to developers. You have the needed expertise on your team to incrementally expand and evolve requirements either via Customer Part of Team or any other practice.

FORCES

Traditional planning is based on fiction—the idea that we can peer into a crystal ball and determine the requirements, dependencies, and time needed in advance of actually doing the work.

- Agile development techniques discourage too much up-front work. Up-front requirements (usually embodied in a specifications document) are incomplete, incorrect, and too precise given the amount of knowledge available at the beginning of a project.[1] Nonetheless, some type of plan and roadmap describing the intended functionality at an appropriate level of granularity are needed.

---

1. You shouldn't measure a cut made with a chainsaw using a micrometer.

- Each iteration must have a set of nonambiguous goals to meet to enable measurable and accurate progress.
- Feedback from iterations and demos should be incorporated into future work. Requirements that are hard to change will hinder effective use of this feedback.
- Software development is a learning activity. As a software product is built, the development team learns more about the problem domain and the solution(s). Requirements will evolve. Detailed, upfront requirements will quickly become stale.
- Estimates are approximations. They are inaccurate.
- Trying to force completion of a project with a nonnegotiable scope and a definite deadline is folly. One of the two must be sacrificed.

THEREFORE

An appropriately coarse-grained set of requirements should be created for at least one project release. (Sometimes themes are outlined for later releases.) This set of requirements should be prioritized by the customer primarily by business value but can be informed by any other information such as risk [Waltzing With Bears], resource availability, and so on. Business value is determined by the customer, not by developers, architects, or project managers. This list can and does evolve and grow as the software development team builds out the software system and consequently learns more about the problem domain, technical platform, and each other.

The backlog is a prioritized list of requirements and can include user stories, use cases, or any other form of requirement. As goals to be met, they should be S.M.A.R.T.[2] Also they need not be of the same level of detail. At a minimum, the top elements on the list should be in enough detail for development and in a granularity that can be completed within an iteration.

There are generally two backlogs: a product backlog that contains requirements for at least one release of a product and an iteration backlog that is populated during a kickoff meeting of an iteration from the top items on the product backlog.

---

2. Specific, Measurable, Attainable, Relevant, and Timely.

ADOPTION

The practice of using backlogs is usually adopted with iteration and frequent release because they set the goals for those two cycles. Because release backlogs are built infrequently, it is difficult for a team to get significant experience doing so. A workshop is generally a good idea. The requirements within the iteration backlog have to be small enough to build within the time allotted in an iteration.

A product backlog is usually created first with coarse-grained requirements such as use case or user story. These items don't need to be detailed enough to develop, nor do they have to be small enough to build in a single iteration. Release backlogs should be built with the involvement of the whole team. The job of the customers is to come to the meeting with a list of requirements to be met. They should understand these requirements enough to describe them verbally—in an overview—to the rest of the team. The whole team—excluding the customers—then proceeds to perform relative effort estimation of each requirement using the Planning Poker practice. Then, armed with initial estimates, the customers proceed to prioritize the work with the help of the rest of the team. The whole team discusses risk, development dependencies, resource constraints, and all other issues that can affect the order of the requirements to be built. In the end, however, it is the customers who set the priority.

At the beginning of each iteration, in the kickoff meeting, the team has to have requirements that are detailed enough to develop (possibly augmented with conversations), roughly estimate, and complete within an iteration. The items chosen for development make up the iteration backlog. Therefore, the customers will need to flush out the coarse-grained requirements ahead of time. This frequently means that they are preparing for the next iteration halfway through the current iteration.

One way to view a team's progress is by viewing the status of the backlog. Therefore, it is helpful to use one or more information radiators to describe what is completed and what remains. Two specific information radiators are of use here: the burn-up chart and the burn-down chart. At a glance, you can see the team's progress.

BUT

Backlogs are a simple, useful practice. However, their very simplicity sometimes makes them difficult to build and maintain because you want to do more! Creating and maintaining a backlog is an exercise in just-enough requirements management and development.

- **Analysis paralysis.** Initializing a release backlog should happen quickly. Often teams can finish such an exercise in several half-day workshops over the span of three to four days. Unfortunately, many who are new to this exercise will find themselves taking weeks and months because they want to specify the requirements to the details they are used to.
- **Estimation paralysis.** Planning poker is not used or, when it is, the team members get into a design discussion/session figuring out exactly how something will be done to estimate the work.
- **Techies take over.** The architects and developers mandate the order of the backlog elements because of risk, technological dependence, or just because they are used to doing so. It is not their responsibility to prioritize the list; instead, they should inform the customers of their concerns and let them decide on the priority. Some may say that technical stories, while not immediately apparent to the business as being valuable, need to be prioritized and accounted for in the backlog. Work toward making that value apparent to the user. If you cannot communicate the value of the tasks, don't do them.
- **Multiple teams (non-cross-functional) have trouble working from one backlog.** This is perhaps the most difficult issue with backlogs. They are meant to have requirements that are built from end to end and taken to the done state. Unfortunately, many teams are not set up that way; they are set up by function, so you will have a GUI team, a DB team, and so on. They are used to build pieces of the same requirement and then integrate them sometime in the future. If you have such a team structure, you may be tempted to create several backlogs, one for each team. But this approach will make it difficult to get any of the benefits of backlogs because you are never really done until the integration is done. The better but much more difficult approach is to work in parallel within an iteration (or two at most) until your team can move toward implementing the Cross-Functional Team practice to take on requirements from end to end.

VARIATIONS

The requirements in a backlog can vary. Teams have effectively included business requirements, nonfunctional requirements, and organizational changes—everything important that they want to accomplish.

The prioritization varies and can include business value, risk, technical dependencies, and any other issues. In general, business value should be the driving factor.

Large companies have challenges managing more than one backlog. This comes up when, as in the "But" section, they have functional teams. It also appears when multiple projects are built concurrently.

REFERENCES

Cohn, M., *Agile Estimating and Planning*, Upper Saddle River, New Jersey: Prentice Hall, 2006.

Schwaber, K., and Beedle, M., *Agile Software Development with SCRUM*, Upper Saddle River, New Jersey: Prentice Hall, 2001.

Chapter 12

PLANNING POKER

Planning Poker is a technique that enables a team to quickly come up with coarse-grained relative estimation of effort. This technique is useful in both release and iteration planning.

BUSINESS VALUE

Planning poker is an estimation technique that enables a team to effectively and quickly estimate the relative difficulty of requirements. This supports building a backlog for both the release and the iteration. Planning poker doesn't really support any business values directly but indirectly affects all business values addressed by a backlog, which includes product utility, visibility, and time to market.

SKETCH

Scott had read about the Planning Poker practice and its use in planning, but somehow he really couldn't see getting together with his team in a few sittings and estimating the requirements for an entire release. So when Caleb facilitated a workshop to do just that to build and prioritize the backlog, it was surprising how many requirements they estimated per hour. They went faster than they ever had before.

Over the next few iterations, Scott saw the effectiveness of theory in practice. The team members were able to modify their expected code-complete date as they discovered how many story points their team was able to complete on a monthly cycle. They also used Planning Poker in every kickoff meeting and were able to plan the work for each iteration in a half-day session.

The gross inaccuracies that Scott expected never materialized. The relative estimations made were good—the team just found it easier and more natural to estimate this way. The estimates were also durable because when team velocity changed, the time needed to complete any requirement changed automatically.

CONTEXT

You and your team want to build a backlog for either a release or an iteration. You have planned a workshop to do this and have invited the whole team.

FORCES

- "You shouldn't measure with a micrometer what you have cut with a chainsaw." That is, overprecision is wasted effort.
- Estimates are *wrong*. An estimate is, by definition, not equal to the actual value. If estimates were correct, they wouldn't be called predictions; they'd be called facts.
- People are better at relative estimation than they are at absolute estimation. For example, it is easier for a person to sort a group of animals by height. A cat is smaller than a Labrador retriever (dog), which is smaller than a horse. But, if asked how tall at the shoulder height each animal is, our answers would be more error-prone.
- Planning based on estimation is *fiction*. It is a useful fiction, but it is fiction nonetheless.
- Meetings for the whole team are expensive. All work comes to a stop until the meeting is over.
- Meetings with many people can easily get off track and lose their focus.
- Most people find meetings tiring and tedious.
- Every team has different productivity.
- Basing estimates on actual team performance—yesterday's weather— is significantly more accurate than estimates looking forward.
- Developers are (mostly) optimists—they have a tendency to underestimate effort.

THEREFORE

Use a lightweight technique to do your estimation. In release planning, rely on relative estimation instead of absolute estimates (usually in hours).

Planning poker is a voting technique used for estimation. When doing effort estimation, use the Fibonacci series (1, 2, 3, 5, 8, 13, BIG[1]), and for value estimation, use 1, 2, 3, 4, 5, 6, 7. For each requirement being estimated, follow these steps.

1. The requirements expert(s) must prepare before this meeting. They must understand the requirements enough to be able to describe them to those in the workshop. (In release planning, that is usually a high level; at iteration planning, it tends to be more detailed and includes a task breakdown.)

2. Have the domain expert of the team explain the requirement so that everyone has a good understanding of it.

3. Perform calibration. Of the requirements, choose the least valuable effort and rank it as a 1. Use this as your starting point.

4. Perform the following rounds of voting and stop if consensus is reached.

   a. Round 1: No discussion. Everyone votes.

   b. Round 2: Take a few moments to reflect and then vote again without discussion.

   c. Round 3: Team members get to say why they voted the way they did. Keep answers to no more than a few minutes. Everyone votes for a last time.

   d. If Round 3 produced a consensus, that's great. If not, but the votes were close, take the average. Otherwise, put the requirement on a to-do stack to be addressed offline.

5. Repeat for all requirements.

The values estimated for each requirement are relative. They make sense only in context of the particular project under consideration.

ADOPTION

Planning poker works. Suspend your disbelief and run it by the book—in this case, Mike Cohn's book *Agile Estimating and Planning*. Here are a few pieces of advice on logistics.

---

1. If a requirement is larger than 13, we don't bother to estimate it and just mark it as BIG. Requirements in this bucket need to be broken down further into multiple parts.

- Use stickies and a wall to create an information radiator for the exercise. Put a sticky on the wall for the possible numbers—1, 2, 3, 4, 5, 6, and 7 for value estimation and 1, 2, 3, 5, 8, 13, BIG for effort estimation. Every time a requirement is estimated, put it on the wall. The display will be there for all to see when they perform their next estimates.
- If someone is new to the practice, explain the process by showing a set of estimation rounds.
- Make sure to get a big, well-lit room as recommended in the Workshop practice.
- The people who are estimating are the people doing the work—not just the experts.
- Team members estimate how long the entire requirement will take—not just the part they expect to be doing.
- Consider using a digital camera to take snapshots of your results instead of using a planning tool for speed and simplicity. Make the pictures available to the team.
- Keep the teams small and the meetings short. Estimation of each requirement should take no longer than three to five minutes. If you cannot agree, put the card aside and come back to it later.

BUT

Here are some common missteps.

- After doing release planning and creating relative estimates, some team members are eager to map the points to hours. They then start measuring hours per task and points completed per individual. Don't do this. It is too much precision. Calculate your team's velocity (number of points completed) per iteration.
- Don't get stuck on tools. If you are using an Agile management tool, it is tempting to get in a room, turn off the light, and run the workshop with one person at the keyboard asking people for input. Don't do that. It is painful and hinders conversations. It also does not offer any of the benefits of having an information radiator on the wall. Remember, software development is a game of communication and invention. You will hinder communication by fooling with the tool. Transcribe the results later for the tool.
- Hold back from discussions during the voting rounds. Independence and diversity are key to the effectiveness of this technique.
- Get a variety of people to vote—testers, developers, database experts, and so on for effort estimation and marketing, sales, management, customers for value estimation.

- Don't re-estimate the point value of a requirement when it ends up that it will take significantly more or less time than you originally thought. Re-estimating will skew your velocity results.

REFERENCES

Cohn, M., *Agile Estimating and Planning*, Upper Saddle River, New Jersey: Prentice Hall, 2006.

Demarco, T. and Lister, T., *Waltzing with Bears*, Dorset House Publishing Company, Inc, 2003.

Surowiecki, J., *The Wisdom of Crowds*, Anchor, 2005.

Chapter 13

STAND-UP MEETING

The Stand-Up Meeting practice is a daily meeting to provide coordination among team members. It should last no longer than 15 minutes. It is a point where a self-organizing team meets to exchange progress information about the current Iteration.

BUSINESS VALUE

Stand-up meetings create business value in two important ways: reducing time to market and promoting visibility. Stand-up meetings also create natural synchronization points with the customer part of team, which enables frequent customer reviews to improve product utility and quality.

SKETCH

When Dave Developer joined his current project, it was his first Agile project, and he couldn't imagine a meeting every day. He felt the previous meetings were almost always a waste of time, where he had to sit through discussions that weren't always related to his work. Of course, the really important meetings where decisions were made about scope and deadlines did not necessarily include him. So he went to his first stand-up meeting, which was refreshingly short and focused on the iteration at hand. After several meetings, Dave realized that roadblocks to meeting iteration goals were quickly addressed by Scott ScrumMaster. In short, stand-up meetings were relevant to the current iterations work and were not too much of a burden to attend.

CONTEXT

You are in an organization that has started to see software development as an empirical process instead of a deterministic one. Therefore, your team needs constant information about where the current project is so that you and your colleagues can respond to change and control the progress of the software. Your organization is also working to establish and maintain whole-team cohesiveness in the development team. Your team is in the process of improving its communications.

FORCES

- Software projects are empirical in nature and not deterministic; therefore, constant readings of where the project stands are necessary.
- Learning happens every day on a software development project. Learning often happens as a result of a mistaken assumption or incomplete information becoming clear. As new issues are cleared up or discovered, they need to be communicated to the different members of the team.
- Learning is the bottleneck of software development.
- Meetings tend to be long and wasteful because they mix so many agendas—both explicit and hidden.
- It is beneficial to structure meetings and interactions so that they focus on one specific purpose—for example, making sure everyone understands what progress is being made toward a collective goal.
- Documents, e-mails, phone calls, and other forms of communication are prone to errors.
- Agile development teams work collectively. The practice of Collective Code Ownership encourages developers to work on the entire codebase, and the practice of Continuous Integration causes interleaving of work in progress. The concept of "my code" and isolated areas of the system are not prevalent. The practice of Test-Driven Development frequently causes the design of the system to evolve day by day. All these forces of change can easily cause conflicts. A way to quickly and regularly address these conflicts is needed.
- Those involved in a software project fall into two broad categories: 1) people who are directly involved with the delivery of the project and whose actions have a direct and tangible effect on the software system being built, and 2) those who are involved indirectly and have an interest but generally do not perform day-to-day activities that directly affect the software.
- The longer you wait to solve an issue, the more it will cost to solve it.

THEREFORE

The entire development team should meet regularly every day to discuss the progress of the previous day and highlight any roadblocks that need to be removed. It is important to keep the meetings from becoming a burden; therefore, daily meetings should be kept short and to the point. Finally, to keep a meeting short, care must be taken to set specific goals and not to stray from them.

Stand-up meetings are the daily events, described in the previous paragraph, used as feedback for management of an empirical process. The daily meetings give the entire team relevant information to adapt to change and new information within the timeframe of an iteration so that obstacles can be addressed in a timely manner and the goals of the iteration can be met. Stand-up meetings also help establish reciprocal visibility among the different members of the team as they see that the entire group (management, analysts, developers, testers) work together to meet the iteration goals.

A member of the team should be responsible for keeping the meetings on track. In Scrum, the ScrumMaster usually fills that role. In XP, it can be any member of the team, and that person frequently rotates. It doesn't make much difference who performs this task, but it is a role that helps keep this practice useful for all involved. It is customary for the meetings to be conducted standing up to keep them short.

ADOPTION

Any team adopting iterations should perform stand-up meetings. These meetings belong to the feedback cluster of Agile practice patterns. Stand-up meetings are frequently among the first set of practices adopted when a development team starts to introduce project management practices. A typical adoption strategy would be to start off with these practices: Iteration, Kick-off, Stand-Up Meeting, Demo, and Retrospective. These practices are typically adopted together.

To execute stand-up meetings, have one person responsible for keeping them on track. The meetings should have an appropriate and constant time of day to enable attendance of all team members. Start the meetings promptly and aim for attendance as close to 100 percent as possible. Try to keep the meetings under 15 minutes; the exception to this rule is that those new to Agile development frequently need significantly more time in the first one or two iterations. (Stand-up meetings of up to one hour are not uncommon.) Use a speaking token and pass it around; only the person holding the token should speak. Burgeoning conversations on planning or design should be interrupted and scheduled for later discussion after the stand-up meeting. Only pigs should be participating in discussions; chickens can only listen.[1] Interrupt chickens and remind them of this policy politely but firmly. Finally, keep the focus on status and don't let the individual reports turn into travelogues.[2]

BUT

Your meetings can easily go off track. Here are some common smells that indicate that stand-up meetings are becoming dysfunctional:

- Meetings become travelogues; people tell what they did in detail instead of sharing short, concise reports of status and impediments. This detail lengthens the meetings and significantly reduces their usefulness because of loss of focus.
- Meetings become design sessions; the need for design discussions can be recognized inside the stand-up but should be scheduled at another time with the relevant participants.
- Meetings become focused on planning. Planning should be done on iteration boundaries and outside the stand-up meetings.
- Meetings are co-opted by people not directly involved with the delivery process.
- Meetings are not regular and are dropped because little or no value to the meetings is perceived. This removes one of the essential types of feedback for a team.
- Team members are not prompt and miss the meetings. This is common where different team members are used to working remotely or have different work schedules.
- The team is large, and stand-up meetings become chaotic and lose relevance to all team members.

Take all interactive discussions off to sidebar meetings. Anything other than a status report is considered a sidebar. Many of the problems with stand-up meetings can be resolved by having one person facilitate them, firmly keeping the different attendees on track.

---

1. The terms *pig* and *chicken* in this context are derived from a story about a pig and chicken starting a restaurant. Given a menu of bacon and eggs, the pig is committed, and the chicken is merely involved. The suggestion here is that only those who are committed—those who will suffer the repercussions of failure—should speak in stand-up meetings even though all involved may and should attend to gain an understanding of what is happening with the project.
2. People should report their completed tasks, current tasks planned for the day, and any roadblocks that are keeping them from proceeding with their work. They should not tell the team a step-by-step reenactment of the work they did the previous day.

VARIATIONS

Stand-up meetings are frequently dropped with small, co-located teams (usually under five members) that have been practicing Agile for a while and grok[3] the culture. Because the entire team is in one room with a common area, the members are constantly communicating, and a stand-up meeting becomes redundant. Be careful with this; dropping these meetings can be dangerous if it reduces your team's communication and synchronization.

Stand-up meetings are also of limited value if there are no iterations. Teams that have adopted some of the technical Agile practices, such as automated developer tests within a traditional waterfall lifecycle, do not necessarily adopt stand-up meetings. They are still working in isolation from others on their team; therefore, they do not need this practice.

Stand-up meetings usually include the whole development team (all the pigs) and are open to anyone else in the organization who is interested in attending. This usually is good for a team size of less than ten members. As teams and stand-up meetings become larger, the meetings become longer and are not as useful to all the attendees. Resolutions to this problem involve breaking up the one meeting into several meetings related to the area being worked on in the current iteration. This break-up is generally augmented by a hierarchical structure of stand-up meetings, with a weekly stand-up meeting having one representative of each subgroup attend. (This is known as a Scrum of Scrums in the Scrum world.)

Distributed teams will use available technology to have a daily stand-up meeting. Effective techniques include telephone conferences and videoconferences. Teams experiencing a significant time zone difference will have local stand-up meetings with one (usually rotating) representative dialing into the other locations' meetings and reporting to his local team the next morning. The key is not to drop this simple activity.

At organizations where core team members—the pigs—are assigned to multiple projects, stand-up meetings for each project will consume a large part of the development team's time. Maintaining attendance at multiple daily stand-up meetings will cause pain. The general recommendation is to move toward having each pig be on a single development project. When that is not possible, teams must get creative with scheduling to maintain these meetings.

---

3. "Grok" is a reference from Robert A. Heinlein's 1961 novel *Stranger in a Strange Land* and means to fully understand something at all levels.

REFERENCES

Beck, K. and Andres, C., *Extreme Programming Explained: Embrace Change (Second Edition)*, Upper Saddle River: Addison Wesley Professional, 2005.

Schwaber, K., and Beedle, M., *Agile Software Development with SCRUM*, Upper Saddle River: Prentice Hall, 2001.

Yip, J., "It's Not Just Standing Up: Patterns of Daily Stand-up Meetings," http://martinfowler.com/articles/itsNotJustStandingUp.html, 2006.

Chapter 14

DONE STATE

The Done State practice is a definition that a team agrees upon to nonambiguously describe what must take place for a requirement to be considered complete. The done state is the goal of every requirement in an iteration. It is as close as possible to deploying software as a team can come.

BUSINESS VALUE

Defining and adhering to a done state directly affects time to market and visibility. The closer you come to deployable software, the more confidence you have in your progress and the less you have to do to get ready to release. Cost is reduced because you pay for defect fixes early. Of course, the further your team's definition of done state is from deployable software, the more risky your estimates are because you are less confident of your progress and the more you have to pay in time and effort for correcting defects.

SKETCH

Initially, the team agreed on a done state that included all automated developer tests passed and acceptance tests manually run by Aparna and Cathy and verified by the testing team. The first iteration had many uncompleted stories because development was completed only a short time before the end of the time box, and Aparna and Cathy found several defects. The team wanted to count the stories 80 percent done. Caleb strongly discouraged this and was able to convince the team not to do it even though they had only 20 percent completion. The completion percentage was discouraging, and Caleb played cheerleader to keep spirits high.

Over the next two iterations, developers complete the stories in sequence instead of trying to do all of them at once. This resulted in stories being complete earlier, which left enough time for the feedback cycle with testing. The team averaged about 85 percent completion over the next few iterations.

Then, when the team picked up functional testing and started writing executable acceptance tests at the beginning of each iteration (test-driven requirements), the completion rate shot up very close to 100 percent because developers were able to fully test the requirements at their desk. The done state was changed from just passing the automated developer tests to passing both the automated developer tests and the functional tests.

CONTEXT

You are on a development team performing iterations; this implies that you need specific, measurable goals for the requirements to be met at the end.

FORCES

- Reporting on partial work done is error-prone; at worst, we are 90 percent done 90 percent of the time.
- The closer a requirement is delivered to deployable, the less uncertainty your team has about the true state of the system.
- Only functionality that is delivered to the customer has real value.
- The closer a requirement is delivered to a deployable state, the more defects you have found and eliminated.
- Depending on your environment, it may be difficult to get close to deploying.
- Integration in traditional software teams is error-prone and difficult.

THEREFORE

Your team should try to eliminate as much partial work done as possible every iteration. A requirement should be built all the way through, including integration, acceptance testing, and as close as possible to deployment. This will weed out most of the errors and increase your confidence in the team's true progress.

Your team should be consistent, so agree on what it means to really be done; this is the done state. Your goal for each iteration will be to take each requirement to completion as defined by the done state. Finally, a done state is binary. Either it is met or it is not; there is no partial credit. If a requirement doesn't meet its done state at the end of an iteration, it goes back onto the backlog.

ADOPTION

Be aggressive in setting your done state as close as possible to deployment, but also be realistic. Your done state has to be something you can meet in the coming iteration.

- Agree on your done state before the start of your first iteration. Work to get commitment from team members; the whole team will have to work to get a requirement all the way through to your definition of done. Remember, a done state is a goal; therefore, it needs to be S.M.A.R.T. (specific, measurable, achievable, relevant, and timely).
- The done state should push your team members without breaking them.
- Expect getting to the done state to be painful initially. If your team consistently fails to meet the goals of the iteration, use your retrospective to address the issue. Look to fixing other things before scaling back the done state.
- Revisit your done state in your retrospectives when your team is comfortable meeting them. Try to push your done state closer to deployment.

BUT

The done state is an important part of having successful iterations. If the done state is set too low, your team won't see the benefits; if it's set too high, your team will feel the pain and get discouraged.

- A common occurrence is that teams fail to get through acceptance testing because developers complete their work near the end of the iteration and don't have enough time to do full acceptance testing and fix errors that arise. It will be tempting to scale back the done state, but consider working on requirements in series instead of in parallel. That is, don't start working on all the requirements at once, but take a few at a time and work to complete them—using Pair Programming to help—and then go on to the next requirements when those that you are working on have reached their done state.
- If your team is not a cross-functional team, it will be difficult to get close to deployment.
    - If at all possible, go to cross-functional teams.
    - If it is not possible, your done state can go only as far as building, testing, and integrating the particular piece your team is working on. At the same time, plan for teams to be done with their interlocking parts as soon as possible for integration feedback.

- If your done state is too lax—that is, it does not include integration and acceptance testing—your iterations will be dysfunctional. Your team will miss many defects that will have to be fixed later at a higher cost. Important feedback will be missed.
- If you have a customer who places a high value on look and feel and more subjective qualities like usability, it will be important to leave time in the iteration for the back and forth with the customer to fine-tune and reach the done state.
- Some teams decide to have two done states—one for developers and one for the QA team. Therefore, a task is coded in one iteration and tested in the next. This usually creates a planning problem because the true done state is the one after testing, and it is hard to plan for an iteration because there will be an unknown amount of requirements that will fail from the QA done state and fall back to the development iteration.

VARIATIONS

The done state originally evolved out of the general idea of "working software" from the Agile manifesto. But what is working software? In XP, it was originally software that passed unit and acceptance tests. As the community gained more experience with continuous integration in larger projects, the constraints were different, and thus evolved the idea of "as close to deployable as possible."

REFERENCES

Beck, K. and Andres, C., *Extreme Programming Explained: Embrace Change (Second Edition)*, Boston: Addison-Wesley, 2005.

Elshamy, Ahmed Elssamadisy, Amr. Applying Agile to Large Projects: New Agile Software Development Practices for Large Projects. In *Agile Processes in Software Engineering and Extreme Programming*, Proceedings of the Eighth International Conference, XP 2007, Como, Italy, June 18–22, 2007, Springer, 46–53.

Larman, C., *Agile and Iterative Development: A Manager's Guide*, Boston: Addison-Wesley, 2004.

Schwaber, K., and Beedle, M., *Agile Software Development with SCRUM*, Upper Saddle River, New Jersey: Prentice Hall, 2001.

Chapter 15

DEMO

The Demo practice is a show-and-tell presentation and demonstration of the working software built in the Iteration as it ends. It is presented to the stakeholders of the project.

BUSINESS VALUE

Demos increase visibility to the stakeholders, increase product utility by giving the customer a concrete system to evaluate, and support iterations. This means they have a secondary effect on business values directly affected by iterations.

SKETCH

On Caleb the Consultant's advice, the team agreed to have a demo at the end of each iteration—they had agreed to "suspend their disbelief" for a few months until they could judge for themselves the effectiveness of each practice.

The team didn't have much to show at the first iteration. The stakeholders appreciated the teams work but had not really seen anything impressive. The team, on the other hand, found that it took much more work to get the requirements to the point of completeness needed for a demo.

By the third iteration, the stakeholders began to see working user interfaces and were very impressed. They couldn't believe that in six short weeks there was working software! Stakeholders quickly became the driving force behind demos and started to invite others from different departments to attend and see how well their team was doing. The Demo was a key practice that drove other teams to seriously look at Agile development.

CONTEXT

You are on a development team performing iterations and have stakeholders outside the development team who are interested in the progress of the project.

FORCES

Putting requirements and design on paper is good, but it's not enough to gain confidence that an application meets the needs of the organization.

- Confidence is gained by visibility and regular, demonstrable progress.
- Working software gives stakeholders confidence that true progress is being made.
- Partial completion statistics—such as being 30 percent done because the requirements and design are fully complete and reviewed—are faulty. Developers have a track record of being optimistic.
- The work done to get to working software involves removing many defects that show up only in the later stages of development.
- The earlier a defect is found, the cheaper it is to fix.
- Finding and fixing defects is a form of learning, and learning is the bottleneck of software development.
- An envisioned solution is not always as we hope. When the software is built and tested, it sometimes doesn't solve our problem even though it is exactly what we asked for.

THEREFORE

To enable the value of iterations as an incremental delivery mechanism that provides visibility into the true progress of a project, the team should do as much as possible within an iteration to arrive at a releasable increment of the software. At this point, there is an opportunity for feedback from the customer and stakeholders. The team can share the working software and the on-the-ground functionality built so far, and the customer and stakeholders can share their opinions about the effectiveness of the solution so far.

A common way to get this feedback is to have a demo at the end of the iteration with the team and the stakeholders. This hands-on method should only review functions that are completely done and not "almost there" to avoid giving a false sense of completion. All stakeholders and any interested parties should be invited to attend; this is a chance for the team members to display their success to the rest of the organization and get specific feedback in a regular manner. Running a demo regularly builds confidence and trust in the team's ability.

ADOPTION

Getting a demo working regularly can be challenging in the beginning because of old development habits. Getting functionality ready every iteration means that the code must be completed, tested (at least acceptance tested), and integrated.

- Work in vertical slices so that the demo shows something end to end.
- Many in the early iterations will not have much built and may be reluctant to demo something small. Do so anyway to get into the habit of regularly reviewing your work.
- The pain that you will feel is normal. Keep doing demos, and they will be easier over time. They will get your team and stakeholders into a healthy rhythm and provide feedback.
- Don't be discouraged by the lack of progress and pain in the beginning. That is normal.
- Regularly invite stakeholders even if they don't show up. Demos should be part of an iteration's regularly scheduled tasks. Give the stakeholders the iteration calendars and emphasize the critical need for their feedback during these demos.
- Keep the demo short; remember, you only demonstrate one iteration's work.
- Have one or two people execute the software to keep things simple.
- Speak to the attendees—especially the managers—beforehand and let them know that their feedback is welcome but that they need to be careful with their criticism so they don't demoralize the development team. This problem can also be mitigated by having the stakeholders closely involved with the team effort—co-located if at all possible or at least regularly visiting the team.
- Take notes of the comments that stakeholders make. This is your feedback, and it is one of the main reasons you are having the demo. Use these notes to have conversations offline.

BUT

A demo every iteration is not something that most development teams are used to.

- Demos will probably be technically challenging in the beginning because you are not used to taking requirements to full completion so regularly. Work on automating the manual parts of preparing for a demo. After a few iterations, setup should take no more than 30 minutes.
- The feedback you receive might be conflicting. The demo is not the place to resolve these issues. Take them offline with those involved and resolve them. Then report back to the team in the stand-up meeting.
- Some teams demo features that are not done and have not met the done state. Don't do this. It is a slippery slope, and you are giving a false measurement to your stakeholders. You and your team will grow by facing the fact that things were not done and doing something different the next time.
- Many of the stakeholders are busy people in upper management. Depending on your organization's culture and the frequency of your demos, you may have little or no attendance by stakeholders. Talk with the stakeholders in person and see what can be done to have them attend. Here are some ideas.
    - Keep demos short—no more than 30 minutes.
    - Let the stakeholders know that their attendance will help keep morale high.
    - Have them attend no more than one demo every month even if your iterations are shorter.
    - Have them send a representative as a last resort. Representatives are significantly less effective than the stakeholders.
- Sometimes teams drop demos because of the lack of stakeholder availability. They think, "We don't need to demo the work to ourselves." Do your best to get the stakeholders involved. If they will not attend or send a representative, go ahead and drop the demo. Sending a representative may be a smell if the representative adversely affects communication to the stakeholder by filtering the information.

VARIATIONS

In organizations with more than one team running demos, it becomes too much work for the stakeholders to attend all meetings. Therefore, have a science fair; get all teams to run their demos in one large area at the same time. The stakeholders can then see each project's progress over a set period.

REFERENCES

Larman, C., *Agile and Iterative Development: A Manager's Guide*, Boston: Addison-Wesley, 2004.

Schwaber, K., and Beedle, M., *Agile Software Development with SCRUM*, Upper Saddle River, New Jersey: Prentice Hall, 2001.

Chapter 16

RETROSPECTIVE

The Retrospective practice is a meeting held at the end of a major cycle—iteration or release—to gather and analyze data about that cycle and decide on future actions to improve the team's environment and process. A retrospective is about evaluating the people, their interactions, and the tools they use, whereas a demo is focused on evaluating the product that has been built.

BUSINESS VALUE

Retrospectives are key to adapting all the development practices to your particular environment. They can augment and enhance all the practices; therefore, they affect all types of business value indirectly. So for example, effective use of retrospectives can increase quality to market when the team diagnoses an ineffective use of pair programming, which, in turn, produces higher quality software.

SKETCH

Caleb the Consultant introduced retrospectives to the team as a lightweight review at the end of every iteration. The idea was to get the team members involved in their adoption strategy and really evaluate the practices that worked for them. Caleb had always indicated that Agile was no silver bullet and the team should evaluate the practices for themselves.

So for the first few iterations, the retrospectives were focused on having the team members directly asking themselves what was working and what wasn't working with the new practices.

In one such meeting, the iteration just completed had a significant number of uncompleted user stories. The remaining user stories were almost to the done state; they just had to clear QA. The team members were tempted to call the user stories partially done or extend the iteration length to finish the work. Instead, with Caleb's urging, they decided to try another strategy. They put the stories on the backlog, and the next iteration they decided on a strategy of quickly completing user stories sequentially and getting them to the done state early. This required all the team members—customers, developers, and testers—to minimize their work in progress and pair program.

The early retrospectives, along with a coach, helped the team members tailor their adoption efforts and quickly learn from their mistakes. Later, after the team became proficient with this new way of working, retrospectives were varied to reflect other issues.

CONTEXT

You are on a development team that is trying something new, and you want to determine whether you are getting the desired results and what, if anything, needs to change.

Or, more broadly, you are on a development team that has just completed a significant cycle and wants to make the next one better.

Retrospectives have been called the desert-island skill of Agile development. That is, if you were on a desert island and could only choose one skill for your team to have for success, it should be the retrospective because you can use it to derive any other practices or skills you need to deliver software. So in a sense, the context is the universe of software development.[1]

FORCES

- There is no silver bullet. Every software development team and project is different.
- The most effective teams adopt the software development practices that are most relevant to their situation and then tailor them for the given context.
- Leaders frequently know the goals but have not communicated them regularly and effectively to the team, while those in the trenches understand the reality of the situation much better than management. Agile teams, therefore, are cross-functional and self-organizing teams that are aware of the organization's goals for the project.
- To adapt effectively, self-organizing teams need feedback about the software they are building and the way they are working.

---

1. Although I made the assertion that retrospectives are the desert-island skill, I wouldn't recommend throwing everything else out. It will probably take years to reinvent the development practices. We don't want to reinvent the wheel!

- Teams have a more complete and accurate picture of the current environment as a whole than any one member of the team.
- Teams also make better decisions than individual experts given certain conditions such as independence and diversity [Surowiecki].

THEREFORE

The core of Agile development is feedback. But it is not enough to collect the feedback data. The data must be analyzed, and then one or more actions must be taken accordingly. For the action to be effective, your team members must understand the current environment and have clarity on one or more goals they want to reach.

Therefore, to effectively tailor the software development practices to the ever-changing environment of your development team, your team should get together periodically to discuss the progress that has been made and the challenges encountered.

One way to do this is to run a Workshop pattern at the end of every iteration and release. As in all workshops, the team should understand the goals of the meeting. Is it to look for improvements to the current process? To find ways to deliver faster? To understand and alleviate the greatest pains for the team? Set the stage by agreeing on what the team wants from this meeting. This is a chance for the leaders to share their views and help the team members understand the context of their efforts within the bigger picture.

Next, it is extremely beneficial to gather data with respect to the environment—that is, how have we done? Only after reaching clarity on the previous cycle's progress can you decide how to improve. Here the team members share their individual views so that the whole team understands the current environment.

The next step is to generate insights as a group to leverage the wisdom of the crowd. Be open, encourage conversation and input from all team members, and consider all suggestions [Derby and Larson].

At this point the team can decide what to try from the suggestions collected to address the goals given the current environment. The goals should be small enough to be doable in the upcoming cycle. They should also be addressed at the next retrospective when discussing the current environment. In this way, team members can regularly recognize and respond to changes in their development practices effectively.

Therefore, to reiterate, a retrospective has five sections.

1. Set the stage.
2. Gather data.
3. Generate insight by reflecting on and analyzing the data.
4. Create an action plan.
5. Close the retrospective.

ADOPTION

The best retrospectives are run by skilled facilitators. It helps to see at least one successful and effective retrospective before trying your own. Or bring in an experienced coach to help you. The most effective way to run a retrospective that has a chance of catching on is to take your time. Do not plan for less than a half day for a one-month iteration. If you find that you do not have enough new information to discuss between retrospectives because your iterations are small, save time by having a retrospective every other iteration instead of shortening the length of the retrospectives. It takes time for people to get comfortable and discuss touchy-feely subjects that are the core of the data-gathering phase.

Make sure to have actions and goals that your team members have individually committed to; get their individual commitment. You shouldn't mandate actions if you want to keep your team self-organizing. Create an information radiator with the actions your team has committed to. You can treat these actions as tasks to be discussed at the daily stand-up meeting. Also don't bite off more than you can chew; a few simple actions that are achieved and make the team go forward a small step are better than larger steps that are not realized by the next retrospective.

Finally, mix it up. Use different exercises in each of the major stages to keep everyone's interest up.

BUT

Retrospectives are fragile exercises that can easily lose their value and become burdens or be dropped. Be careful of the following common mistakes.

- These are problems with the agreed-upon actions that set up the team for failure and disappointment. These include
  - Creating a large list of action plans that cannot be met.

- Creating actions that are not achievable and measurable. The actions will not be met, and people will say, "We've been around this block before…"
- Choosing actions that your group cannot address. The actions must be within your group's power to achieve.
- Not following up on the actions. The result is that retrospectives repeatedly come up with the same problems.
- There will probably be discomfort or lack of appreciation of the touchy-feely nature. Understand that this is normal and expected; in today's world, feelings are seen as unprofessional. Retrospective exercises, however, focus on feelings as important data to help teams dig up and find problems.
- These are examples of dysfunctional retrospectives that are of limited benefit:
  - Dropping a retrospective because it doesn't seem useful.
  - Running a light retrospective (10 to 15 minutes), thinking that it is not worth taking several hours to run properly.
  - Not varying the exercises or goals and becoming stale.

VARIATIONS

Unlike most practices in this book, Retrospectives are flexible and have unlimited variations. As long as the basic structure is there of opening the meeting, gathering data, generating insights, creating an action plan, and closing the retrospective, any of a variety of practices can be used to run the meeting.

REFERENCES

Derby, E. and Larson, D., *Agile Retrospectives: Making Good Teams Great*, Raleigh: Pragmatic Bookshelf, 2006.

Kerth, N., *Project Retrospectives: A Handbook for Team Reviews*, NY: Dorset House Publishing Company, 2001.

Surowiecki, J., *The Wisdom of Crowds*, NY: Anchor, 2005.

Chapter 17

RELEASE OFTEN

Release your software to your end customers as often as you can without inconveniencing them. Figure 17-1 shows how the Release Often practice is related to the Continuous Integration practice.

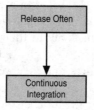

Figure 17-1 The Release Often practice is made possible by building things end to end and removing defects as soon as possible. This is best achieved by practicing Continuous Integration with Automated Developer Tests.

BUSINESS VALUE

The most obvious business value addressed by this practice is time to market—the fact that you can release often means that you can get functionality out the door quickly to maintain an edge on your competitors or catch up quickly.

Furthermore, software that is used by your customer is the ultimate test of product utility; therefore, releasing often gives you an opportunity to frequently improve this business value. It motivates making all of testing, integration, and deployment automated to keep them from taking too large a part of your development cycle, so it indirectly improves the quality of the software you are building.

Finally, releasing often does wonders for building stakeholder and customer confidence. It also is a great way to build trust and reduce the Us Versus Them smell.

SKETCH

The first release of the team was a full year in the making. Over this year, team members adopted and adapted many Agile practices, including Self-Organizing Team, Test-Driven Development, Iterations with Backlogs, Kick-off Meetings, Stand-Up Meetings, Demos, Retrospectives, Continuous Integration, and Functional Tests. Their release was remarkable in terms of how painless it was to go from development to a product that was ready to roll out to their Web site. It took about six weeks of working out the kinks, load testing, and doing all members could to break the program.

The team was happy, and so was the organization; by all measures, the release was a success. The team members picked up right where they left off and started working the next release. In the meantime, they kept an eye on customer feedback about their release. It seems one of the areas they put the most effort into—their Righteously Right Search—was annoying many of their customers, and they were going to popular search engines instead.

This became the topic of their next retrospective, and they decided that they really should have had feedback much earlier in the process. After reading about Amazon and eBay and how those companies slowly and continuously modified their Web sites and functionality, they decided to do the same. The team members had enough confidence in their development ability to release often. They started to release to the Web site every third iteration.

And as for their search engine problem, they ended up gutting their own search engine and delegating out to other search engines. They were not a search company and could not compete with them on accuracy or relevancy. Instead, they built their own database of searches run from their site and used that to help prioritize their backlog.

CONTEXT

You are on a project where releasing often will enable you to produce revenue earlier. Having new features available frequently will not inconvenience your customer base.

FORCES

- Feedback from released software is more valuable than any other type of internal feedback with respect to product utility.
- Getting to the point of releasable software requires comprehensive integration and acceptance testing.
- Without automated developer tests and functional tests being run regularly as part of continuous integration, getting ready for a release is extremely time and resource-intensive.
- Some applications are more amenable to extra features being added regularly than others; likewise, some customers are more comfortable with using new software than others.
- A team that has the ability to release often has a greater ability to get to market quickly and compete rigorously with competitors.

THEREFORE

If your organization is in a position to make money from smaller releases, you would be crazy not to do so! Therefore, you should know or find out if getting your software to your customer in smaller pieces will

- Be marketable and sellable
- Not inconvenience your existing customers
- Give you a competitive advantage

If all three of these issues are acceptable, consider your development team's capability to release often. Is your team comfortable with automated developer tests, functional tests, and continuous integration? If so, you are ready for the next step—releasing often.

ADOPTION

If your team has a done state that is close to deployable software and has automated developer tests and functional tests being run regularly with continuous integration, you are close to having deployable software.

- Pull as many of your organization's procedures for release into continuous integration as you can to minimize the effort of releasing and schedule your releases appropriately.
- Work with sales and marketing to let them know what you are doing and support them in making the most out of this new capability.

BUT

Be aware that releasing often is not for every organization or team.

- If your customers have a large rollout procedure, it will be inconvenient for them to deal with frequent releases of your product.
- If your team is not practiced enough—has not built those Agile muscles by performing automated developer tests, functional tests, and continuous integration—you might be setting your team up for failure.
- Many times, the technical group drives the practice of Release Often, without regard to what makes sense to the business. Make sure you have buy-in from sales and marketing because they will know best whether this feature is desirable.

VARIATION

Although considerably suboptimal, you can release often without continuous integration and automated developer tests. Just beware that doing so will be extremely painful.

REFERENCES

Beck, K. and Andres, C., *Extreme Programming Explained: Embrace Change (Second Edition)*, Boston: Addison-Wesley, 2005.

Schwaber, K., and Beedle, M., *Agile Software Development with SCRUM*, Upper Saddle River, New Jersey: Prentice Hall, 2001.

Chapter 18

CO-LOCATED TEAM

Teams that follows the Co-Located Team practice work in the same physical space. Their workspace is usually an open area that enables and encourages communication. The informal communication that happens between members of such a team enhances the team's ability to work together effectively.

BUSINESS VALUE

A co-located team is able to recognize and collectively respond to new information effectively, which affects its flexibility. At the same time, this team spends much less time in cycles trying to understand each other correctly. Being co-located gives the team the most channels and the highest possible bandwidth of communication, so it gets things done faster.

Furthermore, osmotic communication—the type of communication that occurs when you just happen to hear a conversation within earshot—spreads knowledge within the team and helps to increase the product's lifetime by indirectly reducing resource bottlenecks.

SKETCH

When Amy joined Scott's team, she had misgivings about giving up her corner office to go sit with the team; she felt that it would be distracting and she would lose the opportunity for "quiet time" for focus. For the first couple of iterations, Amy found herself a little annoyed by all the noise and constant interruptions; people kept coming to her for advice, and she spent most of her time pair-programming or in one break-out room or another having design discussions. She had much less time for herself and found that she signed up for fewer tasks every iteration than she expected.

After a while, as the new work rhythms started to sink in, Amy found that she was doing more good for the team in her advisor role. She was a valuable resource and was mentoring the team, while keeping an indirect eye on the design and architecture of the system as it grew. Whenever she needed personal time, she would go into one of the small break-out rooms, close the door, and get done whatever she needed to get done. The rest of the time was spent with the team energetically building the system piece by piece. She also found that her personal relationships with the rest of the teams grew and, overall, she enjoyed the personal aspects of work just as much as the technical ones.

CONTEXT

Your development team has members who live in the same vicinity or can relocate, and you want to build a high-performance team that can work effectively together. Time-to-market and product utility are critical success factors for your project.

FORCES

- Communication is one of the most vital tools to learning.
- Higher-bandwidth communication is better at getting things done fast. There is a smaller probability of miscommunication, and when they do happen, feedback and response are faster.
- Face-to-face communication is much more productive than any other form, including video-conferencing, phone calls, and e-mails.
- When a team sits together, the members overhear important conversations that they would have otherwise been oblivious to. The team that sits together can recognize important issues much faster and much more easily because of this type of communication. This type of communication is commonly known as "osmotic communication."
- Software is built by people. Personal relationships matter. It is much easier to solve problems in person than remotely.
- Remote teams have error-prone and slow communication that slows down development and often creates an Us Versus Them environment.
- Face-to-face communication helps build trust among team members.

THEREFORE

Don't make building software harder than it has to be. Get your team working in one physical area in an environment that encourages good, clear communication. This practice, Co-Located Team, is often one of the easiest to implement and get right. It enhances any team's working capability—Agile or not. Use co-location to improve your team's communication and build the team members' relationships to help "gel" the team.

Co-locating simply means that the team works in one area. There are several configurations of the work area that support the communication of such a team. The most common of these is the caves-and-commons configuration described in Cockbun [Cockburn 2006]. This configuration has an open area—the commons—where the teams work together in an open environment. It also has several break-out rooms—the caves—where one or more people can go to work quietly and privately.

ADOPTION

To effectively have a co-located team, you need to move the entire team—not just the developers—into one physical area. The most effective way to adopt this practice is to create a good collaborative work environment and then let the team members work in the area. They'll figure out the rest. Here are some of the most important things to have in your area.

- An open area for work, commonly known as a bull-pen, with low (or no) dividers between areas where developers work. This area needs to be large, but this is not an invitation to decrease the work area of the team by half.
- A seating arrangement where two can easily work together at a computer.
- A private location for people to keep "their stuff" and have alone time.
- Plenty of low-tech communication media such as whiteboards, stickies, and note cards.
- Break-out rooms with whiteboards.
- Significant wall space on which to hang information radiators.
- Digital camera(s) to quickly save whiteboard information.
- Wireless Internet for interteam visitations and work.
- A computer projector.

There are several wish lists out there for collaborative workspaces, and Hartmann's two articles in the "References" section are a good starting point.

BUT

A co-located team in an appropriate collaborative space can increase its productivity. But be sure to make the space a humane one.

- Avoid stripping down team members' personal space—having a co-located team should not mean extremely tight quarters (no tighter than cubicles).
- Noise is a constant problem—people talk (and some very loudly). Watch out for these problems and encourage the more vocal of your team to be considerate and take conversations to break-out rooms where they won't disturb others.
- Some teams go overboard with the collective idea do things like erasing whiteboards daily. Remember that the key is communication. Do what needs to be done to support your teams' needs; don't just replace one set of rules with another.
- Remember that the main goal of co-locating the team is to improve communication and team building. Keep those goals in mind as you watch the effectiveness of your team. Use the Retrospective practice to debug the effectiveness of your co-location.

VARIATIONS

Some environments are distributed, and co-location is unrealistic. This has been mitigated by the following approaches.

- Temporarily co-locate the teams for the members to work together, build trust, and hopefully have higher-bandwidth communications later.
- Use high-bandwidth communication mediums such as video conferences.
- Reorganize teams using the cross-functional pattern to reduce dependencies among distributed teams.
- Use nonambiguous communication techniques, or tests. The Test-Driven Development and Test-Driven Requirements clusters of practices are most effective in this case.

REFERENCES

Cockburn, A., *Agile Software Development: The Cooperative Game (Second Edition)*, Boston: Addison-Wesley, 2007.

Hartmann, D., "Co-Located Teams vs. the Cubicle Farm," www.infoq.com/news/collaborative-team-space-study.

Hartmann, D., "Designing Collaborative Spaces for Productivity," www.infoq.com/articles/agile-team-room-wishlist.

Chapter 19

SELF-ORGANIZING TEAM

The practice of running a Self-Organizing Team yields a team that is in charge of its own fate. Management gives the team goals to achieve, and the team members are responsible for driving toward those goals and achieving them. Self-organizing team members recognize and respond to changes in their environment and in their knowledge as they learn. A self-organizing team is frequently a cross-functional team as well. Figure 19-1 shows the relationship of the Self-Organizing Team practice to the Retrospective practice.

Figure 19–1   A Self-Organizing Team is most effective when a retrospective is used to give the team feedback on its progress.

BUSINESS VALUE

A self-organizing team is one that does what it takes to get things done to meet the goals of a project. Such a team, by its very nature, requires less management intervention and direction. This practice directly affects flexibility and the team's ability to respond to change. Self-organizing teams also excel at extending a product's lifetime by effectively working together to share knowledge. This practice goes hand in hand with retrospectives as a supporting practice that enhances all others by making the team more productive.

SKETCH

From the start, Scott's team was self-organizing. With his background in management, Scott was delighted to stop trying to tell the future and focus on helping the team move forward through true servant leadership. The rest of the team took to the new responsibilities easily. The feedback points of stand-up meetings and retrospectives gave them plenty of opportunity to see change coming, and they worked well together to clear the obstacles and make appropriate course corrections.

One of the many examples happened early on in the development cycle; the first few iterations did not meet most of the team's goals. By the time developers were done with the work, it was close to the end of the iteration, and there was little time for testing and even less to fix defects found in testing. The team attacked this issue with a two-pronged approach: 1) they did the work in sequence instead of in parallel, and 2) toward the end of the iteration, the whole team ran acceptance tests with Cathy and Aparna supervising. This willingness to do work that is not officially in your job description is a common occurrence with self-organizing teams.

CONTEXT

You are assembling a development team, and you want to make it high performing. You trust that your employees are experts in their field and do not need hand-holding to do their work. You understand that micromanagement is less effective than setting goals for people and empowering them to meet those goals.

FORCES

- Management is aware of strategic goals for the projects.
- Often the truth of an issue is at the ground level. The people on the ground have a better grasp of a problem and are better equipped to solve it.
- "Plans are nothing; planning is everything."[1] Planning enables the team to understand the problem and set goals. The plans themselves become stale quickly as execution begins. Therefore, teams must respond to the reality on the ground instead of following a plan.
- Software development professionals are highly trained knowledge workers. They are more qualified to make decisions regarding how best to do their jobs than their managers.

---

1. Dwight D. Eisenhower. Involving every team member in planning has the benefit that every member understands the tactical goals of the project. Such concepts were critical to the successes of D-Day where bottom-up leadership (squad and company commanders) pulled their teams together and achieved goals while top-down command was offshore or out of theater.

- The most effective team members overcome obstacles and changes in environments and requirements as they arise instead of getting stuck and waiting for someone else to solve the problem. They are aware of these changes when they happen and respond to them appropriately.
- It is demoralizing and frustrating to professionals when they can see a solution to their problems but official processes and procedures impede that solution.
- Trust is a two way street. Giving a development team the power to solve its own solutions builds trust in management, while constant visibility and delivery on commitments build trust in the team.

THEREFORE

Management should communicate with development teams by setting goals instead of assigning and mandating tasks. Teams have the most information and the right skills to achieve these goals. They are responsible for figuring out how achieve those goals. They should communicate their progress regularly to management via demos, information radiators, and early notification of setbacks and alternatives to enable management to make good strategic decisions. Trust will be built through honest, visible communication and doing all that you can to meet the goals.

Teams that adapt to meet goals are self-organizing teams. The individual team members are aware of the goals of the project and work together to meet them. When obstacles arise in a stand-up meeting, they collectively solve the problem without concern for whose job it is. They have regular retrospectives where they spend the necessary time reflecting on their progress and process and adapt. A self-organizing team has the potential for greatness.

ADOPTION

Successful self-organizing teams have members who are responsible, as defined in Chapter 2, "Personal Agility for Potent Agile Adoption." Therefore

- Nurture your relationship with management.
    - Get acceptance from management to work this way and agreement from them to communicate with the team by goals instead of tasks to perform.
    - Display important information radiators such as burn-down charts and passing tests to provide visibility. Augment these with demos to reinforce your commitment to meeting goals that you have agreed upon.

- Communicate challenges and slips early and do not hide them from management. Take responsibility to solve these problems whenever possible.
- Get the right people and encourage their participation.
  - Review what it means to be responsible, as defined by Avery's Responsibility Process Model in Chapter 2, and get a commitment from team members to act from a position of responsibility.
  - It would be great if the entire team had personal agility, but that is not always the case. Do your best to have at least two to three members who have this attribute or are willing to learn and practice responsibility.
  - Make sure to get everyone's point of view in stand-up meetings and retrospectives. Don't let the extroverts take over and the introverts lurk.
  - Try to make your team a cross-functional team to improve your chances of successfully responding to problems as they arise.

BUT

Self-organizing teams are usually a huge step forward but, like all practices, they have their challenges.

- Some experts are too few as a resource to assign them to only one team, and they must be shared. This means that they can easily be a bottleneck when nobody else can address an issue. One of the best ways to address this is to always pair with the experts when they work on your team to incrementally transfer knowledge to the team and reduce dependency on them.
- Watch out for abuse. This happens occasionally when the members of a team do not have the integrity and discipline to work toward the goals they have committed to. Remember that trust is a two-way street; therefore, expect a self-organizing team to provide visibility and transparency through information radiators, demos, and constant feedback. If team members are quiet, encourage them to communicate. If they don't communicate, it may be worth taking a closer look into their progress.
- Beware of local maximization. Remember, a team's goals should be directly related to the business goals of the organization. It is easy for a team to become focused exclusively on its iteration and release goals and cause/exacerbate an Us Versus Them smell. Be sure to stay connected to the larger picture and respond to the global context.

VARIATIONS

Self-organizing teams tend to be cross-functional teams because this improves their ability to respond to issues as they arise. However, this is not always the case, especially in organizations that have a long history of working in functional teams with extreme specialization. In those instances, each group focused on one area is a self-organizing team. They gain many of the benefits of using the Self-Organizing Team practice but are more constrained when it comes to the issues they can address because many lie outside their circle of influence.

REFERENCES

Avery, C., *Teamwork Is an Individual Skill*, San Francisco: Berrett-Koehler Publishers, Inc., 2001.

Beck, K. and Andres, C., *Extreme Programming Explained: Embrace Change (Second Edition)*, Boston: Addison-Wesley, 2005.

Derby, E. and Larson, D., *Agile Retrospectives: Making Good Teams Great*, Raleigh: Pragmatic Bookshelf, 2006.

Schwaber, K., and Beedle, M., *Agile Software Development with SCRUM*, Upper Saddle River, New Jersey: Prentice Hall, 2001.

Senge, P., *The Fifth Discipline: The Art and Practice of The Learning Organization*, NY: Currency, 2006.

Chapter 20

CROSS-FUNCTIONAL TEAM

The team that utilizes the Cross-Functional Team practice is one that has the necessary expertise among its members to take a requirement, such as a use case or user story, from its initial concept to a fully deployed and tested piece of software within one iteration. For example, a user story can be taken off the backlog, elaborated and developed, tested, deployed, and whatever else needs to be done for that story to reach the done state. Figure 20-1 illustrates the relationship between the Cross-Functional Team practice and the Collective Code Ownership and Pair Programming practices.

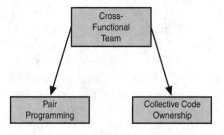

Figure 20–1 The Cross-Functional Team practice relies on collective code ownership to enable different team members to build end-to-end functionality and pair programming to reduce the problems of experts as bottlenecks.

BUSINESS VALUE

Cross-functional teams primarily affect time to market by enabling true iterative and incremental development. In other words, they work by fully building small increments of the software a piece at a time that can be deployed at will. Cross-functional teams also indirectly affect product utility by creating executable, testable software every iteration that the customer can use for evaluation and feedback. By building out functionality fully every iteration, you enable planning to deliver at any time and minimize the work in progress, which increases flexibility. Finally, this practice positively affects the quality of the software if the definition of the done state includes a fully tested requirement.

SKETCH

The different team members had mixed feelings about working on a cross-functional team. Tim Tester was looking forward to working more closely with Aparna Analyst instead of working through stale documents and trying to figure out exactly how the software was supposed to work for adequate testing. Scott ScrumMaster saw a big challenge in getting this group to work well together because the team members came from such diverse experiences and working environments. He felt there was great potential and also a huge risk if they did not communicate well and gel as a team. Amy Architect felt that this wasn't going to be the best use of her time; she was a valued architect and traditionally spent minimal time with each team in the beginning helping to set the architecture and design and leaving the rest of the work for the developers and testers.

Caleb had helped teams through this before and had been working with the organization to encourage it to form this team and prove/disprove the productivity and quality gains that were expected. As he expected, there were no problems at the start. Things went much smoother than everyone expected; people tend to work well together when given the chance. The team was able to complete work from end to end every iteration. The demos at the end of every iteration showed the rest of the organization that steady progress was being made. Over the first six months, the team gelled, and productivity grew at an unexpected pace.

Over those six months, the team members stepped up to the plate and performed duties that were not traditionally their roles. Amy pair-programmed with the developers, and Tim worked with Aparna in the analysis cycle to better understand the business and helped her when the team decided to move toward test-driven requirements. The team kept busy, did what needed to be done, and did it together.

CONTEXT

You are on a development project that has quality and time-to-market issues. There is a significant hardening cycle at the end of each release indicating unresolved integration issues. Or perhaps you have a need for your product utility to improve significantly and you have decided to do so through small inspect-and-adapt cycles; therefore, you need a fully working system at the end of each iteration. Building a slice of functionality end to end in your system requires the diverse expertise of many different people.

FORCES

These are some common scenarios in today's development environment.

- Taking a requirement and developing it completely into working software takes the expertise of many different people: a customer who understands the problem domain, possibly an analyst to help elaborate the details of the problem, one or more developers with different expertise to build different parts of the system, and frequently a DBA to support the database, testers, and technical writers.
- Traditional methods that create "slices" of the work to be built out or assembled in a later date typically suffer from the following.
    - Documents used to communicate intent are misread and misunderstood.
    - Working pieces don't come together easily and create a large integration burden.
    - Found errors take significant time to cycle back to be addressed.
- Traditional teams have "experts" that work on multiple projects at once. They are extremely specialized, and there would not be enough of them to go around if they were part of only one team.
- Task and context switching between multiple projects detrimentally affects focus and efficiency.
- Software ownership and pride are common and fit naturally with being split up by expertise.
- Partially done work has no value.

THEREFORE

To learn fast and catch as many errors as possible early, you and your team should build functions all the way through—as close to deployable as possible—which forces you to address issues in all phases of software development iteration by iteration.

To maximize flexibility, you must be done with a piece of functionality before you move to the next. To be done—reach a done state that includes integration and testing—the necessary expertise must be present on the team, and the team must be able to work together closely to resolve issues quickly.

Have your whole team be a cross-functional one that has the expertise to build the software all the way through every iteration. This will allow you to do just that and improve flexibility, quality, and time to market.

ADOPTION

Two issues come up when trying to go to cross-functional teams: 1) the initial formation of the team is difficult given the way things are done presently, and 2) once the team is together, it is not usually possible for everyone to be busy 100 percent of the time, which runs against the grain and current best practices concerning efficiency.

As with all learning, you must slow down before you can speed up. If your organization currently runs multiple projects using the traditional approach of having experts in certain areas and sharing these experts among the different teams, you come up against a problem: "If we give you this expert for your cross-functional team, she will no longer be available for the rest of the teams." And that's usually that. Unfortunately, not having a cross-functional team usually means that you won't be able to set an appropriate done state. It will impede the use of Agile iterations. So here are some common ways that people have gone from their functional teams to cross-functional teams.

- Have experts available to pair-program. The first option involves having the expert be part of the team and keeping her available to other teams in pair-programming sessions only, so that the expertise is transferred over time. The second option is using the mirror image, which involves contacting the expert to pair-program with a member of the team—although this frequently causes resource bottlenecks when the expert is unavailable.
- If pairing is not in the cards, consider frequent brown-bag lunches to disseminate expert knowledge to the rest of the team.
- Gradually cross-functionalize your team. Make your team as diverse as possible today. Be on the lookout to recruit needed experts and be prepared for someone to drop what he is doing and pair-program with him when he comes to help.
- Take what you can. If you can get an expert on a part-time basis only, take it!

BUT

Cross-functional teams not only go against current organizational structure but also against many personal working habits. Watch out for these smells and address them quickly. All of them are personal matters, so you have to be creative in addressing them.

- Developers are used to owning their code. The code is their "baby," and they don't want anyone touching it. That attitude can easily form bottlenecks where everything stands still because nobody can touch code that is not theirs.
- Nobody owns the code. The Collective Code Ownership practice is misused, and the quality of the code suffers.
- Many feel threatened working in a cross-functional team where others can learn what they know, and they may feel they are less valuable to the team and organization.
- Watch out for "not my job" syndrome. Because bottlenecks occur in different areas and at different times, team members are called upon to help each other. For example, the whole development team may need to test the system with the testers. Some may feel that this is degrading, lower-status work or the type of work they left behind, making them uncomfortable.

VARIATIONS

A cross-functional team is frequently called a whole team because it is not just developers, but developers, testers, customers, and everyone else involved in building software.

Cross-functional teams that transition from active development to maintenance wind down the team to a fraction of its original size. The most successful of these teams relies on an apprenticeship model and a large suite of automated developer tests and functional tests. The maintainers are part of the original team or have apprenticed and pair-programmed during a several-iteration transition phase.

REFERENCES

Beck, K. and Andres, C., *Extreme Programming Explained: Embrace Change (Second Edition)*, Boston: Addison-Wesley, 2005.

Cockburn, A., *Agile Software Development: The Cooperative Game (Second Edition)*, Boston: Addison-Wesley, 2007.

Poppendieck, M., and Poppendieck, T., *Implementing Lean Software Development*, Boston: Addison-Wesley, 2007.

Chapter 21

CUSTOMER PART OF TEAM

The Customer Part of Team practice is just that—a customer is part of your team. The customer should know the details about the problem to be solved. This team member's main responsibilities involve the overall usefulness of the product being developed. Does the software solve real business problems? Are the solutions usable and useful? Are the right trade-offs being made? Is the prioritization of the backlog appropriate?

BUSINESS VALUE

This practice is perhaps the most significant one in terms of achieving a product that is useful to the business—that is, product utility. Time to market is also affected by this practice because the customer as part of the team is key to prompt and realistic feedback on the deliverables, reducing the likelihood of major time-critical surprises. Flexibility is improved because the customer is there to guide the team in making appropriate trade-offs.

SKETCH

Cathy, who had been in the software business for several years, was to have the role of the customer. She had helped many teams understand the domain of the business to build useful software. Her experience prior to this team was mainly in writing and validating requirements, which required patience and an eye for detail. She would also work with several teams at a time because they really only needed her in the start-up phase and in delivery.

Cathy was skeptical when she was asked to join Scott's team full-time as the customer. What would she do for the entire development cycle after the requirements phase was up? And if the team was going to work in small cycles, how would she keep busy? She could easily write up enough requirements to keep the whole team busy for that time.

Needless to say, Cathy was busy the entire time writing and prioritizing user stories and having conversations with the team to clarify and explain. She also found herself learning to write test scripts with Tim as the team adopted functional tests and, later on, test-driven requirements. She never realized that she had been underspecifying her requirements before!

Cathy had caught the Agile "disease." She would never go back to the old way of working. Cathy built strong relationships with her team members, and they let her drive and prioritize the requirements. When technical issues and dependencies came up, they did not enforce one way of doing things—as had always been done on other teams—but explained the issues to her and let her decide on the ultimate priority of work. This resulted in the software being delivered on time, even with the eventual surprises, because the really important parts were built and solidified early on.

CONTEXT

You are on a software development project in an organization that would like to improve product utility.

FORCES

- Solving the "problem right" is different from solving the "right problem"; no matter how technically apt your solution is, it is useless if it does not address the needs of your customers.
- Learning is the bottleneck of software development; in many contexts, a large part of that learning involves refining and changing the initial requirements of the system.
- Many potential customers are reluctant to join a software development team thinking that it is the software development team's responsibility to figure out what needs to be done and build the software; they don't realize how error-prone that technique is in most instances.
- Customers may not know what they want, but they can recognize what is useful when they see it.
- Customers are not usability experts or software experts; they are domain experts.
- Product companies have a large and possibly diverse customer base.
- Software projects have a limited and focused customer base.

THEREFORE

Because product utility—the usefulness of the software you build—is important to your organization and because there is much to learn about what will best help your customer, you should strive to get early and frequent feedback from the potential users of the system.

There are several ways that this is done in practice. One of the best ways to do this is to have significant and regular customer involvement throughout the development of the application.[1] This is so effective that it was listed as the primary reason for success of software projects in the 2006 Standish Report.

Therefore, get a domain expert to play the role of customer on the team.[2] Give this person responsibility for creating and prioritizing the requirements. Inform the customer of any technical risks, constraints, and other information that may be relevant to the order in which things are built, but in the end, allow the customer to prioritize the work.

With the customer part of team, the demos at the end of every iteration are an opportunity for evaluation and feedback with respect to product utility.

ADOPTION

Product organizations and those that have individual projects seem very different at first look, but they are actually very similar when it comes to the practice of Customer Part of Team:

- Product
  - You probably already have an HCI expert for usability who runs experiments and focus group sessions to help decide what the UI should look like. This person also probably works up front, at the beginning of the project. Have this expert build models incrementally instead and continue working throughout the development cycle.

---

1. Another common way is to have a Human Computer Interaction (HCI) specialist on the team who will work to run focus groups and experiments to come up with the user interface upfront. These are complementary practices.

2. This does not mean to have a developer play the role of the customer. It means the customer has to be more than just a "user" of the system—he has to be an expert in the business domain.

- Your analyst/domain expert/marketing expert—the person(s) who currently provides the requirements—needs to be more involved. He probably already has a full-time job. Get the group who supplies the requirement to commit one person of their group to the project to play the customer role.

- Project
    - You have a client you are building the system for, and that client is investing a lot of time and money to get software to help it do its job better. Tell this client about the Standish report for 2006 [Standish Group]. The research clearly shows that user involvement is the number-one reason cited for project success.
    - The client you are building the software for will probably be amenable to dedicating one of its team members to working as the customer part of the team on a part-time basis. Take this opportunity and work closely with this person to support his efforts.
    - Get other members of the client organization to attend the demos to make sure you are on track.

Other adoption considerations include the following:

- This is not an all-or-nothing practice. Push as hard as you can to get a full-time customer as part of the team—but take what you can get. The important thing is to get the customer involved in prioritizing and providing regular feedback as you build the system.
- If you cannot get a customer as part of the team, consider having a person on your team play the role of customer as proxy. That person will have the responsibility of the customer with the added responsibility of communicating heavily and directly with the client to validate the work being done. This role is often referred to as a customer proxy.
- Realize that the ultimate test for product utility is releasing the software and having people use it, so consider releasing often to augment this practice.

BUT

Here are some challenges with the customer being part of the team.

- Many analysts take up the role of the customer as part of the team because they are domain experts. This is great, but they should beware of the added responsibilities and constraints.
    - The customer builds incremental requirements and needs to get out of the habit of eliciting large upfront requirements.
    - The customer needs to be available to the rest of the development team for clarifications and conversations; this becomes a more time-consuming task than it is traditionally.
    - If the team uses functional tests or test-driven requirements, the customer has to learn the testing language and be more precise in his requirements.
- Clients often "sacrifice" the junior person of their team to be part of the development team. Unfortunately, this can handicap the project right away because the customer cannot properly perform prioritization and clarifications and cannot respond appropriately to feedback. Remember: The Customer Part of Team practice is there to help the team "solve the right problem," but if this person does not know enough, the product utility will be at risk.
- Stakeholders are often management and not subject matter experts. They make equally bad customers as the junior person being sacrificed. They don't have the time and are not accessible. The best place for a stakeholder to participate is the iteration and release demos.
- Customers who are part-time and are not available to answer questions put the team meeting their goals at risk every iteration. One way to mitigate this is to adopt test-driven requirements to reduce the ambiguity of the requirements.
- The customer changes. The new person doesn't have the same expertise or point of view. There will probably be a change in the prioritization. Remember that documents are not enough unless they are evocative. The apprenticeship model works best. The new and old customer should work together for at least two iterations before making the handoff.
- Many distributed teams have customers in a different location from the development team. This makes communication and resolution of information error-prone. Mitigate this issue by communicating through tests instead of written specifications—that is, adopt test-driven requirements as a communication mechanism for requirements.

VARIATIONS

- In Scrum, the Product Owner is the same role/practice as Customer Part of Team.
- When you cannot agree with the true customer to join the team, you can have a customer proxy. This person will have the responsibility of the customer with the added responsibility of communicating heavily and directly with the client to validate the work being done.
- Product teams regularly have both HCI and domain experts. They often work together to play the customer as part of the team role because they bring different required skill sets to the table.
- The customer is accessible rather than co-located with the team. Accessible in this case means that the customer promptly answers any e-mails and is able to join any meeting on demand.

REFERENCES

Beck, K. and Andres, C., *Extreme Programming Explained: Embrace Change (Second Edition)*, Boston: Addison-Wesley, 2005.

Elssamadisy, A., "Human Computer Interaction (HCI) and Agile Compatibility," www.infoq.com/news/2007/06/hci_agile, accessed November 2007.

Hartmann, D., "Interview: Jim Johnson of the Standish Group," www.infoq.com/articles/Interview-Johnson-Standish-CHAOS, accessed November 2007.

Schwaber, K., and Beedle, M., *Agile Software Development with SCRUM*, Upper Saddle River, New Jersey: Prentice Hall, 2001.

Standish Group, "CHAOS Report," 2006 (can be purchased at www.standishgroup.com/chaos_resources/index.php).

Chapter 22

EVOCATIVE DOCUMENT

In the Evocative Document[1] practice, documents are created that evoke the memories, conversations, and situations of those who wrote the document. These documents are more meaningful and representative of a team's understanding of the system than traditional documents.

BUSINESS VALUE

Evocative documents help prolong a product's lifetime by accurately representing the team's internal model of the software and allowing that model to be handed down from master to apprentice. The better understanding of the system over time also reduces the maintenance cost of the system over time because appropriate changes reduce the deterioration of the software.

SKETCH

Aparna and Dave were on their way home from a week-long UML training course and discussing what they had learned. "UML certainly provides a rich and detailed tool for describing our software," Dave noted. "But it can still be misleading," Aparna responded. "Remember our discussion about the customer class?" "I do," said Dave, "and I remember how we got into that discussion of what 'is' is—when people started using our UML description as if it were a customer." "Oh yes, and that guy in the back talking about Alfred Korzybski and 'the map is not the territory'—that was weird," Aparna added. "But he was right, really," continued Dave. "No matter how much detail you get in your UML model and templates, something is always missing. The model is never the real thing." "And our understanding of what the real thing is keeps changing and changes from one context to another," Aparna said.

---

1. Based on a paper presented at PLoP 2006 and coauthored with David West.

"How can we put all of that in a model?" "Well," Dave suggested, "we probably don't need to if we can find a way to remind ourselves of everything we know about something when we need it." "How would we do that?" Aparna asked. "Remember that icon on the wall of the seminar room," Dave responded. "Remember when we asked the facility manager about it and she talked for half an hour about its meaning and history and everything." "Sure do," said Aparna. "One simple symbol evoked a huge amount of memory. Maybe that is the secret…"

CONTEXT

You are on a software development project where product lifetime and reducing the cost of software are important. You are building a system to last for several years. Documentation isn't working; as a document is passed from one person to another, much of the context and value are lost and, as a result, the maintenance team's understanding of the code base constantly deteriorates. This makes your software system calcify.

FORCES

- Literate and legalistic societies and organizations share a deeply held, though often unconscious, belief that written documents are representative in nature.
    - A contract is the agreement among parties (and not just a representation). The blueprint is the building, albeit in a different format.
    - The specification is the software artifact desired. This belief is so strong in the arena of software that many feel it should be possible to formally and mechanically transform specifications into an artifact with no interpretation or ambiguity.
- Documents that are built collectively—by having a conversation—are much more valuable to those who were part of the conversation. These documents evoke memories of the conversation, its context, and much more than what is merely written on paper.
- Agile development is the embodiment of group "theory building" as described by Peter Naur [Naur 1985]. That is, the software we build is directly related to a mental model—the "theory"—that the programmers share. Traditional documents fail miserably in imparting this model to others. Naur suggests that the only successful way to share this model is through apprenticeship.
- Agile practices, more than any other kind of development practices, require the creation of a rich and easily accessible external memory.

- Representational documentation is notoriously limited and has a long track record of failure in supporting "theory building" and acting as an "external memory."

THEREFORE

All documentation should be evocative rather than representational. Anyone who has read a good novel is familiar with the notion of an evocative document—one that enables the reader to "recall to mind" thousands of sensations, emotions, and even details of time and place that the author could not possibly have included in the text of the novel.

This is how you can truly preserve the shared knowledge and understanding of the team and pass it along to new members. There is no "one way" to put together such a document, so the distinguishing factor in an evocative document is that it is a reminder of the real information and knowledge in a person's head. It is not the knowledge itself, and it is not directly representational.

ADOPTION

A team that relies on evocative documents spends more time in face-to-face conversation and less time building and maintaining documents. The documents they keep tend to be simple and only comprehensible to those in the conversation; therefore, to transfer the knowledge behind the document to someone who was not there, the conversation and context have to be repeated and the document built from scratch. What is gained by this is a much better transfer of knowledge within context that ultimately leads to more proper understanding of the application and reduced maintenance costs.

More specifically, evocative documents tend to have the following characteristics.

- They're informal. They might be 3×5 cards rather than syntactically correct and detailed UML diagrams.
- They're based on natural language, both in terms of the natural language used by the team for communication inside and outside the office, but also in terms of the domain-driven vocabulary of the project.
- They're rich in references to people, time, and place.

> - They're contextual in nature. Photos that are rich in color and detail communicate much more than simple UML diagrams.

Evocative documents are an external memory to a previous conversation. They have value to those who took part in the conversation. To share such a document with someone who was not part of the conversation, the person who wants to understand the document must reconstruct the document from scratch with someone who *was* part of the original conversation. This means that evocative documents are not very scalable. (The problem is that traditional documents aren't either; we just assume they are and are unaware of or ignore the information loss and corruption.)

BUT

Your documentation has probably slipped into representational form and is no longer evocative if the following are true.

- It takes longer to produce the documentation than it does to comprehend and use it.
- Anyone in the organization begins to express a belief that the documentation has intrinsic value and not just utilitarian value.
- Documentation that is highly stylized and that uses precisely defined and context-free syntax (for example, UML) will almost certainly be perceived as representational rather than evocative. However, it need not be, as long as it brings up a shared conversation or experience.
- There is any kind of movement to make the documentation archival.
- Specialists are employed to produce the documentation. The exception to this rule are technical writers (who should really be more novelists than tech writers) charged with producing manuals and books for users of the software who were prevented from participation in its creation.

VARIATIONS

Agile modeling, as originally described by Scott Ambler, is a form of just-in-time modeling. People model to have a conversation and then take a digital photo of that model to remind them of the conversation. This is a form of evocative document that uses highly stylized languages such as UML.

One last note on evocative documents: They point out a limitation of our current culture and what many of us take for granted. Accepting the value of evocative documents means rejecting the notion of accurately communicating detailed information in context by writing them down. You have to have a conversation; the document is there only as a reminder. As the eminent American philosopher Dr. Phil says, "How's that working for you?" How have the reams of requirement, design, and planning documents been working?

References

Ambler, S., and Jeffries, R., *Agile Modeling: Effective Practices for Extreme Programming and the Unified Process*, Wiley, 2002.

Larman, C., *Applying UML and Patterns: An Introduction to Object Oriented Analysis and Design and Iterative Development, Third Edition*, Boston: Addison Wesley, 2005.

Korzybski, A., *Science and Sanity: An Introduction to non-Aristotelian Systems and General Semantics (Fifth Edition), Brooklyn:* Institute of General Semantics, 1994.

Map-territory relation, Wikipedia, http://en.wikipedia.org/wiki/Map-territory_relation, accessed November 2007.

Naur, P., "Programming as Theory Building," *Microprocessing and Microprogramming*, 15:55, 253–261, North Holland, 1985. (Also reprinted in Cockburn's *Agile Development*.)

Chapter 23

USER STORY

To enact the User Story practice, you simply create an evocative document for requirements. A user story is a high-level description of the requirement to be built. It usually fits on a 3×5 index card and is a "promise for a conversation" later between the person carrying out the Customer Part of Team practice and the implementers.

BUSINESS VALUE

The User Story practice enables flexibility because a small fraction of time is originally invested to create user stories for the backlog. The team is then free to reprioritize them in response to new information or changes in the environment without wasting much work-in-progress. A user story forces a conversation to take place to flesh out the requirements; thus, there is less noise in a developer's understanding of the requirements. Consequently, the product utility is improved, and the cost to build the software is reduced.

SKETCH

Aparna and Cathy were a little suspicious of the effectiveness of user stories. Many of the new Agile practices seemed counterintuitive. The user stories were easy to write and looked a lot like high-level use cases, which eased a little of their discomfort. Surely, they were going to go back and extend them as they had previously done with use cases.

As it turned out, they didn't go back and extend the user stories. Instead, they had lengthy conversations with the rest of the development team throughout the iteration to explain their work. This kept them busy a large percentage of their time, but the communication was much more natural, and it was faster and more effective than writing a full document. The downside was they had to re-explain the basics every time a new developer worked on a task. The rest of the development team, however, vastly preferred the conversations and ready access to Aparna and Cathy as customers over traditional documents.

What was really good about user stories was the fact that there was so little invested in them in the time before development. This made it somehow easier for Aparna and Cathy to change their minds about prioritization, and even the requirements themselves, when they discovered new information as the team progressed. In the end, Aparna and Cathy felt that user stories made a significant difference in how readily the team changed course effectively.

CONTEXT

You are on a development team that has adopted Iterations and Backlog practices. The backlog for the release needs to be filled with low-fidelity requirements.

FORCES

- Evocative documents are preferable to representational documents.
- A backlog for the release is populated with high-level requirements. Those requirements are not fleshed out until they are close to implementation.
- Conversations are more valuable as a communication medium than any form of document.
- Using something physical in a conversation, such as an index card, engages our tactile senses. Cards can be moved, organized, ripped up, and so on. Conversations using cards are more memorable and more creative because they engage more of our senses [Heohn 2007].

THEREFORE

To originally populate the backlog, do not spend too much time researching every aspect of the requirements, but rather headline them. This will be enough for prioritization and relative estimation exercises when you initialize the backlog.

Then, when these requirements come close to implementation as they filter to the top of the backlog, rely on conversations more than you do on representational documents. Therefore, documents that are produced upon conversations will have more meaning and will be evocative.

To encourage conversations, write down just enough information to remind you and others what the subject is. For those who have not participated in a conversation on the topic, the text will not have much value and will thus prompt them to find the right person to talk to.

These high-level requirements written on index cards that are a "promise for a conversation" are known as user stories. A sample user story follows. It is based on advice in Cohn [Cohn 2004].

> *Story: Publish news with future date*
>
> *As a news editor, I want to be able to post news stories with a future date. I should be able to view and review the news story on our site and have our readers see it only on the date of publication.*

ADOPTION

User stories are used throughout Agile development as the elements of the backlog, units for estimation using planning poker, and evocative documents that remind you of conversations that have taken place explaining the intricacies of the requirements. Here are a few ideas about how to apply user stories effectively.

- Mike Cohn [Cohn 2004] has written an entire book on employing user stories that would be a good candidate for a reading circle.
- Start using user stories in your workshop to create the release backlog. As the customer, your job is to know enough details of what the requirements are to be able to write a short description that fits on index cards. Those index cards are your user stories.
- When large user stories filter to the top of the backlog, they need to be ready for implementation within an iteration. Break up large user stories end to end instead of splitting the stories along technical lines so that each smaller user story is a vertical slice of functionality.
- Keep in mind that the user stories are meant to be evocative documents and promises for conversations, so have those conversations to explain the requirements.

BUT

User stories rely on leveraging tacit knowledge because of their evocative nature; therefore, they have all the pitfalls documented in the evocative document practice. In addition

- Don't mix the problem description with the solution. A story is a problem description. This means that the problem rarely contains a user interface.

- Stories are meant to have meaning and value to the user. If they do not, they may be too small. Remember to take a feature from end to end.
- Stories also must fit within an iteration. Do not try to develop one over multiple iterations and break it up into smaller ones.
- "Quartering the chicken" is sometimes a problem when breaking larger user stories into smaller ones. Look for natural joints in functionality to make a vertical slice. See Elssamadisy and Schalliol [Elssamadisy and Schalliol 2002] for an example.
- User stories are not the answer to everything. They are good at describing business features; they are not good for specifying the user interface, nonfunctional requirements, and so on.
- User stories do not have enough detail for creating functional tests, but the tests should be linked to the stories.

VARIATIONS

Many view user stories as use case scenarios in summary format; that is, their scope is the same as scenarios, but the text is brief. Indeed, when functional testing is practiced, the tests for user stories look remarkably like use case scenarios.

REFERENCES

Cohn, M., *User Stories Applied: For Agile Software Development*, Boston: Addison-Wesley, 2004.

Elssamadisy, A., and Schalliol, G., "Recognizing and Responding to Bad Smells in XP," *Proceedings of the 24th International Conference on Software Engineering*, 2002.

Hoehn, D., "The Renaissance of Paper," *Agile Journal*, www.agilejournal.com/articles/articles/the-renaissance-of-paper.html, 2007.

Jeffries, R., "Essential XP: Card, Conversation, Confirmation," www.xprogramming.com/xpmag/expCardConversationConfirmation.htm, accessed November 2007.

Chapter 24

USE CASE

A use case describes a business workflow of measurable value to the customer. The Use Case practice describes the behavior of the system in response to external events and action by describing the systems response.

BUSINESS VALUE

Use cases affect product utility by communicating requirements clearly. A use case is more effective if it is an evocative document and is built collaboratively; it is less effective if it is a representational document and is used as the primary form of communicating requirements.

SKETCH

Aparna's previous experience as an analyst involved writing many use cases to describe how the system was to perform. Upon joining the team and starting to use user stories instead, she thought she had seen the last of use cases. Indeed, for a long time, her use case experience was useful in how she thought about the system, but the form and documentation were never used on the project.

Then the team adopted functional testing, and Aparna immediately recognized that these tests are similar in form and content to use case scenarios—just with concrete numbers. As she and Cathy started to regularly write functional tests for the user stories, they naturally grouped stories together, as several stories comprised different aspects of one piece of functionality. For their sanity, Aparna and Cathy started writing use cases as logical introductions to a family of functional tests. The functional tests fleshed out the alternatives that a use case documented.

CONTEXT

You are on a development team that wants to improve product utility, but user stories are too light given your team's context or your organization's culture.

FORCES

- Expertise on a development team is distributed among its members. Most often those with the knowledge of the domain are not the ones who have the technical knowledge to build the system. They must communicate and collaborate to build the system.
- Evocative documents are better suited for the communication and collaboration needed to build a software system.
- User stories are more naturally evocative documents, but they are also alien to many organizations' cultures.
- Use cases have a longer history and are more easily accepted.
- Use cases are historically representational documents and not evocative documents. They can, however, be evocative; it all depends on how they are built.
- Use cases can easily be evocative documents if they are created during a conversation between the customer and other members of the team.
- Use case scenarios—threads of execution through a use case that take only one route through the many alternatives—are excellent candidates for functional tests.
- Use cases are generally too large to fully develop in one iteration.

THEREFORE

A development team should use evocative documents to communicate and collaborate around requirements. Because your environment is not ready for a drastic change to user stories, or you already have knowledge and experience with user cases, consider use cases created in workshops where your developers and customers build them together for context instead of just "throwing them over the wall." A use case describes a business workflow of measurable value to the customer. A use case describes, in detail, what the system will do—not how—in response to external events and actions.

ADOPTION

A use case is a form of requirement that describes behavior. This tends to be the natural way for us to think. We tend to tell stories of how something works to describe why a particular structure is necessary. Remember the last time you were reviewing a class design diagram. Didn't you explain relationships among objects using as a background their use?

- Utilize Workshops to discuss and transfer requirements every iteration. (This is generally done in the kickoff meeting.)
  - The customer should prepare requirements and flesh out his understanding of what is needed individually so that he is ready to explain and elaborate the requirements at the workshop.
  - Build the use case scenarios together using a collaborative medium—such as a whiteboard—as you have a conversation about the requirements. The scenarios you build become evocative documents to those in attendance.
  - Only review an iteration's worth of work.

- Because use cases are large, they are frequently broken up into scenarios; scenarios are different sequences of behavior that make up a use case. For example, the "happy path"—where execution happens with no errors—is a scenario. Scenarios are at the granularity of requirements that you will be commonly concerned with in an iteration.
- If functional tests or test-driven requirements are adopted, the use case scenarios should form the basis for all your tests.
- Consider conducting a reading circle to review Cockburn's *Writing Effective Use Cases*.

BUT

Use cases are an artifact of the pre-Agile days that have significant value. However,

- Use cases are large chunks of functionality; an entire system may have only 10 to 15 use cases. You can easily get "sucked in" and flesh out more of the requirements than are needed, which creates significant work-in-progress that can easily become stale as your team learns more about the problem domain and system constraints. This is dangerous. When using use cases, create them incrementally as you would with code. Start with the main success scenario and then iteratively add alternatives and exceptions.

- Use cases can easily be built and used without conversations. If you find yourself writing or consuming use cases without conversations, you are reducing the opportunities for feedback, validation, and learning while building the system.
- Use cases can easily be used as representational documents; therefore, much can be missed. Try to make use cases evocative documents by constantly having conversations as you build them and explain them.

VARIATIONS

Functional tests are executable use case scenarios.

REFERENCES

Cockburn, A., *Writing Effective Use Cases*, Indianapolis: Addison-Wesley Professional, 2001.

Larman, C., *Applying UML and Patterns: An Introduction to Object-Oriented Analysis and Design and Iterative Development Third Edition*, Upper Saddle River: Prentice Hall PTR, 2005.

Chapter 25

INFORMATION RADIATOR

An information radiator is an object—often a chart—that is placed in a common area where members of the organization regularly see it. That object "radiates" information every time someone sees it. The Information Radiator practice helps communicate important data/issues/context about the team, the project, and its progress.

BUSINESS VALUE

An information radiator primarily improves visibility. Also, by acting as a conduit for important information, it indirectly affects a team's ability to recognize and therefore respond to change, which improves flexibility.

SKETCH

The team's practice of test-driven development had made a real improvement in the quality of the code so far, but there was still a lot of improvement to be done. Aparna still saw many issues fall through the cracks, and by the time she got to reviewing the work that Dave had completed for the iteration, the two of them would go into overdrive to get the user story completed or just miss completing it all together.

Recently, Scott put up a storyboard chart (a type of information radiator) in the common area. Aparna saw that Dave's work was completed and ready for testing halfway through the iteration and was reminded of it every time she passed the chart. She picked up the work Dave had completed, found one or two issues, and notified Dave. Dave had the issues fixed in a couple of days, and the user story went through to completion smoothly. It was funny how such a simple chart placed so that both she and Dave saw it many times a day helped them finish the card on time.

CONTEXT

Your team is a self-organizing one that responds to events as they happen instead of following a plan.

FORCES

- The whole team needs consistent and continuous information about factors that inhibit/enhance the process of delivering business-valued software.
- Traditional forms of project documentation are (rightfully) perceived as overhead, generally inaccurate, and incomplete.
- Information that is accurate, exceedingly easy to update, and understandable "at a glance" is exceedingly valuable for its effectiveness to communicate important data.
- Indirect communication is sometimes more effective than direct confrontation.

THEREFORE

Display the main indicators of progress, roadblocks, and action plans for all to see—whether they want to or not. Make the information visible from a distance—do not just put up single-sheet printouts—to enable those walking around, visiting, and so on to easily see it. Choose your locations carefully; they should be high-traffic locations for the people who need to or want to read the information.

Getting the right information to people affects their actions. This is a powerful technique for introducing change, encouraging discipline, and understanding context for the entire team.

ADOPTION

Almost all Agile methods discuss and advocate the use of various forms of static information radiators. The idea of "big visible charts" is common vocabulary and addresses, but does not explicate, the same issue as the Information Radiator practice.

- If you have trouble thinking of what to do, visit your local elementary school and look at the walls of the classrooms; they are filled with pictures, signs, and reminders of what is important in class.
- Every aspect of a project's state of interest to any member of the whole team is an appropriate subject for an information radiator.

- As a rule of thumb, the contents of any given information radiator should be limited to one to three distinct aspects of the project state.
- Updates to the content must use nominal effort (such as moving a user story from one column of a progress chart to another during a stand-up meeting) or be automatically generated as a byproduct of development efforts (such as tests written, tests passed).
- Information radiators should be "large format"—that is, large posters, whiteboard diagrams, or any other equally visible and interpretable form.
- Information radiators should be consistent with the pattern of Evocative Documents.

BUT

Simply posting a series of "facts" about a project's state is insufficient to satisfy the constraints imposed by this abstract pattern. "Smelly" information radiators can exhibit one or more of the following symptoms.

- Voids in the information exist, indicating that individuals or roles are persisting in their predisposition to secrecy. Some members of the team still believe that they can avoid or transfer to others accountability for failure.
- Too many charts reduce the effect of the information radiators because people tend to tune out too much information. Remember, you want to effect actions by providing vital data.
- Team members fail to see any value in one or more of the information radiators in use. In other words, progress is being measured but not in a meaningful way. The information does not lead to improvements in the development process.
- Updates are not performed in the same time frame as they occur and when they are of use. This usually means that the updates require far more than nominal effort to make or they are not automatically generated. Overtime, erratic productivity, and declining team morale are secondary symptoms of this problem.
- Too much information is presented. Remember, this is an evocative document, and its power is in quickly reminding people of greater context and information. Too much information often dilutes or confuses the issue at hand.
- The chart is too small and cannot be seen from a distance and at a glance. This reduces the information radiator's capability to "radiate" data to passersby.

VARIATIONS

Information radiators are also known as big visible charts. Some common ones include the following:

- **Storyboard.**[1] This is a chart that has all the user stories signed up for in the iteration and their status. As stories progress, they go into development, and then testing, and finally completion. At a glance, you can see the current state of all the requirements for the current iteration. It provides an opportunity for people to help move things along if they are stuck.
- **Burn-down.** This chart shows the number of requirements completed over time. Every time a story is completed, the chart is updated. The burn-down chart gives everyone a chance to see the long-term progress of the team over time and a reasonable projection into future productivity for planning.
- **Continuous integration status.** It is important for the continuous integration build to pass at all times and to be fixed quickly when it fails. The status is frequently shown as a web page on a computer monitor in a common area, but some teams get creative by hooking up traffic lights, lava lamps, and, in one instance, a dancing skeleton to indicate the status.
- **Impediment chart.** This clearly identifies all roadblocks in the way of the team and who is responsible for addressing them.
- **Build monkey.** As a negative incentive to breaking the build, some teams buy a small doll to indicate who last broke the build. The doll is placed prominently in their work area until someone else breaks the build. (Be careful with this one; it can easily upset people.)
- **Happy face/sad face radiator.** Use these simple indicators to radiate important touchy-feely information. For example, a customer satisfaction radiator can be used to indicate current customer satisfaction.

REFERENCES

Cockburn, A., *Agile Software Development: The Cooperative Game, Second Edition*, Boston: Addison-Wesley Professional, 2007.

---

1. Don't confuse this usage of storyboard with its original film and television usage where it was used to plan scenes. In the Agile community, a storyboard is used to show progress, not to do planning.

TECHNICAL PRACTICES

Chapter 26

AUTOMATED DEVELOPER TESTS

The Automated Developer Tests pattern is a set of tests that are written and maintained by developers to reduce the cost of finding and fixing bugs—thereby improving code quality—and to enable the change of the design as requirements are addressed incrementally. Disciplined writing of tests encourages loosely coupled designs.[1] Furthermore, these test suites are easily executable—usually by a single click—and are considered part of the build process.

There are two types of automated developer tests: test-first development and test-last development, which are each described in their own patterns in Chapters 27 and 28. The Automated Developer Tests pattern covers the commonalities between test-first and test-last development. When you are working in a team environment, automated developer tests require collective code ownership. These relationships are illustrated in Figure 26-1.

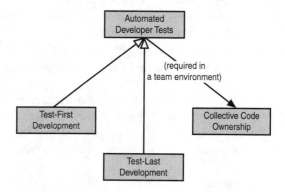

Figure 26–1 The relationship of the Automated Developer Tests practice to the Test-First Development, Test-Last Development, and Collective Code Ownership practices

---

1. Automated developer tests do encourage loosely coupled design; however, test-driven development does so much more effectively.

BUSINESS VALUE

Automated developer tests help increase quality to market by catching errors early in the development cycle. Flexibility and product lifetime are improved by creating a "safety net" of tests and enabling refactoring. The previous values are obvious, but what is not as obvious is that automated developer tests also reduce the time to market and cost of development by shortening the development time. This is accomplished by decreasing a developer's time in debugging loops by catching errors in the safety net of tests and increasing his courage to constantly refactor the code, which reduces the inertia that typically builds up from overgeneralized solutions and code duplication.

SKETCH

Waterfall Will and Uthman UpfrontDesign joined Scott ScrumMaster's Agile development team at the beginning of their third release cycle. Scott's team had two spectacular successes under its belt, and some of the developers went to other teams to "spread the Agile disease." Will and Uthman came from traditional development backgrounds where testing was done by the QA department and developer tests were only written ad hoc on an as-needed basis.

As Waterfall and Uthman joined Scott's team, they practiced pair programming with others on the team who had a disciplined testing regimen. Some of them, like Cindy Coder, wrote their tests first and practiced test-first development while others, like Dave Developer, usually wrote unit tests after doing some coding. But both of them always had their tests done before checking code into the code repository.

Because Scott's team was a self-organizing one, its members chose not to enforce writing tests but highly recommended that developers write tests for all the code base to support the fact that there were no subteams; every developer had access to and permission to change any part of the code base.

Uthman and Will ran headfirst into this problem as they took on the invoicing subsystem of their application. They paired to incrementally build upon the invoicing system (which unfortunately had no tests) and were happy with the design and flexibility of the functionality. Aparna Analyst was also pleased with the work they added and signed off on the work being done since it passed all her (manual) acceptance tests. Dave and Cindy were pairing to modify how the "charge" object worked (which the invoicing subsystem used heavily). They also added their work to the system successfully. As Aparna was preparing her work for the next iteration, she noticed that the invoices produced by the system were no longer working. When Will and

Uthman discovered this issue, they went to Cindy and Dave and asked, "Why didn't you tell us you were making such significant changes?" Dave and Cindy replied, "Where were the tests? We rely on tests to tell us if we've broken anyone's functionality."

That was an annoying lesson in one of many aspects of automated developer tests. Will and Uthman played a significant role in the next iteration, rewriting the invoice code to make it work with the new charge code and adding developer tests.

CONTEXT

This particular pattern is effective in many contexts. Any or all of the following are environments that will benefit from this practice.

- You are on a development project that needs to significantly improve its quality (reduce its bug count).
- You are on a development team that has decided to adopt the Iteration and Simple Design practices. You need to evolve your design as new requirements are considered.
- You are on a development team that wants to build code using a distributed team. The lack of both face-to-face communication and constant feedback causes an increase in bugs.
- You are on a development team that is practicing Collective Code Ownership. You need to compensate for the fact that not everyone knows the entire code base but may touch any part of the system at any given point in time.

FORCES

- Checking in code to the source tree to be tested by QA significantly increases the cost to find and fix a bug.
  - Both a QA person and a developer must find the bug and communicate via a tool to document the work being done.
  - Bugs often go back and forth between QA and development until the problem is clear enough to be reproducible.
  - The time for a bug to be found, discovered, and fixed is usually at least one order of magnitude greater than if the developer had discovered and fixed the bug before checking in the code. By then, other developers have had time to check out that faulty code base and build upon it.

- Fixing one bug frequently causes another bug. Cycles and chains sometimes occur where one bug causes another that in turn causes another, ad infinitum.
- Complex parts of the system tend to have more bugs than others. Their bugs also tend to be recurring because not everyone understands the code base.
- Systems are designed to be general so that when requirements change, the system can accommodate the changes. Unfortunately, this extra flexibility doesn't come free—there is a cost to the extra complexity. Every time a developer works with a complex piece of code, he must take time to understand it and time to properly use it. This is known as cost of design carry.
- Band-Aid fixes are made because changing the design of the system is prohibitively expensive. In changing one thing, you're likely to break something that depends on it. This eventually leads to code duplication, poor and brittle design, and less maintainable code. It takes a long time to get the corrected code through QA before release, and even then problems get through. Hence, we minimize the number of things our fixes affect out of fear.

THEREFORE

Reduce the overall effort for finding and fixing bugs by finding them earlier. Have developers test their code more rigorously. Automate that testing and make it available for all other developers so they can test for bugs that may have been introduced by their changes but outside of the tests they just wrote. Introduce a practice that has all developer tests running before checking any code into the source repository. Help make complex systems more understandable by documenting them. Also ensure that the documentation changes with the system; the best way to do that is to make documentation executable (well-written tests). Finally, whenever a bug is discovered, write a test to reproduce that bug. Add it to the test suite, and then fix that bug and check in both the fix and the tests to the code repository. You have now ensured that that particular bug will not come back because any developer who reintroduces it will fail your test and not check in the code until it is fixed.

If you are working in a team environment, some of the code you write may eventually break existing tests. After all, one of the main benefits of a test is to act as a safety net and warn you when you break assumptions made by other parts of the system. Remember that you have to get all tests passing before you check in your code change; therefore, you have to change the affected parts of the system to pass the tests. Both collective code ownership and pair programming are helpful in solving this problem.

By introducing automated developer tests and making them easy to run by grouping them in test suites, you can address all the problems introduced in the "Forces" section. Be aware that once you have started writing tests regularly, you will see a change in the way that developers attack problems on their team. They will be much more confident and courageous and will make design changes when needed, relying on the tests that have been written to catch their mistakes. Therefore, you must be diligent in writing good tests for all your code, or you might find yourself in the position of Will and Uthman in the sketch at the beginning of this pattern.

What are good tests? That is a nebulous question that is almost as difficult to answer as "What is good code?" Tests are best treated as any other code—not as second-class citizens—so adhere to everything you know about good design. The best way to learn is to start writing tests. Learn by doing and read what others are writing. Pay close attention to all the problems that occur and modify your test-writing technique to avoid those problems.

ADOPTION

We will not cover exactly how to write a developer test, but many books do this in great detail. Instead, we will cover the steps that you need to perform so that you and your team have the maximum likelihood of successful adoption with this practice.

1. Commit as a team to the discipline of writing tests.

   a. Realize that this is first and foremost a human issue and not a tool issue.

   b. Agree that tests are just as important as production code.

   c. Agree that it is better to miss a feature completion than to have a feature complete without tests.

   d. Agree to be patient. Depending on your current project, it may take anywhere from two to six months for this practice to become a habit and for the real benefits of automated developer tests to become obvious.

2. Find a tool that is easy to use. The ease should be with respect to the amount of effort it takes to write a test and not whether you have to write that test.

    a. JUnit and TestNG are available for Java. NUnit and Visual Studios built-in testing tool are available for .NET. CXXTest and CPPUnit are available for C/C++.

    b. Use automatic test-generation tools for auxiliary testing and not the primary form of testing. If you rely only on test-generation, you will lose the thought process that goes along with making code more "testable" and the gain of more loosely coupled, better designed code.

3. Treat your test code as you would your production code. Tests should be well designed also.

4. Get as much help as you can on this.

    a. Bring in an experienced consultant or two if you can.

    b. Try to enlist the help of others at your company who have successfully participated in projects in which they have been disciplined about either test-first development or test-last development.

    c. Buy several copies of books specifically on TDD andtg5 xUnit testing. (Recommendations are provided at the end of this chapter.) Encourage your development team to take time to read these books.

    d. Get involved with online communities and local user groups focused on TDD, Agile development, and so on.

    e. Don't worry about mock objects and pure unit testing initially. (If you don't know what these are, don't worry about it because they are unimportant at this point.) As a starting point, write tests for each nontrivial method in each class. There is no need to write a test for simple getters and setters.

5. Adopt collective code ownership to support team development. This will enable you to always fix tests when they are broken.

6. Consider adopting pair programming as a support practice to ease the learning curve for the team. It is easier to be disciplined about tests when you are working with someone else.

7. Start writing tests with the current iteration. Expect a slowdown of up to 50 percent if you are working on a new project. If you are on a project that already has a large amount of untested code, your slowdown will be more pronounced. Your testing time will go down over time to about 20 to 30 percent of the total development effort. You will eventually hit a "critical mass" point where existing tests can help you write new code. This will speed up your overall development time. Believe it or not, you will develop faster even with the testing overhead!

8. Within a few iterations, your team will come up against the problem of setup data. As you write objects that rely on other objects, which in turn rely on even more objects, the amount of code written to "set up" for a test increases. There are two approaches to this problem:

   a. Pull out the common setup code into common classes. These classes are responsible for creating classes and test data; they are a special type of factory. They also create business objects in a given state. Martin Fowler gives a brief overview and links to the original ObjectMother paper presented at XPUniverse 2001 at www.martinfowler.com/bliki/ObjectMother.html. Object-Mother is a common evolution of complex setup code. Your tests are always exercising real business objects, which is good. On the other hand, the ObjectMother creates a maintenance burden that can easily become unwieldy from supporting too many special cases. Tests based on this solution may become brittle because one test relies on many business objects. They also can become slow, and slow tests aren't run. Be careful.

   b. Use mocks and stubs to keep away from the complexity of ObjectMother. Mock objects and stubs are placeholders for the business objects under test. They can be used to cut off the thread of one object pulling another several objects for testing purposes. A good paper describing the correct use for mocks and stubs is "Mock Roles, Not Objects" (www.jmock.org/oopsla2004.pdf), which was written by the group who created the jMock framework. Mocks can be used to make your tests much more readable and less fragile. On the downside, mocks are a form of duplication. A proper mock object mirrors the business object it mocks, which can be dangerous. If the business object changes, a mock must change also; if it does not, a test will continue to pass even though it should really fail.

c. Both approaches—mocks and ObjectMother—work well. The important part is consistency. Agree as a team on an approach and follow it. This will make it easier for team members to work with each other's code.

d. Always use mock objects and stubs to test classes that communicate with external systems.

e. If you are new to this type of development, start with Object-Mother to keep from adding too many new tools at once. After the team is comfortable with automated developer tests, it can shift to mock objects.

9. Keep your tests running fast. The entire suite of tests should run in no more than 10 minutes; otherwise, developers will stop running all the tests before checking in code.

10. All tests should be running and passing all the time—no excuses.

BUT

There are several ways that new adopters of this practice go wrong:

- This practice is fragile. It needs everyone on the team to be on board.
    - If one person breaks a test and does not fix it, it is much easier for others to do so. That one break—usually with a "it's not in my part of the code" or "I'll get to it later" comment—is the beginning of the end for automated developer tests.
    - Developers must get used to fixing tests that they break even if they did not write them. This means they need to touch parts of the system they are not used to working with instead of creating a bug in the bug tracker and moving on.
- The fact that tests are written says absolutely nothing about the quality of the production code. Badly designed code can be written in any language and using any technique. Tests encourage loosely coupled code, and a good developer writes better code using this technique. But bad code can still be written; consider adopting pair programming or performing regular code reviews of the tests if you have this problem.
- Tests sometimes end up as second-class citizens. When creating the tests, we break all the rules of good design. What this inevitably ends up causing is brittle and hard-to-write tests. Treat your test code as you would your production code and refactor it when the design is

no longer adequate. Be mindful of coupling and cohesion and all the other principles you already know and practice.

- Writing tests—especially for existing systems that have been written without testing in mind—is hard. Don't give up. Figure out how to put in tests incrementally. Be prepared to slow down significantly before you start speeding up again in your development. Pick up a copy of *Working Effectively with Legacy Code* by Michael Feathers for some suggestions on how to proceed.

- Sometimes teams will check in something that breaks a test. They don't fix it, thinking they'll get to it later. That one broken test becomes 10, and then 100, and then 400 broken tests within a few iterations. This is unacceptable. You've just lost one of the major advantages of this type of testing: catching bugs early and keeping other bugs from being introduced based on faulty code. You are also desensitizing your team to broken tests. Fix bugs immediately. Pull all the broken tests into their own suite and convince your team not to break any more tests. Any broken tests should force an immediate rollback. Incrementally start to migrate the broken tests to the functioning test suite by fixing them and then moving them to the live test suite.

- Code coverage becomes an overly important metric. Managers drive development from code coverage. Although using code coverage to indicate areas of code that need more attention is valid, using code coverage to drive development is not. It can (and often is) easily "gamed."

  - The fact that a test calls a method says nothing about the quality of that test. Code coverage statistics are often mistakenly used as test-quality statistics—they are not.

  - The relationship between tests and methods on a class should not be one to one but many to many if indeed we are writing tests to verify the code's conformance to requirements. Coverage encourages a one-to-one form of testing. Write a method and then make sure you have a test that exercises that method.

VARIATIONS

There are two types of automated developer tests that are patterns in their own right, but they address the forces described here adequately. The two types of automated tests reflect a general pattern—of which they are two specializations—that provides a context and a set of forces that can be addressed by both test-first development and test-last development.

Instead of using collective code ownership to share code, some teams adopt pair programming. They have specialized team members, and it is unrealistic for them to have everyone learn enough to modify all parts of the code. Their solution is to rely more heavily on pair programming and have a culture that encourages this. The problem here is obvious; you've just put more tasks in the lap of some of your bottlenecks. This type of pain needs to be resolved, either by augmenting the staff or by giving in and moving toward collective code ownership.

This practice is also known as automated unit tests in the community. The reason I've chosen the word *developer* instead of *unit* is that there is a debate about whether they should be true unit tests—tests that exercise only one class at a time. Calling the practice developer tests or unit tests is not important for adoption. In fact, it is easier not to write true unit tests until you get your feet wet. At that point, you will have enough information to make your own decision about unit testing.

REFERENCES

Automated developer tests are discussed in books on test-driven development and books written specifically for JUnit (the leading unit-testing tool in Java). Michael Feather's book in the following list is about testing and test-driven development with existing systems.

Astels, D., 2003. *Test-Driven Development: A Practical Guide*, Upper Saddle River, New Jersey: Prentice Hall, 2004.

Beck, K., 2003. *Test-Driven Development: By Example*. Boston: Addison-Wesley, 2003.

Feathers, M., *Working Effectively with Legacy Code*, Upper Saddle River, New Jersey: Prentice Hall, 2005.

Jeffries, R., *Extreme Programming Adventures in C#*. Redmond, Washington: Microsoft Press, 2004.

Massol, V., *Junit in Action*. Greenwich, Connecticut: Manning Publications, 2004.

Rainsberger, J.B., *Junit Recipes: Practical Methods for Programmer Testing*. Greenwich, Connecticut: Manning Publications, 2004.

Chapter 27

TEST-LAST DEVELOPMENT

The practice of Test-Last Development involves writing tests after *writing the code to support the requirements for a particular task. These tests exercise the system after it has been built. Beware of using this practice—it is easy to use but has many pitfalls, and the entire pattern is considered a smell by many in the community.*

BUSINESS VALUE

Test-last development addresses the same business values as indicated in automated developer tests. These values are quality to market, flexibility, product lifetime, time to market, and cost.

SKETCH

When Uthman UpfrontDesign joined Scott ScrumMaster's team along with Will Waterfall, they agreed to pair program with other developers on Scott's team and do their best to pick up the development practices that the team had adopted. One of those practices was to create automated developer tests for each piece of code written.

After a few iterations of pairing with others on the team, Uthman and Will paired up on the invoicing subsystem. Because they were new to the automated developer testing practice, they planned to write tests after writing some code (test-last development). They designed and coded and added to the existing invoicing subsystem incrementally. It turned out that this was a piece of the code that had absolutely no tests, and because they had already completed the code (close to the end of the iteration), they called the task done and skipped the tests instead of marking the task as incomplete. The next iteration, they signed up for more work on the invoicing system. Unfortunately, it came down to the wire, and tests were dropped. (This was an independent system anyway, so they weren't hurting anything by not adding tests. As long as they were working on the subsystem, it would be all right.)

Therefore, when Dave Developer and Cindy Coder modified a piece of the system that the invoicing subsystem depended on, they ran and passed all the tests and checked their code. The invoicing system silently stopped working. Aparna Analyst noticed this as she was running the system to prepare for the next iteration's invoicing requirements and told Will and Uthman. Needless to say, they were upset, and when they confronted Dave and Cindy to ask them why they weren't more careful, they got a, "Well, our code ran all the tests. How were we supposed to know your invoicing work would fail?"

This particular incident cost Will and Uthman a large portion of the next iteration to correct and back-add the developer tests that they should have written earlier. On the bright side, they picked up the discipline of always writing their developer tests. To keep from making the same mistake again, they wrote their tests more incrementally; that is, after every development step, they wrote the tests for the code they had just written.

CONTEXT

You are on a development team that has decided to implement automated developer tests; therefore, the context from that pattern applies. Furthermore, most of the members of your team have no experience with test-first development, and you want to adopt a practice that is not completely different from what they were used to previously.

Or maybe your company has purchased a tool that helps with creating developer tests. The generation of tools for developer testing can only generate tests for code that has already been written.

FORCES

All the forces listed in the Forces section in Chapter 26, "Automated Developer Tests," apply, as does the following.

- Writing tests for existing code has a smaller learning curve than learning to write tests before writing the production code.

THEREFORE

Develop your production code in small steps. After every small step, write a developer test using your tool of choice to exercise the code you have written. Collect the tests that you and others write in test suites so that they can be run in groups easily. Do not check any code into the source repository that has not been fully tested. Run all developer tests before checking in your code base to make sure that you have not broken anyone else's tests with your change.

This type of development is not only about tests; it is about the production code that results from this practice. Production code will be, by design, more testable. The testability will drive a design that has far less coupling than code written without this in mind. The code produced, including the tests, reduces the cost of change. The design will be modifiable instead of something static that we will only Band-Aid for fear of introducing more bugs than we fix.

ADOPTION

The adoption strategy in the parent practice pattern, Automated Developer Tests, is sufficient to cover the adoption of test-last development. Be aware that this practice is less effective than test-first development but easier to adopt because it does not seem backward, as test-first development does. Test-last development is usually less effective for the reasons mentioned in the next section, which are unique to this practice.

Many have used this practice as a stepping-stone toward test-first development to get their feet wet with disciplined testing. Many more have started this practice and dropped testing altogether.

BUT

This type of testing is not new. In fact, developer tests written in this manner were around long before their emerging popularity with eXtreme Programming. It didn't catch on because of the touchy-feely issues that follow, so beware.

In addition to all the problems listed in the "But" section in Chapter 26, the following problems are unique to test-last development.

- Testing is dropped during crunch time. Although this is a problem in both test-last development and test-first development, it is much more common with test-last development because the code is seen as done before the tests are written. The approach taken by Will and Uthman in the earlier sketch is not uncommon.
- Testing is seen as an overhead, and the practice is sometimes dropped as a whole.
- Instead of developing your code with a mind toward testing, your first priority is to get the feature completed. Then you come in after the fact and try to consider how you can bolt on a few tests. If you find yourself here, seriously consider adopting test-first development instead.
- Tests are biased toward the solution. A developer writes the code, which is a solution to the problem defined by the requirements. The tests should logically make sure that the code conforms to the requirements but often simply make sure that the code conforms to the code.

REFERENCES

Astels, D., 2003. *Test-Driven Development: A Practical Guide*, Upper Saddle River, New Jersey: Prentice Hall, 2004.

Feathers, M., *Working Effectively with Legacy Code*, Upper Saddle River, New Jersey: Prentice Hall, 2005.

Massol, V., *Junit in Action*. Greenwich, Connecticut: Manning Publications, 2004.

Rainsberger, J.B., *Junit Recipes: Practical Methods for Programmer Testing*. Greenwich, Connecticut: Manning Publications, 2004.

Chapter 28

TEST-FIRST DEVELOPMENT

The Test-First Development practice involves writing tests before writing the production code that will support and eventually pass that test. Tests resulting from this practice tend to reflect a developer's understanding of requirements because there is no design at its inception. The production code written to satisfy the tests tends to be loosely coupled and simple, which are both excellent design qualities.

BUSINESS VALUE

Test-first development addresses the same business values as indicated in automated developer tests. These values are quality, flexibility, product lifetime, time to market, and cost. In general, although test-first and test-last development address the same business values, test-first development is more effective and harder to adopt.

SKETCH

Uthman and Will joined Scott ScrumMaster's development team earlier this year. As they pair programmed with others on their team, Uthman and Will got a taste for automated developer tests and had their own run-in with what happens when someone does not write tests for his code on an Agile team. (See the sketches for automated developer tests and test-last development.)

After fixing the invoicing system code that they had coded without tests and back-filling the tests for that part of the system, Will and Uthman decided to do one more iteration together on some invoicing tasks. They decided to try to write their tests first. Although they had done this previously with others on the team on other tasks, they had never led an effort themselves, so they struggled. It was difficult and awkward to come up with tests for code that hadn't been written yet. They ended up talking through a design on paper and whiteboard, discussing both the static and dynamic structures, and then writing a test for the virtual solution they came up with in their heads. At the end of the iteration, they had a small piece of working production code that was tested. But they were far from happy with their experience.

On the subsequent iterations, Will went back to test-last development and was disciplined in writing tests incrementally with the production code. Uthman, on the other hand, decided that there was something to this test-first development and tried to pair with as many people who were already doing test-first development as he could. He picked up a copy of Kent Beck's TDD book and went through the exercises. He suspended his disbelief because he saw that there were many highly respected people who were using this practice exclusively. He also learned about mock objects via the Mock Roles, Not Objects paper and learned to use JMock effectively. After several slow iterations, the light bulb finally went on for Uthman, and he was hooked!

The next time Uthman and Will teamed up on a set of tasks, Uthman drove development in a test-first manner and explained to Will what he was doing. When Will drove development, he developed in a test-last manner. Uthman felt that the quality of tests was much better with test-first development when comparing the results of the test-first and test-last approaches, but he kept that thought to himself.

CONTEXT

You are on a development team in an environment that matches the context of the automated developer tests pattern. Furthermore

- You want to get the most benefit out of the developer tests.
    - You want to increase your development speed.
    - You want to increase the benefit of tests in creating and promoting loosely coupled designs.
    - You want to have full test coverage of your requirements instead of test coverage of the design.
- You may have already adopted test-last development and have noticed that tests are not always written—especially during crunch time. Unfortunately, this is when you need tests the most.
- Your team is willing and able to struggle through an awkward stage while this practice becomes natural (usually one to three months).

FORCES

Test-first development resolves all the forces documented by automated developer tests. The following forces are also resolved by test-first development:

- Tests that are written after the code are more likely to never be written. In crunch time, it is easy and common for developers to move on to the next development task before writing the tests for the current task.
- Tests written after code drive code indirectly. A developer writing production code keeps the fact that he must be able to test this code in the back of his head while developing. So in that way, the design is affected by the tests to be written.
- Unnecessary code—code that does not directly address a requirement by the user—is written, which is a form of waste.
- Tests written after the production code is written are usually biased toward the code when they should be validating the solution as the solution to the problem. That is, a developer test should verify that the production code written satisfies the requirements. When the production code is written first, the developer has not necessarily solved the problem, and tests written after the fact likely just exercise the production code. All this really verifies is that the code written works as the developer thinks it should. The requirements could have gone by the wayside untested.
- Tests written after code may or may not test all the requirements that drove that code to be written.

THEREFORE

Write your developer tests *before* writing the production code to support the requirements. At this point, because you have not yet solved the problem by writing the production code, the only information available to you will be the requirements. By forcing yourself to write a test, you will need to make decisions about classes that will support the required functionality. You will make design decisions to support the requirements at hand. Your test, therefore, will mirror these requirements and be a form of executable requirements. This test should be failing—probably failing to compile, too. That is as expected.

You will then write the production code to satisfy the one test you have written. You have already made decisions regarding responsibility assignment to classes, and now you only write the code needed to make that test pass. The test you wrote earlier will drive the creation of classes, methods on those classes, and their relationships to other classes in your system (that is, object-oriented design).

Once you have made the test pass, you now have a passing test and production code that satisfy the requirements. You have not written one line of code that has not been driven by requirements. If you are strict about never writing code without a failing test to drive that code, you have requirements coverage, which means that you have a test that exercises each requirement supported by your code. It also means that you have not written any wasteful code; you have only written code that addresses a concrete requirement.

The last step is to **refactor**—that is, to modify the structure of your code without changing its behavior. You have the passing test that verifies the behavior; therefore, any change you make that does not break the test you have written means that the behavior is still the same. Do not add new functionality, but feel free to make your code more efficient and maintainable by cleaning up any sloppy work and use the existing tests to ensure that the behavior is the same after you've done your cleanup work.

What we have just described is the Red-Green-Refactor loop in the Test-Driven Development pattern.[1] It is a mandatory part of test-first development.

ADOPTION

Some people have successfully adopted test-first development on their own. Many have written about their experiences in online articles, conference papers, and blogs. They are the minority. By far, most of us who have successfully adopted this practice have done so with outside help. Here is how to go about doing this.

1. (Required) Commit to learning this practice as a team and being patient while individuals on your team internalize this practice. Agree to suspend your disbelief for at least two months and plan for a significant slowdown in development speeds of up to 50 percent (75 percent if you are on a project with legacy code that was written without tests in mind).

---

1. Automated developer tests and especially test-first development are big parts of test-driven development, although they are only part of TDD in a team environment.

2. (Recommended) Send your developers to a TDD immersion class.[2]
These types of classes are typically 80 to 90 percent hands-on work
using the test-first development approach and other practices under
experienced practitioners'/instructors' tutelage. These classes give the
attendees a good headstart in a controlled environment.

3. (Highly Recommended) Bring in help until this practice catches on.
(An outside consultant is best, but if you have internal resources that
have successfully practiced test-first development, they can carry out
this task). You need someone who has been there, done that with respect to these practices. They need to be able to pair with the developers to help them learn this technique hands-on. Typically, you need at
least one person per four or five developers for at least one week out
of every month for several months. This expert will be there to keep
morale up, show ways that tests can be written, and help the team
adapt and adopt this practice to your particular environment.

4. (Highly Recommended) The parent pattern, Automated Development Tests, encourages you to adopt pair programming, which is
important in easing the learning curve.

BUT

This is one of the most difficult practices to adopt of all the commonly
known Agile practices. All the problems listed in Chapter 26, "Automated
Developer Tests," apply here also. In addition, this way of doing development
is backward and nonintuitive for many developers. It takes significant practice for the light bulb to go on regarding why this is a superior method of development. Developers must suspend their belief long enough to figure out
how to perform test-first development efficiently. This practice has a high
drop-out rate.

VARIATIONS

Teams use test-first development as a form of requirements documentation.
The tests are written by someone who has face-to-face contact with the cus-

---

2. Many are offered by consulting companies in an open enrollment or onsite format.
Check www.valtech.com, www.objectmentor.com, and others. Get recommendations from people you know in the community who have attended any of these
classes. Do your best to get into a class where the instructors have real-world development experience.

tomer and then given to the developers who are to build the production code.

REFERENCES

Test-first development is synonymous with test-driven development in published works.

Beck, K., *Test-Driven Development: By Example.* Boston: Addison-Wesley, 2003.

Feathers, M., *Working Effectively with Legacy Code*, Upper Saddle River, New Jersey: Prentice Hall, 2005.

Jeffries, R., *Extreme Programming Adventures in C#.* Redmond, Washington: Microsoft Press, 2004.

Massol, V., *Junit in Action.* Greenwich, Connecticut: Manning Publications, 2004.

Rainsberger, J.B., *Junit Recipes: Practical Methods for Programmer Testing.* Greenwich, Connecticut: Manning Publications, 2004.

Chapter 29

REFACTORING

The practice of Refactoring code changes the structure (the design) of the code while maintaining its behavior. The relationship of Refactoring to other practices can be seen in Figure 29-1.

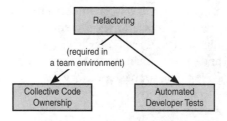

Figure 29–1   Refactoring depends on collective code ownership and automated developer tests to work well. Collective code ownership is needed because refactoring frequently affects other parts of the system. Automated developer tests are needed to verify that the behavior of the system has not changed after the design change introduced by the refactoring.

BUSINESS VALUE

Refactoring increases flexibility and the product lifetime by enabling and encouraging developers to change the design of the system as needed. Quality to market and costs are reduced because continuous refactoring keeps the design from degrading over time, ensuring that the code is easy to understand, maintain, and change.

SKETCH

Uthman UpfrontDesign jokingly told people that he was considering changing his name to Rashid Refactoring after a few months on Scott Scrum Master's team. As he learned about other Agile practices such as Pair Programming and Automated Developer Tests, he became aware of an option that had never been open to him before. He could redesign his code when requirements were changed or added. After reading *Refactoring: Improving the*

Design of Existing Code by Martin Fowler and with the automated developer tests present, he learned how to incrementally change the design of his code to accommodate new information.

Uthman no longer put together elaborate designs at the start of a new piece of functionality. This wasn't really as bad as he had thought because he found himself doing a little design each day. The practice of Refactoring had quickly replaced Up-Front Design as his favorite practice.

CONTEXT

You are on a development team that is using automated developer tests. You are currently working on a requirement that is not well supported by the current design. Or you may have just completed a task (with its tests, of course) and want to change the design for a cleaner solution before checking in your code to the source repository.

FORCES

Some problems are a natural result of software development.

- Traditionally, software gains entropy over time. Requirements change, and the software is Band-Aided with less-than-perfect solutions because of the increasing cost of making a change to the old, fragile code base.
- Quick fixes quickly build up a design debt that charges interest daily in the form of code that is more difficult to understand and modify.
- Code duplication is almost inevitable to avoid changing working code and possibly introducing a bug.
- Requirements are added and modified, and the current design is no longer a good solution to the problem.
- Software development is a learning process, and the design decisions that make sense today are poor when seen with tomorrow's information.

THEREFORE

Incrementally change the design of the code instead of proffering a quick and dirty fix. Do not add new functionality and change the design at the same time because that complicates the issue. Instead, change the design of the code while maintaining the behavior. Ensure that you are maintaining the behavior by relying on automated developer tests and functional tests. Start with a passing set of tests, change your design, and fix any broken tests by changing production code (not the tests). At this point—from passing tests to passing tests—you have changed the design and maintained the behavior. This process is called refactoring.

Refactoring is a simple and elegant activity. It is best when practiced regularly—before and after every task. That is, before you start a new task, read the existing code and determine if it will support the requirements of the task you are working on. If it does not, make the necessary change(s) to the design before starting on your task. At this point, go ahead and code the task and its tests. After you are done, re-examine the resulting design. If the design can be improved, go ahead and improve it by refactoring the design again so that you do not leave any design debt for the next person down the line.

ADOPTION

This is one of those just do it! patterns (well, almost). One of the things to keep in mind is that Refactoring is a practice and not a tool, although tool support helps. Here is how you should go about adopting this practice.

1. Start automated developer tests until you are comfortable with the discipline of writing tests for all your tasks. Do not attempt to refactor any piece of code until there are adequate tests covering the particular segment to be modified.
2. In a team environment, adopt collective code ownership on your team. Agree how to handle broken tests from refactoring in a timely manner.
3. Pick up a copy of *Refactoring: Improving the Design of Existing Code* by Martin Fowler and a book about test-driven development that is exercise-driven (see the test-driven development chapter for a large list of good books on the subject).
4. Start. Perform the steps as described. For every task, inspect the design to see if it needs to be changed to accommodate the new work. After completing the work, inspect your own solution and clean it up if needed. Be disciplined in refactoring mercilessly—that is, before and after every task if applicable.
5. Run a biweekly study group to share different refactorings that have been performed.
6. As you become comfortable with the canonical refactorings as defined in Martin Fowler's book, be courageous and make significant changes. Work toward large design changes that you and your team have known were needed when appropriate. Get a copy of *Refactoring to Patterns* by Joshua Kerievsky and run a study group based on that book to expose yourself to larger refactorings.

BUT

Refactoring is one of the most powerful practices in a developer's toolbox. Nevertheless, here are some things to watch out for.

- Don't get carried away and refactor just for the sake of refactoring. Remember, refactoring delivers no direct business value. By definition, refactoring maintains behavior, making it completely transparent to users. Therefore, refactoring without a requirement that causes the code being refactored to change is wasteful from the customer's perspective.
- Many missed small refactorings build up over time, causing the need for large refactorings. Large refactorings are much more difficult to perform. Therefore, be diligent in constantly refactoring your code and cultivate your sense of code and design smells.
- Beware of code ownership and pride causing commit wars once something is refactored. This problem is a dysfunction of the collective code ownership practice that is required to successfully refactor within a team environment.
- In a team environment, you will eventually refactor code that causes tests that you have not written to break. Some who are new to Agile practices may check in this code and rely on the developers who have written the tests to fix the broken ones. In this path lies the danger of breaking down the Automated Developer Tests practice. It is unacceptable to check in code that breaks existing tests. Make sure to practice collective code ownership in a team environment so that you are able to pass all the tests after performing a refactoring.

VARIATIONS

We know that the majority of the cost of software development goes into maintenance and not the initial creation of a software system. It then makes sense that we focus on making our systems maintainable.

Traditionally, we design with tomorrow in mind—that is, we build a flexible system so that when new requirements come, the design does not have to change to incorporate the new requirements. But there is a hidden cost in this solution: A general design is more complex. We pay for that complexity every time a developer has to understand and use that code. One of the most common techniques for sharing these flexible designs is via design patterns.

Erich Gamma, in the 1995 edition of *Design Patterns: Elements of Reusable Object-Oriented Software*, promotes this type of solution.

In an interview in the summer of 2005, Gamma stated that his thinking had evolved, and he now starts with a simple design to meet the requirements at hand. When new requirements emerge, he is able to refactor the solution toward a design pattern. Therefore, he does not have to increase the complexity of the design until it is absolutely needed.

This, of course, brings us to the variation of refactoring toward patterns instead of using design patterns upfront. In this way, we merge the benefits of both techniques. *Refactoring to Patterns* by Joshua Kerievsky is full of examples of how to do this effectively for common problems in today's development environment.

REFERENCES

Fowler's book is a reference that should be on every developer's bookshelf. Kerievsky's book is useful when you have gained experience in refactoring and want to learn to focus your refactoring toward well-known design patterns.

Fowler, M. et al., *Refactoring: Improving the Design of Existing Code*. Boston: Addison-Wesley, 1999.

Kerievsky, J., *Refactoring to Patterns*. Boston: Addison-Wesley, 2005.

Venners, Bill. 2005. "Erich Gamma on Flexibility and Reuse: A Conversation with Erich Gamma," Part II. www.artima.com/lejava/articles/reuse.html.

Chapter 30

CONTINUOUS INTEGRATION

Continuous Integration is the practice of performing a clean build, conducting full integration, and running all tests every time a change is committed to the code repository. This is accompanied by frequent integration of each developer's work into the code repository.

BUSINESS VALUE

Continuous integration reduces time to market and increases quality to market by finding integration bugs early and often, thus eliminating hardening iterations and the rework that goes along with it. Continuous integration also increases visibility of the progress of the project by making it explicit to the development team and stakeholders.

SKETCH

Bob BuildMaster had been reading about continuous integration and noticed that many of the problems this practice was purported to solve were present in his project. So he spent some time over the next several weeks fully automating the build. At that point, he ran a nightly build and made the results available on a Web page where the entire team could see the results.

Bob then sat down with Scott ScrumMaster, Cindy Coder, and Dave Developer to show them what he had done and to get their buy-in. They came to an agreement that they would solve build problems as soon as they found them. Cindy and Dave also agreed to work with Bob to get all the automated developer tests they had written to be part of the nightly build.

After a few iterations, the development team started relying on the nightly builds that ran all the developer tests. By removing all errors as soon as they discovered them, the entire team became more aware of integration problems and their causes. Bob also made the build script available to all developers to perform a local integration before checking things into the code base.

With that success, the team decided to do full continuous integration, and Bob dedicated a large portion of the next three weeks to installing and configuring a CI tool, reducing the build time to just under ten minutes.

Context

You are a member of a development team that has decided to reduce the risk associated with hardening iterations. Or maybe you are on a development team that is adopting Automated Developer Tests as a practice and want to keep the build passing all tests. Or perhaps you are on a development team that is introducing functional tests and want to make sure that the team is incrementally adding new functionality without breaking the old.

Forces

Many problems in today's typical software development life cycle are directly addressed by continuous integration.

- Integration has been traditionally seen as difficult and risky. This usually drives several practices to buffer against this risk of uncertainty. (These practices are suboptimal.)
  - Subteams work independently and stub out work to be done by other subteams to avoid the need for integration.
  - Subteams start out with a detailed design of their subsystem boundaries to ensure that their subsystems will come together smoothly (which is almost never the case).
  - Have hardening iterations at the end of a development cycle to figure out and address the mistakes in assumptions your teams have made.
- Integration becomes exponentially more risky with time.
- Lack of integration typically masks a large set of bugs. Many of these bugs can be serious and can be symptomatic of significant design mismatches in the system.
- A bug indicates an error. If that error goes unseen and uncorrected, other code that relies on the error is built upon incorrect assumptions.
- Successful integration is a prerequisite to successful functional testing.
- In the Agile community, integration includes a fully working system—that is, a fully working system involves compiling, deploying, and testing—not just a successful compile.

THEREFORE

Instead of shying away from integration because it is so painful and pushing it to the end of a release cycle, embrace the pain. Pain—in software development—means that something is not working well; we should use that feedback to fix the problem instead of ignoring it. By taking this approach, we fix the problem, and the pain goes away instead of just being avoided.

We traditionally think of integration as something we do out of obligation. The only reason we are really doing it is to deliver the system to the client (a pretty important reason), so we do it just before we are ready to release.

By reflecting on the pains of integration, we can get an idea of the values we can deliver by doing integration well.

- Lack of integration is a risk and masks several bugs. Therefore, by integrating more frequently, we can discover the bugs early and often and perhaps avoid many compound errors.
- The difficulty of integration is almost always related to several manual steps and synchronization of different versions of code bases, libraries, and other resources to deliver a working product. There is nothing inherently unautomatable about these steps. Therefore, spend the effort to automate all steps in integration.
- Integration is a form of feedback and information regarding the global state of the system. If we want to be more agile, we want feedback more frequently. Use this information as feedback for the entire team. Don't keep it hidden so that only those responsible for the build know what's happening.

ADOPTION

The steps involved in moving to continuous integration are outlined in Figure 30-1. The first step is to automate your build. This means you must remove all manual processes.[1] Depending on your development environment, there will be different tools to help you do this.[2] This may mean that you will

---

1. Some common processes are checking out the current code base for a build, tagging the files with a build number, generating the database schema, compiling the code, running automated tests, etc.

2. In Java there are several open source projects such as Ant and Maven, in .NET there is NAnt and MSBuild, and there are several build tools (in addition to make) available in the C/C++ environment.

have to change or augment your existing toolset if it does not support full automation (for example, if it requires human interaction periodically with dialog boxes). But this step can be done independently and does not need the full development team's involvement.

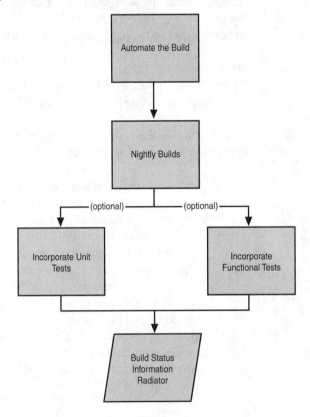

Figure 30–1   Steps in adopting Continuous Integration

Once you have a fully automatic build, you need to get that build running regularly—preferably nightly—and produce a report that is available to the team. One of the best ways to do this is to put up an information radiator[3] that shows the build status. At this point, the entire development team must be brought in and told that the build status will be available daily and that fixing a build must become a priority.

---

3. An information radiator is an artifact that is placed within the development team's work area that is easy to read and understand—it radiates its information to those in its vicinity. Specifically a daily print-out, poster, or monitor to show the status of the build is needed.

You want to get to the point where it is unacceptable for a build to be broken. It must be fixed before any new functionality is added to the code base. The next step toward achieving this is getting your developers to the point where they can completely build the subsystem with a single script before they check it in, to avoid breaking the build. There are two parts to this step: 1) making the build script and the external deployment configuration available to developers locally on their desktop, and 2) making the build run fast enough so that developers can realistically test locally before checking in. Both of these steps have their challenges that, depending on your particular environment, may seem daunting. If this is a nontrivial problem for your team, set up one or more deployment machines where a developer can take the modified code and run full build before checking in the code. Remember that the human practices are more important than the tools. As a team, you need to value integration before check-in—especially during crunch time—to keep from breaking the build.

Once it is possible for developers to realistically perform a full integration build before checking in, we come to the heart of continuous integration: frequent feedback. Developers now have a tool that will let them integrate their new code into the entire system. How will they use it? How often? This newfound tool—full integration on the developer's machine—should be used before each check-in to the source repository. Only upon a successful local integration build should a developer check in code.

As a rule of thumb, developers should integrate as often as possible to validate that their code works with the entire system. How often is that possible? This depends on how they develop software. Practices like Test-First Development encourage a developer to build small testable work; a developer using this practice may check in four or five times a day. Developers who are not already going that fast should strive to reach a daily check-in so that every day they force themselves to get to a point where they can integrate successfully.[4]

At that point, every developer has at least daily feedback on the integration state of the build. For the majority of check-ins, the local integration will go smoothly. A minority will break locally, and the developer will be able to fix the problem before checking in the code. An even smaller minority may pass through the local build check and fail on the official build machine. In that

---

4. Many of us are used to taking a functional piece and working on it for several weeks and then checking it in (and waiting for *Integration* several months afterwards during the hardening *Iterations*). This is usually not because of any restrictions of the problem itself but rather our own way of working. Therefore strive to achieve a daily check-in as a minimum.

case, the team should identify which check-in caused the build to break, roll it back to get a successful build, and fix the problem offline. The local developer scripts should be modified to catch that new type of error that fell through the cracks.

Finally, there are the tests. We have intentionally not talked specifically about tests. Continuous integration, as stated so far, without automated tests, is still extremely valuable. That said, if your team has automated developer tests or functional tests, it should incorporate them into the Continuous Integration practice. The tests should be incorporated as early as possible, as part of or directly after automating the build process. At this point, a definition of a broken build goes from one that doesn't compile or deploy to one that doesn't pass all the automated tests.

BUT

Continuous integration sometimes becomes too slow or too brittle. If this happens, a major side effect is a continuously broken build. This is worse than useless. It acknowledges that something is wrong and does nothing about it. The development team becomes desensitized to the importance of the build process and goes back to ugly stepchild status again. Do what it takes to speed up the tests.

Frequent and long-lasting broken builds are the bane of continuous integration. As long as it is obvious who broke the build, there are usually no problems. How is it obvious who broke the build? If only one person, say Cindy Coder, checked code and the build broke, discovering the culprit is easy. In this case, Cindy is responsible.[5]

But what if Cindy, Dave, and others all checked in code. Who broke the build? Often what happens is that all of them are sure they did not break the build, and they have an important task they cannot drop at this point to investigate the break. Anyway, they ran the build locally, and nothing went wrong, so it must be one of the others. Be forewarned: This is a slippery slope. If you don't fix the problem, four more people will check in and possibly compound the problem. They ran their local builds and all failed, but

---

5. Continuous integration is only valuable if you fix the broken build immediately. Broken builds that are accepted, much like failing tests that are accepted, are worse than not having them at all.

that is because of the earlier failure, not their code, right? Your one test failure, if not fixed promptly, can easily turn into ten broken tests over a couple of days.

So what is the root problem here? The problem is that the build is too slow. If between one build and the next several people are consistently checking in within one build cycle (the rule of thumb is more than three people at a time), the build needs to be faster. If you have a nightly build, this problem is unavoidable. You can mitigate it by having one person—a build cop—be responsible for tracking down build failures and helping developers fix them. If you want to have true continuous integration, you must work to make your build faster.Making the build faster is dependent on your environment so there is no general guidance I can give. Be creative. Remember that builds are no longer the ugly stepchild and deserve your attention just as much as any other part of the development process.

Continuous Integration, especially during adoption, is not a free practice. For many development environments, you need to invest significant time to fully automate the build and bring its time down. The entire development team needs to invest time and effort to keep the build running.

VARIATIONS

Continuous Integration is one of those practices that has caught on even in non-Agile shops because it keeps development environments running effectively and is visible to management. Here are some common variations on continuous integration.

- Continuous integration takes place at an enterprise level. Each project has its own continuous integration tool, and the tools are linked hierarchically so that one build pulls only successful builds from the other.
- A single-code repository is used. As automated developer tests and functional tests are pulled into continuous integration (there is more detail in Chapters 43), greater confidence in the quality of the code emerges. With this greater confidence, the need for isolated integration streams in the source code repository disappears. Teams start to have a single code repository that is always working.

- Functional testing is more time-consuming than automated developer tests because it exercises the system as a whole. Some teams pull these tests out of continuous integration and make them secondary. Because this is a common pattern, it is important to call it out. It is equally important to point out that, generally, teams take this approach too early. By pulling these tests out of continuous integration, you enable them to become stale and fail, thereby negating a large portion of their benefit. If at all possible, I recommend staying away from this solution by focusing on making your build and your tests run faster.

REFERENCES

There are several articles written and available on continuous integration. Any search engine will bring up several tools and articles. The original article, which was updated in May 2006, is Martin Fowler's.

Fowler, M., "Continuous Integration," www.martinfowler.com/articles/continuousIntegration.html.

Duvall, P., Matyas, S., and Glover, A., *Continuous Integration: Improving Software Quality and Reducing Risk.* Boston: Addison-Wesley, 2007.

Elssamadisy, A., "Is Pipelined Integration a Good Idea?" www.infoq.com/news/2007/09/CI_Pipeline.

Chapter 31

SIMPLE DESIGN

The practice of Simple Design is based on the following premises. The complexity of your design should support the current requirements at hand and no more. By keeping designs simple, you can build your software more quickly, maintain it with less pain, and modify the design incrementally by relying on automated developer tests and refactoring (see Figure 31-1).

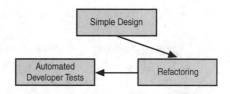

Figure 31–1 Simple Design depends on refactoring to be able to change the design as requirements change, which, in turn, depends on automated developer tests to ensure that a change in design does not introduce a change in behavior.

BUSINESS VALUE

Simple Design is a powerful practice that yields business value in reducing the time to market and the cost of a software product because the team does not pay for what it does not need. It also increases a product's lifetime because a less complex design is easier to understand and has less inertia.

SKETCH

When Waterfall Will joined Scott the ScrumMaster's Agile Development team a year ago, he had many misgivings about the project team and its coding techniques. Most importantly, he had the burning question: Where is the design? He could not fathom how starting with a simple design could ever work. In his experience, a team must set the architecture and design up-front; otherwise, the frequent changes that are required to change the design incrementally incur exponential costs.

Will decided to suspend his disbelief for a few months and give this new development technique a chance. Grudgingly at first, Will had to admit that the simple designs were elegant in their own way. As he observed again and again the resilience of these designs and how they could be easily changed according to new requirements because of the safety net of automated developer tests, he started to enjoy this way of developing. His designs were much leaner overall, and he recognized that this was not really getting rid of the design cycle but making design part of every day's work.

CONTEXT

You are on a development team that is building a software system with one or more of the following needs.

- Requirements change frequently, so your system must be resilient to change.
- Your customer may not know exactly what he wants. You want to be able to give him something to work with as soon as possible to help him make a good decision.
- Your team wants to significantly reduce time to market of your product.
- Your team is working with complex or unfamiliar technologies, and you want to leave major design decisions to the latest possible point when you have become more familiar with the problem or technologies.

FORCES

These are common problems typical to software development that are addressed by this practice:

- Feedback between customers and developers is infrequent because of the large delay between requirements and working software.
- Functionality is complex, and developers have a tendency to go off track and come back to the customer with an incorrect solution.
- A significant portion of development in an overdesigned application goes into understanding and using the built-in abstractions—even if they are not used.
- Design complexity has a cost of design carry that is paid every time a developer has to understand, use, or test the complex code. If this complexity is for tomorrow, we still pay a cost today. Unfortunately, tomorrow never comes for much of the complexity we developers build into our software.

THEREFORE

In the Agile community, we believe that building complexity in hopes of reducing the cost of change for the future is a false hope. Generalizations provide much more flexibility than what is strictly needed by the current requirements. In the Agile community, this type of generalization is known, derogatively, as Big Design Up Front (BDUF).

We are not fortune-tellers and cannot foresee all the changes. The up-front design is not free; the extended generalizations made to allow for change are more complex and harder to understand and maintain than a simple design. The cost of carrying that design far outweighs the benefits gained.

The design should only be complex enough to meet the requirements of the current iteration. Your design should be a simple one that has no generalizations for needs that will come in the future for two reasons: (1) you really don't know what the requirements will be two years down the road, and putting in those generalizations will incur a cost of design to carry over those two years, and (2) by enabling refactoring via automated developer tests, you have reduced the cost of change (see Figure 31-2) and will be able to cost effectively make the changes when new requirements dictate them.

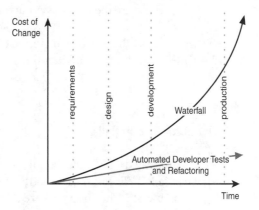

Figure 31–2   Cost of change curve for Waterfall and TDD

ADOPTION

So how do you apply Simple Design?

1. Nonambiguously determine what the requirements are for the task at hand. Get clarity on your goal before you start.
2. Determine what the solution will look like. You can do this by writing the tests first and letting them drive the solution or, more traditionally, by coming up with a design before starting to code. Either way, do not include generalizations for requirements that you see coming down the road. Play dumb and assume you aren't gonna need it (also known as YAGNI). You will be able to refactor later on if you really need the complexity.
3. If the solution uses existing code that is not general enough for the new requirements, refactor the code to make it amenable to the addition of the new functionality. Rely on existing tests to verify that you have changed only design and not behavior.
4. Add the new functionality to form a solution that is only as complex as needed to meet the new requirements.

Don't practice simple design without the ability to refactor and evolve the design. Refactoring cannot be done effectively without a set of automated developer tests. These are the necessary practices for simple design.

To effectively adopt the practice of simple design, most developers must suspend their disbelief[1] for several iterations to observe it working effectively.

BUT

Watch out for these pitfalls.

- A team may drop simple design when some paths lead directly to where a BDUF would have led them. They see the constant refactoring as a waste. They don't realize that most of the BDUF still leads to overgeneralization; conversely, most simple design leads to less complex designs.

---

1. Most experienced developers have problems building a simple solution only for the requirements at hand. Years of generalizing and designing ahead for future flexibility makes most developers very hesitant to trust that a design will be changeable without an exponential increase in effort later on.

- A team may interpret simple design as the design that takes the least time. Frequently that includes cut-and-paste solutions. This is *not* simple design; it's bad code.
- Teams frequently do not adopt simple design because, in their opinion, it cannot possibly work. It goes against all their expertise and good sense. We highly recommend that teams suspend their disbelief as Waterfall Will did in the sketch of this pattern. Two to three months of practicing simple design regularly will make a believer out of a team!

VARIATIONS

These are some common groupings of simple design with other practices. Both of the examples that follow are instances of the evolutionary design cluster.

- Test-first development, simple design, refactoring. Write the tests, build the simple design to pass the tests, and then refactor the simple design to make it more appropriate.
- Simple design, test-last development, refactoring. Come up with a minimal design to meet the requirements at hand, develop the code based on that design, write the tests to exercise the code just written, and then refactor the design to better fit the (code) reality on the ground.

REFERENCES

Simple design comes directly from eXtreme Programming.

Beck, K., *Extreme Programming Explained: Embrace Change*. Boston: Addison-Wesley, 2000.

Beck, K. and Andres, C., *Extreme Programming Explained: Embrace Change, Second Edition*. Boston: Addison-Wesley, 2005.

Chapter 32

FUNCTIONAL TESTS

Automated functional tests (also known as automated acceptance tests) are tests that exercise the requirements. They are generally written with the help of the customer and in the language of the business domain. They usually exercise a large part of the system and integrate several subsystems. Automated functional tests are complementary to automated developer tests. Figure 32-1 shows the relationship between the Functional Tests and Customer Part of Team practices.

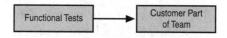

Figure 32–1 Automated functional tests are executable requirements that the customer should write.

BUSINESS VALUE

Functional tests primarily increase value to market and visibility of the software development team's progress by drastically improving the communication and validation of requirements. These tests also help to increase product lifetime, reduce the time to market, and reduce the overall cost of the system because it is a form of testing and feedback.

SKETCH

Caleb joined Scott ScrumMaster's Agile team as a part-time consultant to help the team take the next step in improving its software development process. After two weeks on the team, Caleb noticed that a significant number of the user stories were not passing approval by Cathy Customer and Aparna Analyst. Upon further investigation, Caleb saw that there were typically one or two days of hardening after a developer marked his tasks complete because of misunderstandings, mistakes, and omissions in the requirements-to-code translation.

Caleb had seen this before. Although the team members were practicing TDD, which helped them solve the problem right, they still had minor problems in solving the right problem. Iterations were forcing these mistakes to be caught and fixed regularly, but there was definite room for improvement.

Over the next several iterations, Caleb had the team members read *FIT for Development* by Rick Mugridge and Ward Cunningham and helped them use the FIT tool to introduce a set of automated tests as requirements instead of user stories. The team members were slow to adopt automated functional testing, but after five or six iterations of hard work and encouragement, they had reached a critical mass of tests and experience. The hardening period went away, development speed increased, and even the design quality improved!

CONTEXT

You are on a software development team, and you want to significantly improve the utility and quality of your software product. That is, you want to write code with fewer defects that doesn't just solve the problem right but also solve the right problem. You and your team are also willing to put in a serious effort to gain this improvement. You are willing to revisit the existing design and architecture and change them to facilitate these improvements. You are also willing to slow down so that you will eventually speed up in performing these tasks.

FORCES

These are common problems in software development that are addressed by this practice.

- **Increased bugs as intermodule dependencies grow.** Unit tests can keep individual classes fairly free of bugs, but they do not address intermodule bugs. Furthermore, as the code base grows, the number of potential intermodule bugs grows faster.
- **Not knowing when a task is done.** Almost everyone has experienced a project that was declared done and which then continued for weeks or months afterward.
- **Misunderstood requirements.** Frequently, especially on distributed, international teams, traditional requirements are misunderstood because of cultural differences. What may be clear to one party is often unclear to the other party.

- **Imprecise requirements.** One of the reasons that projects drag on after they are declared done is that the original requirements were imprecise. Verbal and prose requirements do not provide enough detail for coding. Developers guess what the customer meant and call the project done. But if the developers guessed wrong, the code has to be reworked.
- **Contradictory requirements.** Many done projects get stuck in the testing phase because of bug cycles. An example of a simple cycle is that when bug A is fixed, bug B appears; and when bug B is fixed, bug A reappears. But the cycle is rarely that obvious, especially if A and B are in different parts of the system or take a long list of manual steps to reproduce.
- **Outdated requirements.** The longer running the project, the more likely that at least some of the requirements have fallen behind the code. Let's be frank—have any of us really had requirements that were 100 percent up to date after a year of development? Outdated requirements can be more nefarious than no requirements. If there are no requirements, developers will try to extract them from the customer, the code, or the unit tests, all of which are likely to provide fairly up-to-date information. But outdated requirements are misinformation. They can waste significant time by sending developers down the wrong track.
- **Delayed releases.** As the application grows and the product matures, the testing department cycle can take longer, causing increasingly delayed releases.
- **Slow manual testing.** Manual testing by a testing department takes significantly longer with a large product than a small one. Because manual testing is slow, the feedback about a bug occurs long after the code changes that caused the problem were made. The delayed feedback makes it hard to diagnose which change caused the bug, so fixing a bug found by the testing department takes longer, too.
- **Slow testing being dropped.** If your tests are slow to execute, they get dropped in a crunch. Manual testing is frequently done quickly when a deadline looms, which results in errors going into production.
- **Slow patches.** A side effect of slow manual testing is slow patches for bugs reported in the field. In many development environments, developers have to set up a full database and perform many manual steps to reproduce a bug. And they must reproduce the bug both to diagnose it and to confirm they have eliminated it.

THEREFORE

Introduce a form of automated tests that describe the business process to be coded and treat them as executable requirements. These executable requirements are written by customers at the beginning of each iteration and provided to the developer(s). This is one of those practices that, unfortunately, is tool-dependent. You need a tool that is usable by nonprogrammers, such as FIT (http://fit.c2.com/) or FITNesse (http://fitnesse.org/). The precision required to write executable tests requires customers to be unambiguous and go to a level of detail that they may be unaccustomed to achieving, so they may need help from either testers or developers. Define these types of tests as functional tests—that is, business process tests that are co-owned by customers and developers and can be automatically executed.

A functional test contains the information that a customer would normally use for acceptance testing after a developer has written the code. A functional test can be seen as a use case scenario with specific values entered. So, for example, let us assume that we have the requirements for an online grocery store application, and the current requirements for this iteration include getting the inventory management to work correctly. Here is a sample FIT test that can be used as requirements. (Don't be intimidated by the table format. Take some time to read the tables and consider them as requirements.)

Item Inventory Management Tests

Load Basic Data to Be Used for Tests

To start off, let's load a standard set of items from an external source into our persistent store. Therefore, our tests coming afterward will have a nontrivial baseline of data.

fit.ActionFixture		
start	com.gemba.post.service.tests. fit.ItemInventoryFixture	
enter	inventory	./src/com/valtech/post/service/tests/fit/inventory.txt
check	total items	10

Okay, we have ten items. Let's be sure we have the right details.

ItemInventoryDisplayFixture		
upc	description	price
2458	Chocolate	0.75
1234	Cola	0.99
9034	Toothpaste	2.34
3214	Milk	2.34
8743	Eggs	2.35
0987	Olives	2.43
1233	Apples	1.12
8745	Paper Towels	3.45
9457	Canned Soup	1.24
2345	Cheese	5.65

Now, with successfully loaded items, let's do some catalog maintenance.

ActionFixture		
start	ItemInventoryFixture	
enter	select	2458
check	description	Chocolate
enter	description	Dark Chocolate
check	description	Dark Chocolate
enter	add Item	1111
enter	description	honey
enter	price	5.60
check	total items	11
enter	remove item	0987
enter	select	0987
check	upc	0987
check	description	Not Found
check	price	0.01

From a development standpoint, these tests should exercise the system from a layer just beneath the GUI. This is commonly known as the service layer or the system facade. Writing tests at this level exercises almost all the system and business logic. (There should be no business logic in the GUI.) Therefore, functional tests ensure that the requirements have been met. Because the tests are written first, the developer can use them to determine doneness. When the developer writes enough code that the test passes, the requirement has been met.

All the executable requirements need to be written up as part of a test suite that is run often—preferably as part of continuous integration. By consistently running the ever-growing test suite, the system never breaks a requirement that has already been met without a test failing. This means that if any requirements contradict, at least one test will fail, and the developer can go back to the customer for clarification.

Benefits of Automated Functional Tests

Upon successful adoption of functional tests, you can expect the following benefits.

- **The development team has more confidence.** There is a definite sense of confidence that developers acquire when there is a solid test framework that they rely upon. Automated developer tests and test-driven development go a long way toward making developers more confident in their code. This is not merely a warm-fuzzy feeling (which is always good for morale); it enables faster development because developers change what needs to be changed via refactoring. Functional tests take this confidence a notch or two above and beyond automated developer testing. They also improve the confidence of the customers/analysts and testers because they have a direct relationship to the requirements and regression tests. They know a green test is a nonambiguous indication that the related scenario is working.
- **Tests are robust.** These functional tests drive the service layer instead of focusing on business logic. Business logic tends to be fairly stable, so the tests don't have to change much. In contrast, automated tests that hit GUI elements break when GUI elements are rearranged.
- **Errors and bugs are reproducible quickly.** Once a bug is found, a functional test is written, and that bug doesn't come back to haunt us. An automated developer test should also be written around the buggy code, of course, but when developers first begin investigating a bug, they don't know where to write the automated developer test because

they don't know which unit caused the problem. But they (hopefully!) know which use case caused the problem, so they should be able to write a functional test immediately. By writing tests as soon as bugs are discovered, you eliminate the bug-fix-break thrashing that happens when systems become brittle.

When a system moves from initial development to production, the amount of time spent developing new functionality decreases. With a functional testing framework at hand, the business language has already been built, and it becomes straightforward (more than for automated developer tests) to build a functional test that exactly reproduces the error based on the bug report. This enables the developer to have an executable reproduction of the bug that can be used for digging into the code repeatedly without having to keep setting up the environment just so.

- **Testers have time to be more proactive.** If slow manual testing is a force behind adopting functional tests, quick automated testing is a benefit. The consequence is that testers are relieved of much of the day-to-day burden of manual testing of the main business rules. Instead, testers have more time to be proactive, collaboratively helping developers design more testable code rather than waiting to clean up at the end of an iteration.

- **When a task is done, it is visible to all.** Using functional tests does help us know when a task is done, but it's more than just that. Functional testing makes progress visible to the entire development team—customer, analyst, developer, tester, and manager. At any point in time, all passing (and failing) tests can be viewed. With a little effort, business value produced at a functional level can be analyzed for management needs.

- **The design and architecture are better.** Functional tests drive better layer and subsystem separation. Consider the layers of a multitier architecture; since the functional tests execute through the service layer, every bit of business logic that has found its way into the presentation layer must be either duplicated in the test fixture or pulled into the service layer.

Similarly, consider the subsystems of the system—the modules with functional responsibility, such as a module for tax calculations. Any tax logic that has leaked out of the tax module will be duplicated in the test fixture unless it is moved into the tax module. Functional tests help solidify the responsibilities of a subsystem.

- **Analysts think through requirements in greater detail.** Analysts think through requirements in greater detail to achieve the descriptions needed to write a test. For example, an analyst might state that text boxes should be disabled whenever they are not needed. But when he writes a functional test for this requirement, he is forced to get explicit about which conditions cause which text boxes—or really the textual representation of those text boxes in the underlying service layer—to be disabled.
- **Customer-developer communication is improved.** Over time, the discussions of the functional tests help the team develop a common vocabulary and a common vision for the system. (Jim Shore shares his ideas at www.jamesshore.com/Blog/A-Vision-For-Fit.html.) Examples of the development of such collaboration can also be found in Mugridge and Cunningham's *Fit for Developing Software*.

ADOPTION

So how do you go about adopting Functional Tests successfully as a practice?

1. Plan on testers/developers working with customers/analysts to write the tests together for the first few iterations.
2. (Highly Recommended) Get some outside help. Bring in someone who has successfully achieved functional tests within an Agile environment. These are much more than automated system-level tests because they are an integral practice of development.
3. (Recommended) Pick up *Fit for Developing Software* and run a study group including customers, analysts, developers, and testers.
4. Choose a tool and don't build your own. FIT and FitNesse are the most commonly used tools in this space.
5. Plan on your developers building fixtures to support the domain language that the team will evolve. Do not try to short-circuit this by having customers and analysts learn the objects you've already built and the methods on them. This defeats the purpose of creating a domain language for your project.
6. Start with one analyst/customer and one developer for one story on one iteration. Write the test as a use case scenario with explicit values.
7. Incrementally grow the team members who are aware of functional tests.
8. If you are working on an existing project, there is a good chance you will need to do some nontrivial refactoring to accommodate tests. At this point, you need to have adopted automated developer tests to enable refactoring. If your team hasn't adopted these practices, you need to do so to move forward.

9. Do not put functional testing on hold, but write the tests and use them manually until you can effectively refactor the parts of the system needed for testing. Even if tests are not automated, this level of detail can be test driven—that is, the tests can be written down and used by developers to determine doneness.

10. During the transition to functional tests, it can help to assign a developer the role of functional test cop. The cop's job is to track down the developers who break the functional tests, help them see why their code broke the test, and help them fix the problem.

11. (Optional) Pick up Eric Evan's *Domain-Driven Design* and run a study group after you have started to write functional tests successfully. Tie the language that your team is coming up with directly to what is in this book.

12. Plan on a 3- to 6-month adoption period until your team starts to write functional tests regularly.

13. Plan on an adoption period anywhere from 3 to 12 months if this is already a long-running project without tests because you will probably need significant refactoring efforts to enable this practice.

Like almost everything in Agile development, functional tests should be adopted iteratively. Be careful that you keep people ahead of process. That is, iterate to get developers and customers trained and have them build a few functional tests. Then, after the team has a few working functional tests that are part of the build, ask these developers and customers for feedback on the tools and processes. Improve your tools and processes until the developers and customers are happy with functional testing. Then iteratively expand the practice to the team.

BUT

There are valid reasons that functional tests are not widespread in the Agile community. Functional tests are very error-prone. Things can go wrong in two general categories of problem areas. The first is in the adoption itself—and, in that way, this section is similar to all the "But" sections for the other practices. The other significant area is that of the underlying system architecture. If the system architecture is not functional test-friendly, you need to change it.

Implementation Smells

Here are some indicators that your adoption is not going well.

- **There's little or no accountability for broken tests.** If there is no accountability for broken tests, they don't get fixed. In general, there is no accountability if it is difficult to tell whose code change broke the test. This usually happens when the test-run cycle is significantly slower than the check-in cycle of developers; that is, if several developers have checked in their code since the last time the tests were run, it is difficult to determine whose changes broke the tests. So how do you address this problem? Simple. Make the tests run faster.

First, the team must make a commitment to Functional Testing as a primary development practice instead of a secondary one. When it is not an option to drop the tests, teams find creative solutions. The main thing is to speed up the running of the functional tests so they can be run effectively by developers on their local machines before checking in. Here are some effective strategies we have found.

- **Run the functional tests on separate machines.** By grouping tests into related suites, you can easily run each suite on its own machine. This effectively parallelizes the test suite and can increase the speed in proportion to the number of machines used.
- **Functional tests roll back database transactions.** That is, the transactions do not commit to the database. This is a simple but effective idea: Don't commit your database transactions if you are testing end to end. We have seen this practice emerge independently on different projects, and this usually gives about an order of magnitude increase in speed.
- **Refactor the functional tests to thinner slices.** By testing a small scenario within each test instead of several scenarios (or even all scenarios) for a use case, we get a finer granularity by splitting up tests. We have also found that larger tests tend to have more redundancy; breaking them up enables faster individual tests.
- **Group the functional tests by business area.** Grouping functional tests by business area enables a developer to test the subset of relevant tests on his machine without running the full suite. This enables a faster red-green-red test loop and keeps a test suite from slowing the pace of development.

Note that having independent database sandboxes for each functional test run is a prerequisite for the preceding advice. If two functional tests run against the same database, one may report an incorrect failure because of interactions with the data inserted by the other test.

- **Confidence in functional tests is lost.** Leaving tests broken takes away from much of the value of the functional test suite as a safety net that prevents bugs from entering the build in the first place. The tests aren't catching the bugs and helping us keep the code in working order as we would expect. Without this safety net, confidence in the tests is lost. Test writing is reduced and, in the more serious cases, it is deleted and finally dropped as a whole.
- **Small code changes break many tests.** When many tests fail, you normally assume that a big code change must have been checked in. However, if only a small change caused many failures, there must be a large amount of test overlap.

To solve this, have each test focus on a thin slice of functionality. When each test focuses on one thin slice of functionality and does not overlap much with other tests, its more likely that only one or two tests will break when a bug is introduced. It is much easier to diagnose why a thin test failed. Thus, writing tests to exercise one thin slice of functionality in one major system provides the best feedback on that example of a business process.

- **Functional tests try—and fail—to catch unit-level tests.** If functional testing does not reduce the bugs found by your testing group and customers, the problem may be that the bugs are at the wrong level for functional tests.

Functional tests are not a replacement for automated developer tests, even if the coverage statistics look high. Automated developer tests support functional tests by exercising the code most likely to break, even if it is deeply buried in otherwise inaccessible parts of the system under test. Use automated developer tests for unit-level bugs and functional tests for interaction bugs.

- **Functional tests are created without appropriate refactoring.** Business logic is then copied into the fixtures used for the tool, and code duplication causes a maintenance nightmare. Don't do this. Tests are as important as production code. Do not introduce duplication; refactor instead.
- **Feature devotion sets in.** The feature list, tied to functional tests, becomes an up-front requirement. Feedback is lost. You are now back in Waterfall Will's world!
- **Functional tests are used as a meter for progress.** This assumes that all functions are of equal value. They are not. You can easily fool yourself into thinking you are delivering business value because you've just delivered 40 running functional tests. But what if these tests don't really have business value to your customer? Focus on business value.

Architecture Smells

If you are using good tools and techniques and it's still hard to write functional tests, the root problem may be your system's architecture. In particular, if your test fixtures contain business logic, rather than merely translating test specifications into method calls, you will want to consider the smells that follow. We also consider a smell that becomes apparent when it is hard for a functional test to run through a single, complete use case.

Functional tests help push business logic into the correct layer (in a tiered architecture) and the correct functional module. When business logic has found its way into the wrong place, functional tests expose the misplacement.

- **Fixtures contain business logic that mirrors GUI work.** If you find yourself writing fixtures that must perform business logic so that they mirror what is done in the GUI, you may have an architecture smell. A common cause of such duplicated business logic is the use of a canonical three-tiered architecture having presentation, domain, and persistence layers. Such architecture does not always succeed in keeping business logic away from the presentation layer. In fact, it is common for GUIs in this setup to contain control logic.

  For example, a simple GUI to transfer money from one account to another (account1, account2) often does the following in the GUI:

  Account1.withdraw($100)

  Account2.deposit($100)

  This is simple logic, but it is business logic and not view logic. So if your fixture for the transfer(account1, account2) function has this logic in it, you have code duplication with the UI (which is bad), and you have uncovered business logic in the presentation layer (which is worse).

  When you encounter this type of problem, the solution is to pull out the duplicate code in a common place. That place is the service layer, which lies between the presentation and domain layers and contains control logic. In this way, functional tests help to ensure proper separation of business and presentation logic and encourage a new logical layer to hold control logic.

- **The fixture for a module contains business logic that belongs in the module.** There is another way that business logic can turn up in a test fixture—when a functional module fails to contain all the business logic that belongs in it. An example can best illustrate this point.

  Let's assume that one of our subsystems is a tax module that is responsible for doing all tax-related calculations. Before introducing functional testing, we wrote this module and believed we had good functional separation. Unfortunately, over the development of our project, not everyone using the tax module was completely familiar with it, so some precalculation was made outside the tax module depending on special tax-exempt days. This functionality should have been in the tax module; in a sense, the tax modules boundary was breached.

  When functional tests were written for the tax module, we found that the fixture code had to perform the precalculation that depended on the tax-exempt days. At that point, a responsible developer would notice the duplication and refactor the calculation into the tax module and out of the fixture and the non-tax-module code.

Functional tests frequently solidify the boundaries and responsibilities of the subsystems. Functional tests help focus your systems modules.

Functional tests are difficult to run through a single, complete use case. Legacy systems—that is, systems that were not designed with functional testing—can be especially difficult to test. Sometimes they do not let you easily run through a single example of a business process. This is a difficult smell to eradicate, and the solution depends on the architecture.

In some cases, the source of the problem is that a module assumes that multiple use cases are running simultaneously. When you try to isolate a single use case, you discover that you still have to perform the setup for all the other use cases, or the system will crash.

VARIATIONS

Here are several different variations for using functional testing effectively.

- **Business logic in the GUI.** Applications that have business logic in the UI layer—such as Web applications with AJAX—use Web automation tools, such as Selenium and Web AII, to run full, end-to-end testing.

- **Functional tests covering the domain only.** The "Adoption" section focuses on functional tests that execute logic from the service layer through the domain layer all the way down to persistence. Not all functional tests must exercise all these layers, though; in fact, Mugridge and Cunningham, in *Fit for Developing Software*, argue for writing functional tests to exercise the domain logic only. Such tests are still useful, but they do not cover the subsystem boundaries, which are prone to bugs. The domain-only approach is a viable alternative if running end-to-end tests within a developer-check-in cycle is infeasible.

- **Functional tests written by committee.** Customers or analysts should write functional tests because they are in the best position to write requirements. However, testers and developers can join customers and analysts to cowrite tests.

  Testers bring their expertise in test-case development and help write requirements that cover the necessary details. Developers may be needed to help make the requirements executable, depending on the tool. For example, the Framework for Integrated Tests (FIT) tool requires developers to write fixtures before tests can execute. Writing tests by committee happens primarily in the beginning stages of adoption of functional testing, as analysts learn to think like testers and developers build their domain language. In later stages, writing tests by committee tapers off, and the brunt of test authoring falls to the analysts with occasional help from others in the development group.

- **Functional tests written with a unit-testing tool.** Some teams write their functional tests with a unit-testing tool such as NUnit or JUnit. Using an xUnit testing tool covers code adequately but loses involvement from customers and analysts, since the tests are now coded in a language that they can neither write nor read. It becomes the developer's job to translate the requirements into these tests. The status of the tests as passing or failing is also not visible to either the customer or testing group.

  Depending on who writes the tests, they could be a valid variation or a smell. If the customer is technical and is writing the tests, this is a valid variation. But if the customer is somehow telling the developer and the developer is translating that into code, functional tests in xUnit tend to be rather hobbled because of the exclusive focus on coverage. These tests are indeed better than no functional tests but could be considered a smell.

- **Functional tests within a traditional development environment.** So far, documented experience with functional testing is within an Agile development environment, but there is no reason it cannot be used on non-Agile projects. The key point is that the functional tests must be run at a frequency that matches the developer check-in cycle. That way, the source of failing tests can be identified. All the benefits of Agile functional testing are achieved, just at a slower cycle time because there is no continuous integration build. When done in this environment, the emphasis on speed of running tests is reduced because the check-in cycles are typically much longer.

REFERENCES

The practice of Functional Tests, as defined here, is most commonly discussed within the context of the Framework for Integrated Tests (FIT).

Gandhi, P., Haugen, N., Hill, M., and Watt, R. 2005. Creating a Living Specification Document with FIT. Agile 2005 conference.

Marick, B. 2002. Bypassing the GUI. *Software Testing and Quality Engineering*, September/October, 41–47.

Mugridge, R., and Cunningham, W., *Fit for Developing Software: Framework for Integrated Tests*, Upper Saddle River, New Jersey: Prentice Hall, 2005.

Shore, J., "A Vision for Fit," www.jamesshore.com/Blog/A-Vision-For-Fit.html.

Chapter 33

COLLECTIVE CODE OWNERSHIP

Members of the development team have the right and responsibility to modify any part of the code. This defines the practice of Collective Code Ownership.

BUSINESS VALUE

Collective Code Ownership is a supporting practice for many other Agile practices. Nonetheless, it does have a direct effect on increasing the flexibility of your project by increasing the knowledge of software developers, which, in turn, enables them to take more responsibility and ownership to create a full solution as opposed to a Band-Aid approach.

SKETCH

Scott ScrumMaster's team had read about collective code ownership in *Extreme Programming Explained* by Kent Beck but decided not to adopt it. In fact, they felt it would be wasteful and counterproductive to have anyone write GUI code, for example, because they would get some really poor UIs from nonexperts. Or so they thought...

Scott's team members started with iterations and automated developer tests. They quickly found that the old way of distributing work led to a consistent block at the end of each iteration for integration work between the different subsets of the code being done.

After two iterations of several missed goals, the members decided to give collective code ownership a try. This led to several scattered instances of pair programming throughout the iteration for knowledge transfer between the team members. It also led to the goals being met much more easily and a reduction in bottlenecked resources.

CONTEXT

You are on a development team where each developer(s) works on only a given set of components. Examples of this type of specialization are GUI developers, middle-tier developers, and database developers. Developers on your team own the code they write and zealously protect it. They're of the mindset, "Nobody touches *my code!*"

Your team is adopting one or more Agile practices that are moving you away from static designs created up-front to a more fluid design. Your team members have a need to modify more than their traditional piece of code to keep the system working.

Or perhaps you want to reduce the resource bottlenecks in your team. You don't want a single point of failure in your team's expertise. You want to be able to roll people on and off the team over time.

FORCES

Many forces emerge from adopting other Agile practices that are addressed by collective code ownership.

Any form of change to the system can cause other parts of the system to change. Many Agile development practices enable and encourage change. In fact, the subtitle of *Extreme Programming Explained* was Embrace Change, which was one of the early mantras of the Agile community.

- To keep automated developer tests passing for the entire system, developers need to periodically modify parts of the system they did not write.
- Refactoring frequently causes the same issue: the need to modify parts of the system that you did not write because they depend on the part of the code you have.
- Evolutionary design is severely limited if you cannot change parts of the system you did not write.
- A team of specialists is susceptible to resource bottlenecks and therefore is less able to react to change quickly.
- Continuous integration forces the entire system to be running and integrating all the time. Therefore, changes that affect multiple parts of the system must be fully resolved before that code is committed to the source repository.

THEREFORE

To enable the agility of many Agile practices, developers must be empowered to change any part of the system as needed. This should not be attempted without a safety net of tests—via automated developer tests—to support developers in unfamiliar territory. The code becomes communal and mutually owned by the team. When a task requires a change in one part of the system that propagates to another part of the system, a developer should be encouraged to make the entire change or seek out help for that change if needed. This practice—of everyone owning the code and being allowed and encouraged to change it when needed—is called collective code ownership.

ADOPTION

You will find that collective code ownership is pulled by many other practices for support. So don't consider adopting this practice until another practice creates a need for it. Once there is a need for collective code ownership, do the following:

1. Decide the scope of the communal code. This will often be the entire system. However, sometimes it is the subsystem that your team is concerned with if you are one of many teams working on the same software product.
2. (Highly Recommended) Consider adopting automated developer tests as a safety net to help ease the pains as developers become familiar with new parts of the system.
3. Set a rule that developer A cannot refuse to help developer B if developer B needs help on a part of the system that developer A is an expert in. That way developer B can make safe changes to parts of the code he is not familiar with yet.
4. (Highly Recommended) Adopt pair programming to share the knowledge of different parts of the system. Rotate pairs frequently.
5. Encourage developers to sign up for development tasks in different parts of the system, even if they are not familiar with those parts. This will also help spread the expertise across the team.

BUT

This is another one of those nonintuitive practices that experienced developers have a hard time buying into. In fact, it is a little threatening to someone who feels a sense of security in being the expert in a particular part of the system.

- Developers cannot let go of the "my code" mentality and become protective, defensive, or aggressive when someone changes code that they originally wrote. These are growing pains and should be dealt with on an individual basis.
- Designs thrash because developers are not communicating or respecting each others' decisions. Developers should only change existing designs in response to requirements driving those changes. Frequently, you will find that one of the developers is changing the design back to the right way out of the "my code" mentality instead of writing code to meet specific requirements.

VARIATIONS

On large teams, it may not be feasible to have generalists on the team because of the many different technologies that must be learned. One way to address this is to move from generalists to multipart specialists. Developers learn the technologies and code of the neighboring subsystems of the one they are mainly focused on.

REFERENCES

Collective Code Ownership was one of the original 12 practices of eXtreme Programming.

Beck, K., *Extreme Programming Explained: Embrace Change*. Boston: Addison-Wesley, 2000.

Beck, K. and Andres, C., *Extreme Programming Explained: Embrace Change, Second Edition*. Boston: Addison-Wesley, 2005.

Chapter 34

PAIR PROGRAMMING

Two developers work together at the same computer to build a feature. One developer is known as the driver, and the other is the navigator; the driver is at the keyboard and is building the software to meet the task-at-hand, and the navigator is thinking forward to design implications and reviewing the work being done. The practice of Pair Programming is sometimes described as a continuous form of peer code review.

BUSINESS VALUE

The practice of Pair Programming is an excellent way to improve the quality of the software being built. Pair programming is effective at spreading expertise across the team and reducing resource bottlenecks, which enables the team to respond to changes faster, increasing flexibility. Finally, pair programming is often a supporting practice when you want to learn or adopt difficult practices such as Test-Driven Development or Test-Driven Requirements. It, therefore, indirectly supports business values of these practices as well.

SKETCH

Uthman had initially pair-programmed heavily with Will when they joined the development team. The main thing that he noticed was that the code they produced was of excellent quality. He also found that, after their invoicing debacle (see sketches in Chapters 26, 27, and 28), pair programming had some subtle effect that made both of them more disciplined; neither of them wanted to skip writing a test in front of the other, even with a looming deadline. And when one of them was mentally exhausted or stuck, the other was usually able to pick things up, write the tests, and move on.

CONTEXT

You are on a development team where quality is near the top in business values, or you are going through a period of adopting some of the more difficult technical practices such as Test-First Development or Functional Tests. You have the ability to trade off development speed for quality.[1]

FORCES

- Programmers naturally go for a second pair of eyes when solving a difficult problem.
- Code reviews are one of the few practices that have been rigorously studied in experiments on software development[2] and have been experimentally proven to significantly improve the quality of software.
- Two developers working together on the same task almost always produce a better solution than either of them would have produced individually—even if there is a big discrepancy in their expertise.
- Improved quality in design and implementation has a positive effect on long-term cost of change.

THEREFORE

If your situation matches the context for this pattern—that is, product quality is of extreme importance, or you are adopting one of the difficult practices—have your developers work together to build the system. Working together is a continuous form of code and design review.

---

1. Reported numbers vary greatly. I have found that a team that pair-programs develops at 60 to 80 percent of the velocity of one that doesn't, but they produce significantly better code. This is, however, anecdotal evidence. I refer you to many articles that will disagree with these numbers. Before reading them, especially the experimental evidence, I highly encourage you to review the appendix on experiments to help you evaluate the quality of the papers and validity of the reported numbers.

2. Many studies that are conducting controlled experiments on real-world projects directly show the benefit of code reviews and inspections. The most notable of these are the ones conducted by Adam Porter and his research team. Here are three links to different papers published in *IEEE Transactions on Software Engineering* (two of which are from Porter's research group): http://ieeexplore.ieee.org/xpl/freeabs_all.jsp?arnumber=601071&isnumber=12999, http://ieeexplore.ieee.org/xpl/freeabs_all.jsp?arnumber=585501&isnumber=12691, and http://csdl2.computer.org/persagen/DLAbsToc.jsp?resourcePath=/dl/trans/ts/&toc=comp/trans/ts/2000/01/.

The two developers should be seated at one machine with the goal of building the task at hand—including all developer and functional tests. One person is at the keyboard and is called the driver, while the other person is the navigator and is codesigning, looking forward and contemplating the design, and doing any research needed. The two talk constantly and communicate ideas by passing the keyboard between them. They trade positions frequently; no one person should dominate the keyboard. Whenever they need to hash things out, they do so on paper or at a whiteboard to discuss different designs.

This practice of working together to build a system and being in a constant state of code and design evaluation and review is called Pair Programming.

ADOPTION

Pair Programming is probably one of the most controversial of the Agile practices because management usually sees two people working at the same keyboard as a 50 percent reduction of productivity. Therefore, when you have a chance to pair-program, you really want to get it right. Here is some advice.

- Pair programming is a different way of working and has a few constraints that developers may not be used to.
  - Because people will be working together, they need to be at the office at the same time. This is a constraint that may be unusual for early birds and night hawks working together. Many teams set core hours when everyone must be available.
  - Many personal issues come up, such as politeness, body odor, bad breath, and personal space. Make people aware of these issues from the start, and bring things up in private if problems occur.
  - This practice is exhausting. You should expect people to put in regular work weeks instead of large amounts of overtime.
- Get a commitment from your team to suspend their disbelief for a few iterations and give pair programming a test run. You don't have to have a 100 percent pairing schedule. Many teams start off by dedicating two hours a day for two iterations as the trial.
- Switch pairs. Developers shouldn't be joined at the hip. Changing pairs frequently keeps everyone on their toes. Consider using an information radiator to show who has paired with whom to encourage this switching practice.

- Working together to program a user story is usually a good starting level of granularity.
- Beware that pair programming is slower; if you are not prepared to slow down a bit—usually about 20 percent—don't set up your team for failure. Unlike many practices, pair programming continues to be slower even after the team learns the practice. This is a trade of time for quality.

BUT

To get the most out of pair programming, keep your eyes open for these problems.

- Watch out for keyboard hogging from assertive individuals. Pair programming is about two people working together, not one person looking over the shoulder of the other.
- Don't be joined at the hip; switch pairs regularly to get the full benefit of knowledge sharing.
- Beware of a spellchecking pair, where code reviews are not being done and the navigator is doing nothing more than looking for trivial, syntactical mistakes.
- Don't force pair programming forever. Only do so for the period where people agree to suspend their disbelief. In the end, there are frequently team members who will be uncomfortable working with others.
- Not everyone has a social personality and is willing or able to work with others. Forcing the practice may produce problems in the team and worse results than individual coding.
- Keep an eye out for personal problems. When they occur, you need to figure out what to do as a team. A self-organizing team should handle these problems during its retrospective.

VARIATIONS

Many teams adopt pair programming incrementally, starting out with one or two hours a day and working their way up to pairing all the time.

Some teams find it useful to have two machines per pair. One is the main machine for programming where the driver sits, and the other is an auxiliary—usually a laptop—that can be used for research as the two work together to solve the problem at hand.

Another variation is remote pair programming using one of many existing virtual desktop tools such as VNC and a communication tool for voice or video. Many teams have been successful pairing in this way. It helps get around the constraint of everyone being in the office at the same time.

REFERENCES

Beck, K. and Andres, C., *Extreme Programming Explained: Embrace Change* (Second Edition), Boston: Addison Wesley, 2005.

Belshee, A., Promiscuous Pairing and Beginners Mind, *Agile Conference* 2005.

Cockburn, A., *Agile Software Development: The Cooperative Game* (Second Edition), Boston: Addison Wesley, 2007.

Fields, J., Spellchecking Pair, http://blog.jayfields.com/2007/08/spellchecking-pair.html.

Porter, A. http://ieeexplore.ieee.org/xpl/freeabs_all.jsp?arnumber=601071& isnumber=12999.

Porter, A. http://ieeexplore.ieee.org/xpl/freeabs_all.jsp?arnumber=585501& isnumber=12691.

Porter, A. http://csdl2.computer.org/persagen/DLAbsToc.jsp?resourcePath=/dl/trans/ts/&toc=comp/trans/ts/2000/01/e1toc.xml&DOI=10.1109/32.825763.

Williams, L., and Kessler, R., *Pair Programming Illuminated*, Boston: Addison-Wesley, 2003.

Part 3.3

SUPPORTING PRACTICES

Chapter 35

COACH

A coach is an experienced practitioner of Agile software development who joins the team in an advisory capacity. This person's job is to mentor the team through myriad practices in a hands-on manner. Therefore, a coach may facilitate the first retrospective, pair-program with developers to aid them in learning test-first development, and help the team decide which Agile practices to adopt and when to adapt them if they don't fit the current environment.

BUSINESS VALUE

Having an effective coach helps accentuate any practices adopted. Therefore, this person can positively affect all business values by helping the team get the most out of the practices.

SKETCH

Caleb Consultant joined the team as the coach to help members adopt and adapt practices to improve their software development capabilities. He spent his first weeks working with stakeholders, domain experts, and others to understand the goals and aims of the project and the needs of the organization. During this time, he helped communicate to the whole team the current business values, helped them focus on them, and uncovered many business and process smells.

Caleb then assisted in development of an initial release backlog by facilitating several workshops so the team could build a release backlog. He then joined the whole team and facilitated their first iteration kickoff meeting. He showed exercises for the first few times by example and then stepped back to let others learn and lead. He stayed with the team members through their first release and then left to aid another team.

CONTEXT

Your team is adopting Agile practices and has no previous experience. You would like to adopt Agile practices with the minimum amount of pain and avoid as many wrong turns as possible. You have the funding to bring in an outsider to help the team.

FORCES

- Many Agile practices are difficult and nonintuitive at first.
- People use past experience to help them understand and mold new practices even if that experience is contradictory to the new way of working.
- Traditional development experience often contradicts Agile practices. Evolutionary design encourages the developer not to look ahead and design for future changes.
- Many Agile practices make things painful. For a team trying to adopt iterations that have a done state that includes working, tested, integrated code, the first few cycles are extremely painful and disheartening if you don't see the light at the end of the tunnel.
- Many Agile practices are brittle. If they are not done with discipline, they become detrimental to development. When these practices go awry, it is often hard to determine what to do.

THEREFORE

Find an experienced Agile practitioner who has experience with the full development cycle and is willing to share his experience with the team. This person should be not only experienced but also able to communicate his experience to the team effectively. Finally, he should be able to get his hands dirty and work with the team individually and as a group to teach the practices. This experienced teacher, facilitator, and mentor is called a coach.

ADOPTION

An effective coach can be extremely useful to a fledgling Agile team in its adoption. So how do you find a good coach?

- Finding a good coach is just like finding a good consultant. References from those you know and have worked with are the place to start. Otherwise, treat this search like any hire that your organization typically performs.

- Test the candidate. Have him present an onsite seminar on one or more relevant areas. Many consultants are typically willing to do this at cost.
- Test facilitation skills. Bring the candidate in to facilitate a workshop for determining business value and appropriate practices or to build an initial release backlog.
- Test individual skills. Have the candidate pair-program with one of your developers, build some requirements with the customer, and create some functional tests (even if only in script format).

Once you have found and hired a coach, you can rely on him to help guide you through the Agile wilderness!

BUT

A bad coach can hurt your team and waste your money. Here are some warning signs to look for when searching for your coach.

- He proposes a set of standard practices to adopt all at once without first understanding your particular organization's context. This will affect your team's gain from adopting practices since they will not be targeted to your environment.
- He doesn't ask about your organization's goals and look for smells. This is a manifestation of the preceding problem. The practices will not be targeted to your environment.
- His experience is only one project. It is tempting to ignore this problem, especially if the coach is not a consultant and has just come off a successful project in your organization. The problem here is that he will frequently try to guide you to adopt exactly what had worked for his team previously. Teams are different. Projects have different contexts. What may be appropriate for one team and project may not be for the new one.
- He does not show competence in both facilitation and one-on-one mentoring. No matter how experienced and talented a person is, if he cannot communicate what to do effectively—which frequently entails showing by example first—he will be of limited help.

If any of these points is present, consider looking for another candidate or going it alone.

VARIATIONS

The coach is frequently a consultant who comes to help the team. Not all coaches join the team in a full-time capacity as Caleb did. A common scenario involves the coach coming in for one week a month. That works well for many teams.

Sometimes the coach is not an outsider but an employee of the same organization who has experience with Agile. That also works well, but it is more difficult to see this person as an advisor.

Finally, the coach does not have to be just one person. Augmenting the team with more than one person at a time is common and allows more time for one-on-one mentoring.

REFERENCES

Beck., K., and Andres, C., *Extreme Programming Explained: Embrace Change (Second Edition)*, Boston: Addison Wesley, 2005.

Chapter 36

ENGAGE THE COMMUNITY

One of the best sources of advice, information, and experience is the members of the Agile community. You can engage the community to your benefit through participating in local groups, conferences, mailing lists/online forums, and online publications.

BUSINESS VALUE

The Engage the Community practice provides information that can help you adopt and adapt any of the practices. Therefore, like all supporting practices, this practice magnifies the business value addressed by the practice(s) it supports.

SKETCH

As the team went into its second release, the automated functional tests started to take longer to run. The time steadily crept up to 30 minutes, and then the continuous integration build started to break regularly. People had stopped running the full test suite locally before checking in code.

Bob BuildMaster was a regular participant in several online Agile forums and posted a message describing the team's situation and asking for advice. By the end of the day, he had gathered several suggested solutions. After following up with requests for more detail, he was able to get source code examples.

By the end of the week, Bob had modified the way the team's functional tests run by rolling back all database transactions instead of committing them. This brought the running time of the entire test suite down to five minutes, and the regular build breaks stopped because developers were now able to catch errors locally first.

CONTEXT

You are on a development team adopting one or more development practices. You want to learn how others have addressed issues similar to yours either because you believe knowing this will help you in the future or because you have a specific problem to solve.

FORCES

- Not every wheel needs to be reinvented when tailoring development practices to your environment. There is a good chance that others have encountered the same problems in similar contexts.
- Learning is the bottleneck of software development. The more you learn, the faster and better you will develop software.
- Conversations often yield much more information than the original point or question indicated.
- Approaching others is sometimes intimidating.
- Many local Agile groups meet regularly, but usually during after-work hours.

THEREFORE

Look for knowledge in diverse areas. Rather than solving everything the hard way, perform some due diligence to find out if others have encountered similar problems and how they were able to solve them.

The Agile community is friendly and open. People are responsive, easily approachable, and eager to help—even the really well-known personalities.

Take advantage of this invaluable resource. Get into the habit of reading a few mailing lists or an online news source. If there is a local group that meets regularly, take advantage and meet others. These groups often bring in speakers regularly to address one or more issues of the day. Finally, if you can afford it, go to an Agile conference or one with an Agile track. These are wonderful experiences and opportunities to learn and connect to others.

ADOPTION

So where and how do you start? Where can you meet others locally? Over the Internet? What conferences are worth going to? Here are some suggestions, but they are only a starting point, and the community is continuously evolving:

- Find a local Agile group and attend a meeting. Make an effort to talk to others at the meeting. Bring your business cards and pass them out.
  - Most groups register with the Agile Alliance or the Agile Project Leadership Network.
    - Agile Alliance (http://agilealliance.org/show/1641)
    - APLN chapters (http://apln.sharepointsite.com/Lists/APLN%20Chapters/AllItems.aspx)
  - If you can't find the group at either the APLN or the Agile Alliance, post a query to one of the Agile mailing lists.
  - Most groups have a mailing list. If yours does, you can probably find it by searching at http://groups.yahoo.com. Joining this group will keep you informed of what's happening in your backyard.
- If you find the time and money, attend a conference. There are at least two well-known conferences that are focused on pure Agile methods, and there are many other smaller conferences around the world. Here are a few, but you can find out about many more by getting plugged into online and local groups.
  - Agile 20xx—This is the largest of the Agile conferences and takes place every summer in North America. The Web site is www.agile20xx.org. (For example, www.agile2008.org is the Web site for the 2008 conference.)
  - XP 20xx—This was the first of all Agile conferences and bears the name XP for historical reasons. It takes place every summer in Europe, and the Web site can be found at www.xp20xx.org. (For example, www.xp2008.org is the Web site for the 2008 conference.)
  - XP Day—XP Days are short conferences (sometimes longer than a day) that take place all over the world. These conferences cover Agile development in general, not just XP. They require less monetary and time investment to attend. At the time of writing, XP days are only run in Europe.[1] Timely information can be found at www.xpday.org.
- Mailing lists and online user groups that focus on one or more Agile practices or methodologies include the following:
  - Agile Development Forum (http://forum.agilesoftwaredevelopment.org/)
  - XP (http://groups.yahoo.com/group/extremeprogramming/)

---

1. XP Day North America, www.xpday.info, has been discontinued because of lack of attendance.

- Scrum (http://groups.yahoo.com/group/scrumdevelopment/)
- Test-Driven Development (http://groups.yahoo.com/group/testdrivendevelopment/)
- Refactoring (http://groups.yahoo.com/group/refactoring/)
- Testing (http://tech.groups.yahoo.com/group/agile-testing/)
- Database (http://groups.yahoo.com/group/agileDatabases/)
- Search for more at http://groups.yahoo.com/search?query= agile.
- News sources and magazines are good places to keep up to date but are minimally interactive.
    - *InfoQ* (www.infoq.com) has columnists who write short news articles daily on what is interesting, new, or significant in many software areas, one of which is Agile.
    - *Agile Journal* (www.agilejournal.com) has regular themed issues. Each issue has several articles on one area of Agile development.
    - *Better Software* (www.stickyminds.com/BetterSoftware/magazine.asp) is a subscription-based magazine that covers all aspects of Agile development.

BUT

There is little that can be called out here other than using your common sense in relating to others. With that said

- Participating in mailing lists, local Agile groups, and conferences can be time-consuming and expensive if you are not careful.
- You should be prepared for a high noise-to-information ratio in some of the more active mailing lists.

VARIATIONS

The idea behind the Engage the Community practice is to build relationships with others in the field and mutually support each other. There are as many ways to do this as there are people. There is no right way to do it. This pattern provides a starting point.

REFERENCES

Manns, M. L., and Rising, L., *Fearless Change: Patterns for Introducing New Ideas*, Boston: Addison-Wesley, 2005.

Chapter 37

Reading Circle

The Reading Circle practice is a regular meeting used to discuss, analyze, and learn from a written work and apply it to improve the team's performance. Typically, one chapter is reviewed at a time and related directly to the software project each meeting.

Business Value

A Reading Circle is a supporting practice to help successfully execute, enhance, or adopt an Agile practice. Therefore, like all supporting practices, it enhances the business value of the practice(s) it supports.

For example, the developers may meet every two weeks to go through *Working Effectively with Legacy Code* so they are aware of the different techniques that can be used to add tests to an existing code base. Or all team members may read *FIT for Developing Software* to learn how to write effective functional tests on their way to adopting test-driven requirements.

Sketch

The whole team decided to read *Agile Estimation and Planning* by Mike Cohn. Members had initially listened to Caleb's advice on short planning meetings, but after trying his advice, they felt it was insufficient, and their estimates were too far off. So they went back to their old way of planning and applied it to iterations. This also didn't work out; the planning time was too long, and they started feeling that iterations were too small. (They were two-week iterations.)

At this point, Caleb brought in several copies of *Agile Estimating and Planning* and scheduled a weekly lunch review that was open for those interested. All attendees read the chapter of the week in advance. They spent half their lunch hour reviewing the chapter and the other half discussing how this might be applicable to the way they currently work.

Over time, they went back to a light relative point estimation process and relied on their velocity to determine iteration capacity. This was almost exactly what they had started with and rejected, but by reading the book and discussing it together, they became much more comfortable with the inevitable inaccuracies. (Those inaccuracies were reduced as the team became more comfortable with the practices they had adopted.)

CONTEXT

You are adopting a new practice that is difficult or nonintuitive. Many on the team are interested in learning more about the particular subject. You have found one or more books on the subject.

FORCES

- It is often difficult to find the time and motivation to read a book individually.
- It is even more difficult and time-consuming to relate everything in a book to on-the-ground events.
- Group work is an effective technique for motivation.
- Group work is an effective medium for sharing insights and ideas.
- There are many useful books available to help a team understand, adopt, and adapt techniques for software development.
- Many of the patterns in this book have references to books and articles that can further explain, elaborate on, and detail the practices.

THEREFORE

When adopting a practice is difficult and it is being practiced by multiple members of the team, consider getting together on a regular basis to read a book on the subject. Use the recommendations at the end of each chapter to help you find and choose the books to support the practices.

Teams will have different ideas on how regularly to meet. It should be anywhere between one to four weeks. Agree in advance on the material that will be covered and rotate the privilege and responsibility of facilitating the meeting and doing the extra research to relate the theory to your project.

Each meeting should have two parts: the first to review the chapter to get everyone on the same page and the second to relate the chapter to your project and environment.

ADOPTION

Here are some guidelines to help you make your reading circle successful and pleasant:

- Individuals
    - Get buy-in and commitment from individuals on the team before announcing the reading circle.
    - Give attendees credit and kudos regularly. By participating in the reading circle, they are learning and becoming more effective employees of the company.
- Scheduling
    - Determine the review order of the chapters and publish it for all to see on a wiki, information radiator, or any other appropriate medium.
    - Keep the meeting time between one and two hours. If it is too long, it becomes a burden, and if it is too short, you will not have enough time to have useful conversations.
    - If the chapter being reviewed is long, break it up into manageable pieces and discuss it over several meetings.
    - Meet regularly at the same time and place to make it easy for people to get into a rhythm of preparing, attending, and participating.
    - Send out a reminder the day before. This will help people remember the meeting and motivate those who put off preparing until the last minute.
- Setting and materials
    - Get buy-in from management.
    - Allow company time for preparation.
    - Buy copies of the book being reviewed for those attending.
    - Bring supplies for the conversation. Have a whiteboard, markers, index cards, and stickies available.
    - Include food. Order lunch for the group.
    - Sit in an informal setting, not a classroom. Face each other and have a discussion rather than facing forward and having a lecture.

- Facilitation
    - Keep it egalitarian by facilitating the meeting rather than running the meeting. Change the facilitator regularly. Encourage those who are not team leads to volunteer for facilitation.
    - Facilitators should encourage everyone to speak, perhaps by starting off each part of the reading circle by going around the circle and asking for comments. We are not all extroverts.

BUT

Reading circles are generally a refreshing break from the grind but, like all practices, they can go awry. Here are some things to watch out for.

- If there is no buy-in from managers and they see it as a waste of time, it becomes difficult for attendees to properly prepare. You may want to start off with fewer meetings to keep from overburdening your team.
- Attendees do not prepare by reading the chapter. Make it easier for them to prepare and encourage their preparation. By getting management buy-in and agreeing to allow preparation on company time, you make it easier for individuals to properly prepare. By sending a reminder the day before, you give any individuals who have forgotten another opportunity to read the material.
- Like all open meetings, it is common for extroverts to dominate the discussion. However, this makes it less useful—and many times less pleasant—for everyone else attending. It is the facilitator's job to politely but firmly discourage hijacking of the conversation.
- If some of the team is much more experienced, they can turn a reading circle into a lecture. The rest of the team may be intimidated and participate less than they would otherwise. Again, it is the facilitator's job to politely but firmly discourage hijacking of the conversation.

VARIATIONS

A reading circle does not just have to be about a book; it can also be about a subject. At this point, articles can be agreed upon in advance from the Internet, academic or industry journals, or relevant chapters from one or more books.

Many teams that try a reading circle are disappointed when the book being read is completed. They frequently go on to another book, and another, and another. The reading circle becomes a regular weekly meeting, and the books vary. Team members find this rewarding as they learn more and slowly make a dent in a typical knowledge worker's significant to-read stack of books.

References

Manns, M. L., and Rising, L., *Fearless Change: Patterns for Introducing New Ideas*, Boston: Addison-Wesley, 2005.

Chapter 38

WORKSHOP

The Workshop pattern is a facilitated meeting of all individuals involved in a certain task. Exercises, conversations, and documents are created by the entire group to meet the goals of the workshop. The Workshop pattern is a focused and productive experience that frequently meets the goals much faster than if they had been accomplished through e-mail, phone calls, documents, and review meetings.

BUSINESS VALUE

As a secondary practice, a workshop accentuates the business values delivered by the practices it supports. Workshops are good ways to create a backlog, review the effectiveness of the software process, or review the current architecture of the system. Many workshops are commonly used in Agile and are known by special names such as iteration kickoff, retrospective, and demo.

SKETCH

Caleb's first contact with the team was to facilitate a workshop for creating and estimating the release backlog. He met with managers and got them to agree to organize a full week of half-day meetings with everyone involved directly with the project scheduled to attend. This meant that Mark from marketing, Patty the program manager, and all team members—including analysts, testers, Cathy from customer support, and developers—were to attend.

Aparna Analyst already had a good understanding of the overall requirements. Mark knew the key features that would give the team a competitive advantage, Patty could envision how this particular project fit into a larger suite, and Cathy was aware of the current customer base's pains.

Caleb facilitated several exercises to help the attendees understand the problems at hand, the opportunities for the future, and the overall context within the organization's business strategy. This was novel information to most of the development team; they found it intriguing but couldn't directly tie it to their development responsibilities. However, this information was invaluable later on when the inevitable compromises needed to be made.

Caleb then led the team through relative effort estimation of the requirements, relative value estimation, and finally a prioritization of the backlog. By the end of the week, a backlog for the release had been prepared with a rough guesstimate of release time and an understanding that the estimates would change and scope would be negotiable.

CONTEXT

You have a goal that requires input from multiple people with varied backgrounds and experiences. It is possible to get all the involved parties together.

FORCES

- The best and most creative type of communication is face to face.
- Documents are useful but can easily be misunderstood without a shared experience.
- The higher the bandwidth of communication, the more effective the group work.
- Exercises and shared experiences improve communication and understanding.
- Working on a shared project is more difficult, time-consuming, and error-prone when the communication bandwidth decreases.

THEREFORE

Take the time and effort to get everyone together in the same room to solve problems that need diverse expertise instead of relying on e-mail, documents, phone calls, and other communication methods.

Prepare the goals of the workshop ahead of time and communicate them to all the attendees.

Invite all who have useful information to provide and get their commitment to attend the entire session and participate.

Make sure you have an effective facilitator to help keep things on track and move issues forward when they are stalled.

ADOPTION

The most difficult issue with workshops is convincing the attendees to attend, participate, and take the time for the work to be done effectively. In today's world, people are almost always multitasking, and it is difficult or even unreasonable to block an extended amount of time for participation. Therefore

- Get management buy-in early for leverage in setting up the meeting.
- Set S.M.A.R.T. (Specific, Measurable, Achievable, Relevant, and Timely) goals for the meeting.
- Get a talented facilitator for the meeting. You are investing the time of numerous people in your organization, and you must use their time wisely.
- Have an open space with plenty of whiteboards, markers, flip-charts, and stickies to allow for a good conversation. If the setting has chairs facing forward, reorganize them into a circle or get them out of the way. Find a room that is rated at double the capacity of the number of attendees; you will need to move around, talk, draw, and so on. Do not underestimate the importance of a comfortable area.
- Take a break about every hour because meetings are draining.

BUT

Workshops are most effective with clear goals, diverse attendees, and a talented facilitator. When any of these three major areas is weak, the effectiveness of the workshop will be at risk.

- Do not run the workshop without those necessary for the group to make binding decisions to meet the goals of the meeting.
- Do not run the workshop if you cannot come up with achievable, S.M.A.R.T. goals.
- Get the most talented facilitator you can.

VARIATIONS

Sometimes the people who are needed to attend the workshop are not available, and they send representatives from their group as proxies. This is okay as long as the substitutes have the ability to make binding decisions and quickly get information from their group as needed.

REFERENCES

Larman, C. *Applying UML and Patterns: An Introduction to Object-Oriented Analysis, Design, and Iterative Development (Third Edition)*, Boston: Addison-Wesley, 2005.[1]

Manns, M. L., and Rising, L., *Fearless Change: Patterns for Introducing New Ideas*, Boston: Addison-Wesley, 2005.

---

1. Larman's book suggests a collaborative workshop approach to requirements and design.

Chapter 39

CLASSROOM TRAINING

The Classroom Training practice involves an experienced practitioner teaching the basics of a subject to the attendees. The trainer guides lectures and leads the students through exercises to help them learn about the subject. Classroom training is a helpful step up, but you must realize that students, at best, leave a class ready to learn in the real world. It will take time and real-world application of the concepts introduced to fully benefit from the new knowledge.

BUSINESS VALUE

Good classroom training provides a head start on learning the ins and outs of Agile practices. Classroom training has an indirect effect on all the practices and therefore can be seen to provide business value through the practices it supports.

SKETCH

One of the first things that Xena's initial team did was to attend an XP immersion class that came highly recommended from colleagues outside of work. In this class, Xena and her colleagues spent an intense week learning and practicing the basics of XP and test-first development. Her team members were away from the office and therefore they had no interruptions. The exercises they did in class gave them first-hand experience with pair programming, test-first development, refactoring, and evolutionary design. Together, they built an application from scratch and saw exactly how things work.

When the team members went back to work the next week, they were ready to go. Over the next few months, they practiced and improved their skills. They also engaged the community to continue learning, get advice, and compare notes with others who were also adopting Agile practices.

CONTEXT

You are on a development team that has decided to adopt some Agile development practices and would like to give your team a common baseline and a head start on successfully implementing these practices.

Or perhaps you are considering seriously adopting Agile practices, and there are several decision makers to appease before moving forward. The decision makers do not have the same level of understanding of the benefits of this way of working, and many are skeptical.

FORCES

Many of the issues mentioned here are true outside of the world of software:

- Learning is the bottleneck of software development.
- It is useful for everyone on the team to share a common definition and experience of the practices in the early days of adoption of any practice.
- Guided instruction is more efficient than reading a book.
- A protected environment for learning provides focus and protects against interruptions.
- A small, focused problem is an easier vehicle for learning than on-the-job implementation.

THEREFORE

Learning is the bottleneck of software engineering. If funds and time can be made available, consider sending your team offsite to attend a class in the practices you are considering adoption of.

ADOPTION

Classroom training is an ancient technique. It has survived for a reason: It works. To make the most of this opportunity, you need to find a class that covers the subjects you need in a timely manner.

- Set your goals. Decide what you want to cover. Make the list of topics first.

- Find a class that covers the syllabus you need with an instructor you can trust.
    - Engage the community to get recommendations from people other than the trainers and their organizations.
    - One place you might want to try is the Agile University at http://agileuniversity.org/.
    - Tutorial days at conferences are good places to attend classes to get a feel for good and bad instructors. If you attend a really good class, consider asking the instructor to teach the class to your team.
- When you have identified a candidate company and instructors, make a call to their training coordinator.
    - Many companies modify the content of the classes, provide onsite training, and allow you to choose the trainer.
    - Talk to someone who is technical and can discuss the content intelligently. Find out how much time is dedicated to the areas of the syllabus.
    - The best classes are those that are experiential in nature. Look for a class that has at least 60 percent exercises. Depending on the subject, exercises can comprise up to 90 percent of class time.
- One of the most difficult things is finding time and resources to train the entire team. Do your best because this investment will pay back in saved time and frustration later on.
    - Consider sending the team before or closely after project kick-off since this is one of the quiet times in the lifetime of a project.
    - If the full team is not possible, consider sending members in multiple stages but not too far apart to encourage good communication.
    - Finally, you might consider sending a few representatives and have them teach what they've learned to the rest of the group. If they are learning the technical practices, you can have them transfer knowledge via pair programming; if they are learning people practices, you can ask them to facilitate the different exercises.
- Consider bringing in a coach to mentor the team after the class and help them practice and develop the skills learned in class.

BUT

Classroom training is a big investment in time and money. Be careful of these issues.

- A good trainer is more important than an extra subject or two in the syllabus. Do not be impressed by one or more flashy additions in a syllabus. Start with the most highly recommended trainer you can afford and then see if you can negotiate the syllabus to your liking.
- A bad trainer can make the time spent in the classroom a frustrating waste of time and money. Bad trainers can easily demotivate people and make it more difficult to adopt the practices.
- Uneven training can lead to miscommunications, Us Versus Them situations, and a feeling of haves and have-nots.
    - If everyone will not be trained, do your best to mitigate the situation by getting buy-in from those who will not attend the training.
    - Consider allotting time for those who attended the class to transfer what they've learned through practice.
- Onsite training is often more convenient but opens the doors for interruptions. Prefer offsite training instead. If onsite training cannot be avoided, do your best to shield the attendees from interruptions and staying late after class to catch up with work-related issues. They are already doing their job by attending the class.
- Lack of immediate opportunities for on-the-job practice of the topics covered in class is a waste of your organization's time and resources. Skills learned in class that are not practiced do not stick. Be aware that this will slow things down because the team will start to quickly forget what they've learned in class.

VARIATIONS

Classes are taught in so many different ways that I can't list all of them here. A few useful distinctions include the following.

- **Open-enrollment versus dedicated classes.** Open-enrollment classes give students a chance to meet others in similar situations and exchange information. Dedicated classes, on the other hand, enable more focus on the problem of the team.

- **Experiential versus hands-off classes.** Experiential classes tend to cover fewer topics because students spend a large percentage of the time performing exercises. At the same time, the skills learned in an experiential class are typically learned very well.
- **Classes with toy problems versus those that use your team's project.** Most classes have students work on toy problems to allow focus on the subject. These classes also reduce complexity and make it easier for the instructor. Other organizations teach a class and use your team's actual project. These classes are a little slower paced, but the work done is directly transferable to the project work the team is doing.

If you are aware of these categories and the differences, you can make a more informed decision when evaluating your training and trainers and determining what they can deliver.

Part 3.4

THE CLUSTERS

Chapter 40

AGILE ITERATION

Agile Iteration is a set of synergistic practices centered on an iteration. Together, these practices enable a team to get the most out of the cyclic nature of Agile development and accelerate their team's learning. Agile iterations help a team be agile by cycling to recognize and respond to change. Figure 40-1 shows the practices that make up the Agile Iteration cluster.

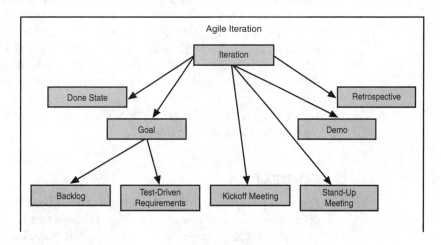

Figure 40–1 The Agile Iteration cluster relies on the Kickoff and Backlog practices and Test-Driven Requirements cluster to set the goal for an iteration. The stand-up meeting adds additional feedback during the iteration, done state, demo, and retrospective to test the achievement of the goal.

BUSINESS VALUE

The set of practices that come together in the Agile Iteration cluster work together to amplify the business values delivered by each. The whole business value delivered is greater than the sum of the parts. An iteration, by itself, helps to provide feedback to the development team from the customer, but it can easily turn into a nonproductive practice and an incremental development instead. The practices in this cluster help keep the iteration effective and are a true indication of the state of the project.

SKETCH

The team started practicing iterations with a backlog, an iteration kickoff, and an ending demo with the customer. This worked well but, after a while, things weren't quite finished at the end of the iteration. The team also had a feeling that not everything was going very well, but it was only a vague, uneasy feeling.

Caleb had expected this and suggested that the team run a retrospective at the end of the iteration. He helped facilitate the first retrospective, and the team members started wrapping their heads around the problems of not being done.

They started practicing daily stand-up meetings and changed the way they were allocating tasks. They started swarming tasks instead of trying to do all of them at once. They went from 80 percent done of 100 percent of the tasks to 100 percent done of 80 percent of the tasks. This was the beginning. The retrospectives continued at the end of every iteration, and a few months later, the team pulled in functional tests and eventually test-driven requirements to tighten up the iterations even more. When the team members were done with a story, it was 100 percent done. The customer and all the stakeholders trusted the teams more and more.

CONTEXT

You are on a software development team that has been having problems with delivery times and quality of work. Time to market and quality may be issues, or maybe it is responsiveness to your client. You may already be practicing iterations, but not everything is being done. Some things are slipping through the cracks. Maybe your bug count is rising each iteration, or maybe you have a sinking feeling that every iteration things are getting a little more off track.

FORCES

Iterative development is nothing new, but sometimes iterations just aren't enough. If issues are not clear and focused at the beginning of the iteration and not resolved at the end of the iteration, they can easily build up. The forces addressed by the Agile Iteration cluster are all of those addressed by the individual practices. The forces listed here are ones that are affected by more than just the sum of the parts.

- The customer-development team relationship is frequently mistrustful. An experienced customer does not trust a development team to be on time with delivery and quality. The customer has been through the 90 percent done 90 percent of the time problem.
- Many things can go wrong within an iteration, including letting bugs through, not being truly done because full integration has not been performed, and communication problems that are not fully resolved. These issues tend to build up over time and become extremely painful.
- Cycles, such as iterations, are most effective with S.M.A.R.T.— Specific, Measurable, Achievable, Relevant, Timely—goals set at the beginning and tested at the end.

THEREFORE

Your team is working together to build software, and the bottleneck of software development is learning. Maximize your learning by doing a little and then checking to make sure that what you've done is correct and constantly making course corrections, as in Figure 40-2.

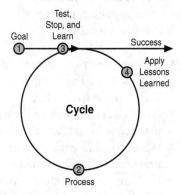

Figure 40-2 An Agile Iteration cluster provides the cycle for a team.

To learn effectively, you must set the goals for the iteration. Use the Kickoff practice to conduct a meeting and create a backlog for the iteration. Set your requirements to be as nonambiguous as possible using the Test-Driven Requirements practice. Then start your iteration cycle. Throughout the iteration, communicate as a team to keep on track to meet your goals and respond to any unforeseen events via the daily Stand-Up Meeting practice.

As you complete each requirement in the backlog, make sure you have removed as many errors as you can by testing, integrating, and doing as many steps as possible to take the development effort close to deployment by using the Done State practice. At the end of the iteration, get feedback on your accomplishments to build trust by giving the customer a chance to see the progress made and an opportunity to learn and improve his understanding of the system being built via the Demo practice. The customer may even change his mind about upcoming functionality based on this new information. Finally, just as the customer took the chance to learn and give feedback on the software your team is building, this is an excellent opportunity for your team to reflect on the way you are working together via the Retrospective practice.

Don't just perform iterations, but perform Agile iterations when possible to get the most out of team cycles.

ADOPTION

An Agile iteration consists of the iteration with all of its supporting practices. Each practice is documented in its own pattern so you find detailed advice on how to adopt each practice there. The adoption advice here is predominantly about sequencing.

- Your starting point for an Agile iteration is the core practice—the iteration itself. The Iteration practice depends on the kickoff, backlog, demo, and retrospective.
- As you start off with an iteration, use the Daily Stand-Up Meeting practice to keep track of the team's progress.
- When you and your team are comfortable with the core iteration practices—usually this takes two to three iterations—start to focus on the Done State practice. This seemingly simple practice may cause significant pain and suffering because of previous habits of leaving integration and deployment issues to the end. Follow the advice given in Chapter 14, "Done State," and incrementally work your way up to at least a fully integrated system with all unit and acceptance tests passing.
- The last practice is really a cluster of practices—Test-Driven Requirements. This is a difficult practice, but it's well worth the time and effort your team will invest. To be able to correctly do this practice, you need to get past any Us Versus Them smells and have a good working relationship between all the members of the development team and

customers. The previous steps of iterations with demos and a done state will go a long way toward building the needed trust. Go to the Test-Driven Requirements cluster to get the details of the benefits and adoption strategies. Once you are successfully performing test-driven requirements, your team will be consistently building and delivering working, tested, (almost) deployable software every iteration and quickly responding to your customer's needs.

BUT

The Agile Iteration cluster does not contain technical practices and does not explicitly address communication in your team. Agile iterations are extremely good at quickly uncovering problems in software development but do not offer specific solutions for solving them. Therefore

- Expect to uncover many ugly and previously hidden aspects of your software development. Ask yourself, "Is this something introduced by the new practices, or am I uncovering something that has always been there?" Solve the problem, and don't quit.
- Realize that although your team is working iteratively, this does not mean you can build your system iteratively. Agile Iterations do not enable your team to evolve your design and architecture. If you want that capability, look to technical practices such as Evolutionary Design and Test-Driven Development. Do not make the mistake of building your system iteratively without the proper technical practices, or you will find you have many extremely painful hardening iterations yet to do when you want to deliver your software.

VARIATIONS

If the practices of Agile Iteration are combined with the Agile Coach and Customer Part of Team practices, you are practicing Scrum. Scrum is the oldest and most widely used of the Agile methods. Scrum is technology-agnostic and can be used with traditional technical practices such as up-front design and architecture.

Agile iterations are frequently coupled with the practices of the Communication cluster to spread the information learned from iterations to the team, its customers, and its stakeholders. The practices of the Communication cluster amplify the learning and allow seemingly difficult problems to be solved.

Finally, Agile iterations are used with technical practices such as Test-Driven Development to enable iterative development of the software and evolution of the design as learning increases. The technical practices accentuate the speed of delivery and add technical agility to the team agility provided by Agile iterations.

REFERENCES

Beck, K. and Andres, C., *Extreme Programming Explained: Embrace Change (Second Edition)*, Upper Saddle River: Addison-Wesley Professional, 2004.

Larman, C., *Agile and Iterative Development: A Manager's Guide*, Boston: Addison-Wesley Professional, 2003.

Schwaber, K., and Beedle, M., *Agile Software Development with SCRUM*, Upper Saddle River: Prentice Hall, 2001.

Chapter 41

COMMUNICATION CLUSTER

A major characteristic of Agile software development is recognizing and responding to change via several feedback loops. Feedback has two main parts: 1) a short cycle to bring information back into the development process and 2) effective communication of that information to those who need to know and can act upon it. The Communication cluster (see Figure 41-1) is a collection of practices that enables this communication, without which the recognize portion of recognizing and responding to change is ineffective. The right people who can respond to that change have to know about the need for it to be able to respond to it.

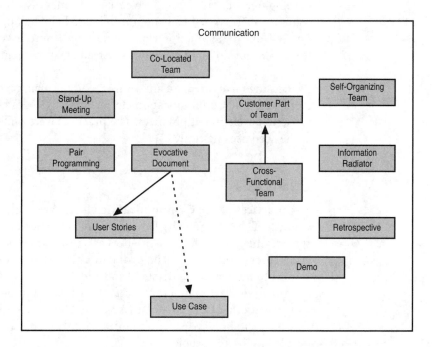

Figure 41–1 Practices in the Communication cluster are about team members spreading and discussing relevant information to those who need to know. Most of the practices are independent and can be implemented alone.

BUSINESS VALUE

Like all clusters of practices, the business value delivered is greater than the sum of the individual practices. Specifically, the values of visibility, flexibility, and time to market are significantly enhanced.

SKETCH

Scott's team had already been a co-located team and had become a self-organizing team with a customer part of team as soon as the members had jumped in the Agile pool. When they started practicing iterations, daily stand-up meetings came into the picture, and as they met daily and started removing impediments, information radiators that indicated progress and current barriers came in as a handy tool.

Over time, the team built an internal culture of excellence and focused on improving the quality and flexibility of their code by practicing test-driven development. Because Test-Driven Development is a difficult practice, the team members started pair programming to help it along. They also focused on the Done State practice, which required them to have a cross-functional team to be able to build by features instead of components.

By focusing on different business values and the main practices to implement them, all of the Communication clusters practices became part of the team's software development practices. The practices were pulled in incrementally as the need became clear.

CONTEXT

The practices of the Communication cluster are useful in many different contexts. The commonality between them is the need for information to be spread, which frequently materializes as a problem to be solved by someone else. Others cannot solve the problem unless they know it exists and can work with the team to understand and address the issues. So if your team frequently finds itself saying it is our fault or it is not in our hands—that is, if you are suffering from a case of Us Versus Them—consider the practices in this cluster to build trust, communicate information, and bring in the right people to solve the problem.

FORCES

The forces for each practice are individually called out in their own chapters. These are generic forces that point to this family of practices as a solution.

- Lack of trust builds from lack of understanding; understanding starts with communication and dialog.
- The most simple of problems seems difficult if you don't understand the problem or its context. Frequently, someone else on the team or in the organization has the understanding needed to solve the problem. The trick is finding that person.
- Blaming someone else for the problem is futile. If the problem is someone else's fault, you do not have the solution, and you can't do anything about it.
- The majority of employees want to do what's best for the well-being of the organization they work for. Once they understand how they can assist and how it is for the organization's benefit, they will gladly help out when a problem arises.
- Distributed teams have a greater need for good communication.

THEREFORE

Whenever an Us Versus Them problem comes around or your team finds a particularly difficult task to complete, look for help from others. Often the problem can be solved by finding the person with the right skill and experience. Communicate your problem to those who need to know. All the practices in this cluster help to get information to those who can effectively do something about it.

- **Co-Located Team.** Enables all team members to listen in on important conversations by osmosis.
- **Self-Organizing Team.** Enables individual team members to leverage the information they know to solve a problem instead of relying on the manager to dictate the solution.
- **Stand-Up Meeting.** Gives a self-organizing team the status of current work-in-progress and an opportunity to eliminate impediments early.
- **Customer Part of Team.** Brings in someone who intimately understands the business value of the software project and presents an opportunity to respond to the inevitable surprises in development by reprioritizing and changing requirements and scope.

- **Cross-Functional Team.** Enables the team to build features to completion and dig up any problems early.
- **Information Radiator.** Serves as a mechanism to inform the team and all the stakeholders of current progress and issues. Helps build trust through visibility and creates a nonthreatening opportunity for those outside the team to understand key issues about the team. These conversations are excellent opportunities for those outside the team to give useful input.
- **Pair Programming.** Provides an opportunity for developers to share and spread their expertise. Difficult problems are solved better and faster through this constant form of code review.
- **Evocative Documents.** Serve as effective communication media because they act as an external memory for the team of previous dialogs and conversations that have much more value in communicating about the project than traditional documents that are passed over the wall to others.
- **Demo.** Provides an opportunity for all stakeholders to have their say and give useful feedback and for the team to build trust with everyone else.
- **Retrospective.** Presents an opportunity to discuss topics outside of the software that affect the team's effectiveness and morale.

ADOPTION

All the practices in the Communication cluster have their own Adoption sections that detail the fine points of adopting each practice. Nonetheless, it is worth noting the following issues when considering any of these practices.

- Communicate goals, not expected action. This allows the others in the group to consider and discuss other ways that the same goals may be met. Adhere to the advice in the Goal practice.
- Describe the problem, not your expected solution. It is a subtle but common mistake to start discussing the solution to a current problem. Discussing the solution is limiting and will hinder your ability to leverage the expertise of others.

BUT

The practices in the Communication cluster are some of the most effective practices in the Agile team's toolkit. Use them liberally and don't underestimate their value.

- These practices generally do not offer solutions to the problems at hand; they rely on individuals and teams to solve the problems. These practices are often underestimated because of this fact and are too touchy-feely for the average technical team.
- Remember the lesson in Chapter 2, "Personal Agility for Potent Agile Adoption:" You only have control over your own actions. Communication practices can help you get the right information to the right person, but that is all.
- Note that a Use Case practice may be considered an evocative document if used as a reminder of previous conversations and not a representation of reality. If your team is using this form of requirement documentation, make them evocative documents.
- Distributed teams have a greater need for good communication. The effectiveness of these practices will suffer with distributed teams, so consider adapting the practices or using more of them if you are on a distributed team.
- Tools almost always hinder communication. Be careful when using software development tools. Use them only when the face-to-face, low-tech alternative is not available.

VARIATIONS

The Communication cluster of practices is rarely adopted as a unit, and that's okay because you should only adopt what you need for your environment. On the other hand, with the exception of self-organizing team, the Communication practices are almost always adopted with another Agile practice as a supporting or enabling practice.

Finally, communication practices are low-tech practices that rely on face-to-face communication and tacit knowledge. Many tools on the market claim to support these practices. They are most effective with distributed teams and are a hindrance with co-located teams.

REFERENCES

Beck, K., and Andres, C., *Extreme Programming Explained: Embrace Change (Second Edition)*, Boston: Addison-Wesley, 2004.

Cockburn, A., *Agile Software Development: The Cooperative Game, Second Edition*, Boston: Addison Wesley, 2006.

Derby, E., and Larson, D., *Agile Retrospectives: Making Good Teams Great*, Raleigh, North Carolina: Pragmatic Bookshelf, 2006.

Schwaber, K., and Beedle, M., *Agile Software Development with SCRUM*, Upper Saddle River, New Jersey: Prentice Hall, 2001.

Tabaka, J., *Collaboration Explained: Facilitation Skills for Software Project Leaders*, Upper Saddle River, New Jersey: Pearson Education, 2006.

Chapter 42

EVOLUTIONARY DESIGN

To engage in a truly iterative development process (not just a waterfall process with time slices), the design of the system must evolve as new requirements are built out. This is achieved by starting off with a simple design and changing that design only when the requirements force that change. The mechanism that enables changing a design is refactoring, which is, in turn, enabled by automated developer tests. Figure 42-1 shows the relationship of the Evolutionary Design pattern to the practices of Simple Design, Refactoring, and Automated Developer Tests.

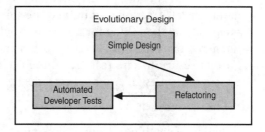

Figure 42–1   Evolutionary Design is built upon the practices of Simple Design, Refactoring, and Automated Developer Tests.

BUSINESS VALUE

Evolutionary Design, like its main practice, Simple Design, reduces time to market and the cost of the software product. The synergy between the practices and focus on changing the design as needed accelerates these values more than the individual practices and increases the flexibility of a product. Furthermore, evolutionary design increases the product's lifetime.

SKETCH

Amy Architect was part of Scott ScrumMaster's initial Agile project. She was a hands-on architect who frequently coded with developers on her team. She knew there was no architect role on Scott's team and looked forward to the challenge. The rest of the team was glad to have her join them because of her experience and talent in building software.

Because they knew they were going to move fast, the team members decided to perform iterations and to practice simple design. Of course, they also knew that to effectively be able to change the simple design later, they would need automated developer tests, so they started with test-last development because test-first development was too alien.

This was the team's first Agile project, so they, out of habit, deferred to Amy on design decisions and came to her often for advice. She was more than happy to help, but she had a habit of going to a generalized design to enable flexibility (as many of us do). The result was that the designs were elegant, but they were too complex for the requirements at hand. After a few iterations, Amy was pairing with Jim Jr. Developer, and she was trying to explain how the particular design used the Template Method design pattern to enable a family of algorithms. Jim didn't really get it, so to show him she took away the abstraction and inlined the solution. Oh! I get it. So we did this template method thing for the future? But I thought we were doing simple design. They took out the complex design and put in the simpler and more direct solution. The tests continued to pass because Amy and Jim had changed the design and preserved the behavior (that is, they refactored the code).

That got Amy thinking about how much time was devoted to dealing with complex designs. She noted how easy it had been to make the change from the complex to the simple design and how the tests had given her confidence that the system still worked. So she started to remove complexity whenever she was pairing, and she and her pair partner would encounter code that was overabstracted. After a few more iterations, the design became leaner and, to Amy's surprise, it had complexity in different places than she would have guessed initially.

The software development team still came to Amy for advice on design, but the advice she gave differed from what she had given previously. She always gave the most obvious solution and only suggested generalized ones when they were mandated by the requirements at hand. Over the months, she watched the synergy between automated developer tests, simple design, and refactoring result in a lean and elegant system that was much more maintainable than anything she would have come up with at the outset. Amy's experience was still very valuable and needed by the team, but it was now more of a guiding hand rather than a dictator's.

CONTEXT

You are on a development project. This is one of those things that are applicable to all types of development projects. The next couple of points about the context are a more obvious fit but are not necessary.

- You are on a development project where time to market is very important.
- You are on a development project that uses technologies that are new to a large part of the team. For example, an ATG-Dynamo group is starting its first JEE[1] Project. It is experienced when it comes to building Web applications but is new to Java and JEE.

FORCES

These are problems with almost all traditional development processes because they primarily stem from up-front design.

- The traditional practice of design up-front is based on the assumption that the cost of change is exponential with time. The disciplined practice of automated developer tests and refactoring reduces the cost of change so that it is possible to change design throughout the course of the development cycle (see Figure 42-2).

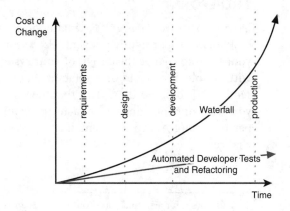

Figure 42–2   Cost of change curve with waterfall and evolutionary design

---

1. JEE is not a typo. Sun renamed J2EE with version 5 of the Java enterprise edition.

- The cost of up-front design involves much more than just a design diagram.
    - The requirements and specifications must be detailed enough to support the design decisions.
    - The design must be created and communicated to the team building the software.
    - Software that is complex enough to implement the design must be created.
    - The cost of design carry for the extra generalizations that may or may not be used regularly accumulates every day for every developer. Each task that developers perform is complicated because they must understand and use the framework built out to satisfy the up-front design.
    - The software built on top of the up-front design implementation is more error-prone because of its complexity.
- Software problems are generally complex. Knowledge is a team's most powerful tool for building software, and it is attained through building the system. You will make a better design decision tomorrow after experience on the project than you can make today because, through the actions taken in building the system, you and your team will learn.

THEREFORE

Do not do up-front design.[2] No matter how much experience you have, don't look forward. Constantly reinvent. Use automated developer tests to enable your team to change the design of your system on an as-needed basis. Start with simple design and only refactor that design when a requirement currently being built needs it. Trust that the tests you have built will warn you if you break anything during a refactoring from one design to another. Do not patch or Band-Aid your system; if a requirement makes a design unsuitable, change it.

---

2. This does not mean that you should not design at all. Designing is a thinking process, and you should be thinking all the time. In fact, when you practice evolutionary design, you will be designing all the time. Just design for the requirements at hand and no more. Have confidence that you will be able to refactor when the time comes.

By using the three practices of Automated Developer Tests, Simple Design, and Refactoring together, you will accomplish the following.

- Deliver faster because you always have the simplest design for the given requirements.
- Capitalize on your learning throughout the project to make better design decisions later. This will produce a design for your system that is much leaner than one created up-front. Because you have a leaner design, your maintenance cost will decrease. The design is easier to understand (simple design) and easier to modify because of the automated developer tests.
- Handle more complex problems successfully because you don't have to deal with all the complexity at once.

ADOPTION

Adoption of the Evolutionary Design cluster follows directly from the adoption of simple design because it requires refactoring which, in turn, requires automated developer tests. So follow these steps.

1. Determine which type of testing you will adopt by reading patterns for automated developer tests, test-last development, and test-first development.
2. Adopt simple design concurrently with automated developer tests.
3. (Highly Recommended) Consider Pair Programming as a helpful practice during adoption of these practices. It helps to have a partner to keep you from slipping when adopting such disciplined practices.
4. Read and prepare for refactoring as indicated in Chapter 29, "Refactoring," and begin to change your designs when your requirements force you to modify your designs.

At this point, you have successfully adopted all three practices. Now you need to focus on the quality of each of them. Are the team members really coming up with simple designs, or are they following in the steps of Amy Architect in the sketch and overdesigning? Is refactoring being considered before and after every task? If not, then although all your practices are present, they are not feeding into each other to cause your design to evolve. Here are some steps you should take until you are satisfied that you are indeed evolving your design.

1. Have a weekly brown-bag design review. Have one developer present some code that he has worked on.

   a. Critique the design from the point of view of simple design.

   b. If the design is overly complex, make suggestions on how to do it differently.

   c. Try to get down to the reasons why the design is not an appropriate level of complexity. Is the reason too much up-front design? Is it failure to refactor before and after a task when needed?

2. Watch out for significant bugs that fall through automated developer tests to QA. If large problems arise from refactoring, such as introducing bugs that are not caught, your automated developer tests are not enough.

But

Evolutionary design is not hacking. It is a disciplined and constant implementation of the three practices in this cluster. Teams frequently loosen up on one of the practices to the detriment of the other two because of their synergistic relationship. These are the most common breakdowns of individual practices.

- Poor automated developer tests directly affect the team's ability to refactor. The design is changed to meet new requirements, all the tests pass, the design is checked in, and everything falls apart. Failing to build a good safety net of tests causes the cost of change to skyrocket because now all the old headaches resurface about finding the bugs, fixing them, and having others build on faulty code.
- Infrequent refactoring means that developers are forcing requirements onto a design that does not smoothly support them. The lack of refactoring means that you will have several Band-Aid solutions, and the cost of change goes back up because the code is now harder to understand and use correctly. Eventually you will hit a brick wall because you started with simple design and have not evolved it. At that point, you will have one or more large refactorings to do, which are significantly more difficult to address.

Evolutionary design can lead to an inconsistent architecture as each group evolves its own solution for similar problems. Teams can address this particular problem in several ways.

- Have an architect of the team be the keeper of the theory of the code. In this role, the architect keeps abreast of the evolving designs by reading code, pairing with different developers, running ad hoc design reviews, and so on. She then cross-pollinates the information and guides the solutions toward a cohesive set—the theory of the code.
- Build out the architecture with a smaller team where it is easy to have a cohesive design/architecture evolve. Have this initial team build broad so it builds a little of everything and solves the hard problems. At this point, grow the team. This is explained in greater detail in the Elshamy and Elssamadisy paper, "Divide after You Conquer."
- Have an architect play a more central role so that all major design decisions go through one person.

VARIATIONS

As indicated in the "But" section, one of the problems of evolutionary design with large projects is inconsistency of design across the team. A technique called Divide After You Conquer is frequently used to mitigate this problem by starting every large project with a small core team that builds out a thin layer of the entire application. This enables the architecture to evolve to meet real requirements. And because it is a small team, consistency is not a problem.

REFERENCES

Evolutionary design is not explicitly called out in the major process books, but it is frequently discussed with simple design. The references, therefore, are similar to those in Chapter 31, "Simple Design."

Beck, K., *Extreme Programming Explained: Embrace Change*, Boston: Addison-Wesley, 1999.

Beck, K., and Andres, C., *Extreme Programming Explained: Embrace Change, Second Edition*, Boston: Addison-Wesley, 2004.

Elshamy, A. and Elssamadisy, A., "Divide after You Conquer: An Agile Software Development Practice for Large Projects," Paper presented at XP2006.

Chapter 43

TEST-DRIVEN DEVELOPMENT

Test-Driven Development is an effective cluster of practices that brings auto-mated developer tests to the forefront of development and subordinates the design to testability. This form of development produces loosely coupled designs that are relatively easy to evolve as requirements change. The practices forming the Test-Driven Development cluster are shown in Figure 43-1.

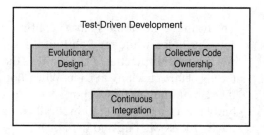

Figure 43–1   The practices that make up Test-Driven Development

BUSINESS VALUE

Test-driven development encompasses almost all the practices in this book. It also, because of the generative nature of clusters, accelerates the business values of the practices. Most notably, test-driven development significantly increases quality to market, time to market, and product lifetime. It also increases flexibility and reduces the cost of development, just like evolutionary design.

SKETCH

Cindy Coder, Dave Developer, Waterfall Will, Uthman Upfront Design, Amy Architect, and Jim Jr. Developer are the developers on Scott Scrum-Master's team. They are practicing test-driven development, and although they did not really set out to be doing the full set of practices, one practice led to another.

Their team started with automated developer tests because it was the most obvious win. Some developers ended up doing test-first development, and others were more comfortable with test-last development. Collective code ownership was quickly pulled in by this type of development to keep all the tests running all the time. Simple design came in later; it was not that obvious a practice to the more experienced developers, who couldn't really fathom not doing a design up-front. But as the tests started to accumulate and refactoring became a reality, simple design became attractive. After several iterations of simple design, the design of the entire system slowly started to evolve and become lean. The set of practices that the team members had adopted had a synergy that made them much more valuable; not only were the team members developing better code, but the entire system was becoming leaner. None of the team had seen this before on non-Agile teams; systems always became worse because of entropy.

The team did not always have a continuous integration build running because it took a while for Bob BuildMaster to get the project building fast enough for this practice. The members did, however, always run all the tests locally before checking in code. When Bob approached them with his plans, they gave him their full support. After the addition of this tool and the capability to run a full integration locally on members' machines, the development process went up another notch in speed and quality.

CONTEXT

You are on a development team that wants to significantly improve its productivity. You want to build the software faster and with fewer bugs, be able to change the design as requirements change, and reduce the overall cost of the software over its lifetime.

You are aware that realizing such a transformational change in your results will require a significant change in the way you build software. You and your team are willing to spend anywhere between three months to a year learning these skills. You are willing to make an investment by requiring less from your development team until these skills take hold.

FORCES

Test-driven development is a cluster of several practices; therefore, all the forces of its building blocks—evolutionary design, continuous integration, collective code ownership—are valid here. That is, test-driven development will ultimately resolve all those forces. But what are the forces that would encourage a team to adopt the full set of practices within test-driven development instead of any of its subsets?

- If testing is not at the heart of the software process, tests may or may not adequately exercise the system.
- Testing is a sampling process. It is infeasible to execute the entire state space of all but the most trivial of programs. Therefore, tests must be written with care to ensure that every test counts.
- Tests, at their best, are a form of executable requirements.
- Some refactorings lead to changes that ripple across the system. For a significant change to be made while maintaining 100 percent passing tests, these subsystem effects must be addressed.
- A successful build should include all possible tests available on the system.
- A team with a solid test base that is always passing has the confidence and courage to make design changes when needed.
- To continuously improve software, Agile practices focus on frequent feedback. There are several successful rhythms. Continuous integration is a hook for running the tests on a build machine.
- In a team environment, evolutionary design can cause challenges as team members make significant changes to the design over time. There is no up-front design spec to be adhered to. A communication void is created by removing the up-front design that is not completely filled with evolutionary design. A team must effectively communicates the knowledge of the current design since it is no longer static.

THEREFORE

To see a significant improvement in time to market, quality to market, and flexibility, and a cost reduction in a team environment, consider adopting continuous integration, collective code ownership, and evolutionary design. These practices are described in Chapters 30, 33, and 42.

Make testing a primary focus of your development effort.

- Make all tests part of continuous integration. Change the definition of a successful build to include passing of all automated developer tests.
- Increase your refactoring ability and speed by introducing collective code ownership. Allow and encourage developers to make the changes necessary to ensure that all tests pass even if they are in different subsystems.

- Focus evolutionary design on tests more than design. Let the tests drive the development. The design will stay simple and will continue to evolve but will be driven solely by tests. By doing this, you will make sure not to write a line of production code without tests. This focus will push your designs to be even more loosely coupled,[1] which, in turn, will increase the lifetime and flexibility of your system.

Upon successful adoption of these practices and cluster with a focus on tests, you will have a team that is delivering software of much higher quality and flexibility at an increased pace for less money. But remember, this hinges on discipline with all the practices and time to learn this new form of development.

ADOPTION

There are two popular forms of test-driven development that differ by the type of automated developer tests done. Test-first development is superior to test-last development but is harder to adopt successfully.

1. Plan for a lengthy period before you get to the point where the different practices are working effectively enough for the generative nature of this pattern to kick in. For small teams on a greenfield project, this may take three months, and for large teams with an existing code base without any tests, it may take up to a year to see full benefit.
2. Have trust in your development team members. Trust them to make the changes necessary and give them the space to learn. Create an environment that rewards the practices you want them to adopt.[2]
3. As a team, start with the adoption of evolutionary design. At the same time, spin off an effort to adopt continuous integration.
4. (Highly Recommended) Introduce Pair Programming as a practice helpful to adopting evolutionary design and its constituent practices. Pair programming will help with the discipline of always writing tests because it is easier to be lazy when you are coding alone. It also provides a natural vehicle for collective code ownership to spread expertise across the team. Use this as an adoption tool. You are free to continue pairing or drop the practice upon successful adoption.

---

1. To test a piece of code adequately, you must isolate it so that all inputs can be controlled and outputs read. This isolation creates an extremely decoupled design.
2. This is a little touchy-feely, but it is really one of the most successful adoption strategies for any practice. How do you create an environment so that your team wants to adopt the practices?

5. When evolutionary design leads to refactorings that break the tests for more than the code being written, pull in collective code ownership.

6. Continuous integration will generally be available before the team is completely comfortable with writing automated developer tests in a disciplined fashion. At that point, introduce the notion, tools, and practice to the full team as described in Chapter 30, "Continuous Integration."

7. When you feel the team has become comfortable with evolutionary design, continuous integration, and collective code ownership, step back and examine your process. Focus the practices around testing even more.

   a. If you are using test-last development, consider moving to test-first development instead. Otherwise, augment the practice with periodic code reviews of tests.

   b. Make sure that the tests drive your design and not the other way around, where your design determines the tests. Writing a test forces the developer to isolate the code under test from all inputs, creating a decoupled design.

   c. Can you read the tests for existing code as a form of documentation? A hallmark of good test-driven development is testing that can be read as documentation of the production code.

BUT

Test-Driven Development is a collection of practices that delivers significant value to the customer. It depends on all team members doing their part to continually and diligently write tests, evolve the design, keep the build running, and work with each other to fix broken tests caused by some refactorings. The problem comes down to this: If any one practice is allowed to slip, the generative nature of this cluster will be lost. Here's what can happen if one of the practices is not done diligently.

- If collective code ownership is dropped, it severely limits successful evolutionary design because the tests broken by a significant design change are not be fixed in a timely manner.
  - This may lead to code check-in with broken tests, which is the greatest of all evils (or at least one of the really big ones) in test-driven development. It leads to the breakdown of 100 percent passing tests and the breakdown of continuous integration that includes the tests.

- It may lead to the code not being checked in and handed over to the person who can fix the tests. This slows down development speed and bottlenecks the person who has the knowledge to fix the broken tests.

- If evolutionary design breaks down or any of its component practices break down, you have just lost at least 50 percent of the effectiveness of test-driven development. See Chapter 42, "Evolutionary Design," for details on keeping it running well.
- If continuous integration breaks down, you lose the ability to quickly know that your code changes are good within the entire system. Evolutionary design continues to function, but at a slower pace.
- Collective code ownership may not be enough to enable fixing of broken tests in an unfamiliar part of the code due to refactoring. Even if the developer is encouraged to change the code, he may not have the expertise to do so. Introduce pair programming to allow the sharing of knowledge.
- What you are doing with test-driven development is building better software. Whether that software actually addresses the customer's needs is not addressed by this cluster. Do not get a false sense of security that you are building software more valuable to the client. Look to other practices such as Functional Testing, Test-Driven Requirements, and Customer Part of Team to help you build software that is valuable to the customer.

VARIATIONS

The main variations of TDD go back to the type of automated developer tests being used (test-first development or test-last development). Test-first development is recommended over test-last development. The details are discussed in Chapters 27 and 28.

REFERENCES

There are several references for Test-Driven Development. Here are a few.

Astels, David., *Test-Driven Development: A Practical Guide*, Upper Saddle River, New Jersey: Prentice Hall, 2003.

Beck, Kent., *Test-Driven Development by Example*, Boston: Addison-Wesley, 2003.

Feathers, Michael., *Working Effectively with Legacy Code*, Upper Saddle River, New Jersey: Prentice Hall, 2005.

Jeffries, Ron., *Extreme Programming Adventures in C#*, Redmond, Washington: Microsoft Press, 2004.

Martin, Robert C., *Agile Software Development: Principles, Patterns, and Practices*, Upper Saddle River, New Jersey: Prentice Hall, 2003.

Chapter 44

TEST-DRIVEN REQUIREMENTS

Test-Driven Requirements call for the customer to provide requirements in an executable format—usually a functional test—at the beginning of the iteration. Test-driven requirements drive the architecture of a system much like test-driven development drives the design. Thus, as shown in Figure 44-1, the Test-Driven Requirements cluster is made up of the practices of Functional Tests, Customer Part of Team, and Continuous Integration.

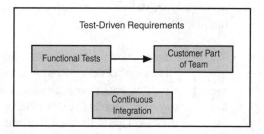

Figure 44–1 The Test-Driven Requirements cluster is made up of the practices of Functional Tests, Customer Part of Team, and Continuous Integration.

BUSINESS VALUE

Test-driven requirements deliver enhanced value to market and increase the visibility of the projects progress significantly by creating a tight loop of communication and feedback between the customer and the development team. Combining functional tests and continuous integration greatly enhances the feedback. Test-driven requirements also address all the other business values as a form of system testing. Therefore, the time to market and total cost of the software system are reduced, the product lifetime and quality to market increases, and the flexibility of the entire application is enhanced. Test-Driven Requirements is a truly valuable cluster of practices that is frequently undervalued.

SKETCH

Aparna Analyst, Tina Tester, and Cindy Coder have been practicing Agile development—specifically Iterations and Test-Driven Development, with Simple Design and Continuous Integration—for six months and have become adept at the practices. They have significantly increased their rate of development and significantly reduced the bug count. The bug count is not zero, however, so there is still room for improvement. At the last retrospective, they recognized this goal.

They decided that what's good for the goose is good for the gander: If TDD helped developers, then taking it a step further and first writing executable and then automated tests for the requirements at the beginning of each iteration would help the entire team. They realized that it would not be completely the developer's responsibility as in TDD; it would involve the entire team. Aparna, Tina, and Cindy volunteered to try this with Caleb the Consultant as their guide and mentor.

The team members are currently nearing the end of the first iteration where they tried this set of practices, and Aparna's head hurts from having to document the requirements so specifically. Tina is pleasantly surprised; these tests look like some of the tests she would have written anyway for acceptance testing after the fact. Cindy realized that putting in the support code to get FIT (Framework for Integrated Tests) was not trivial—maybe it even constituted too much work. She had to reluctantly admit that part of the difficulty in writing the support code was that she had to refactor some business code that had made its way into the UI. Caleb, because he has been around this block before, is content; the work put in to get the FIT tests running improved the architecture of the system and paved the road for future changes as the system evolves. The team members had recognized this problem on their own and found a solution. They were beginning to grok that Agile development is all about continuous improvement.

CONTEXT

You are on a development project with a customer who is willing and able to participate more fully as part of the development team. Or perhaps you have had difficulty managing expectations with your customer in the past and want to build trust by consistently meeting expectations. Your team is also willing to make difficult changes to any existing code. You are willing to pay the price of a steep learning curve. The following issues strengthen the fit of this pattern but are not necessary.

- You are on a distributed development team with the requirements created at one location and the development done at another location.
- You want to significantly reduce the bug count of your code.
- You want to significantly reduce the time to market of your development team.
- You want to build a system that solves the right problem and increases product utility.

FORCES

The forces that are resolved by Test-Driven Requirements are all the forces that are resolved individually by the practices that make up this cluster. These forces are addressed more strongly by the cluster than by the individual practices.

- Functional tests that are not part of a continuous integration build tend to fail silently. When they are discovered, it is not obvious which check-in (of the multiple builds that ran in the background via continuous integration) caused the problem. In this scenario, not all functional tests may be passing because the feedback is not frequent enough. This reduces the quality improvement from functional tests and can lead to them becoming second-class tests.
- Having the customer as part of the team but without functional tests causes errors in translation between requirements and code. The customer means one thing and the developer understands it as another.
- The previous point—errors in translation—is exacerbated with a distributed team where the customer and the developer are not co-located. Cultural differences make this even worse.
- Functional tests tend to fail silently and remain that way without continuous integration.

THEREFORE

Have customers be part of that team that can work closely with developers to write functional tests. Have the customers write their requirements as functional tests instead of your previous method for gathering and specifying requirements. By doing this, you have a concrete, unambiguous method of communication between customers and developers even in distributed, multicultural teams. Also have continuous integration include not only automated developer tests but all functional tests in each build.

Use the tips in Chapter 32, "Functional Tests," to run your tests fast enough for this to be feasible.

A developer's task is to build the part of the system that will satisfy the functional tests and build the needed scaffolding for the tests to execute correctly. Once the new functional tests are passing, the developer will run all the automated developer tests and the functional tests for the entire system locally and, upon success, check the new code into source control. Because functional tests are run by continuous integration, all the requirements built so far by the entire team over all iterations will be tested.

These practices, when used together as described, make up the test-driven requirements cluster. The requirements are written as tests, and the same tight feedback loop found in test-driven development is expanded to include the entire team.

ADOPTION

Adoption, of course, relies on the individual adoption of the practices. You should adopt the Customer Part of Team practice before functional tests. You can adopt the Continuous Integration practice at any time. The Test-Driven Requirements cluster requires more than just the three practices to be adopted. You must actively work to thread them together.

1. For functional tests to really be used as requirements, the customer must learn to write the tests, and this is usually a process that takes time. It also frequently requires help from a technical person; often testers from the QA team or developers can pair with the customer for several iterations until it becomes natural. (See Chapter 32 for more details.)

2. The second part is that a language forms between the customer and the developers via the tests. This is a step-wise process. Plan for this language to evolve as these practices are adopted together. This is strongly related to the concept of domain-driven design described in Evans [2003].

3. Do your best to make all functional tests run with every build in continuous integration. These tests are slower than automated developer tests and need more care to keep them running fast enough without causing continuous integration to break down.

BUT

Like the other technical clusters, test-driven requirements depend on all its practices to be executed well. If any of the three practices have problems, it affects the cluster; therefore, check the "But" section of Chapters 21, 30, and 32.

The most common problem is that of functional tests running slowly. This causes two problems.

- Developers will not run all tests before checking in. Therefore, continuous integration is more likely to break on check-in.
- The continuous integration build will be slow, and tests will fail without a clear indication of who should fix the broken tests.

To get functional tests into the continuous integration, you need to make the tests fast enough. First, the team must make a commitment to functional testing as a primary development practice instead of a secondary one. When it is not an option to drop the tests, teams find creative solutions. The main thing is to speed up the running of the functional tests so that developers can run them effectively on their local machines before checking in. Here are some effective strategies to help you speed up your tests.

- **Functional tests on separate machines.** By grouping tests into related suites, you can run each suite on its own machine. This effectively parallelizes the test suite and can give a speed increase proportional to the number of machines used.
- **Functional tests roll back database transaction.** This is a simple but effective idea: Don't commit your database transactions if you are testing end to end. We have seen this practice emerge independently on different projects, and it usually increases speed.
- **Functional tests refactored to thinner slices.** By testing a small scenario within each test instead of several scenarios (or even all scenarios) for a use case, you get a finer granularity for splitting up tests. Also larger tests tend to have more redundancy; breaking them up enables faster individual tests.
- **Functional tests grouped by business area.** Grouping functional tests by business area enables a developer to test the subset of relevant tests on his machine without running the full suite. This enables a faster red-green-red test loop and keeps a test suite from slowing the pace of development.

Note that having independent database sandboxes for each functional test run is a prerequisite for the preceding advice. If two functional tests run against the same database, one may report an incorrect failure because of interactions with the data inserted by the other test.

VARIATIONS

A variation illustrated in Figure 44-2 is that of test-driven requirements using xUnit tests when the customer is technical. With a technical customer, tests as code may be more appropriate and natural than spreadsheet-like solutions with FIT and FITNesse. This technique can be seen as a smell instead of a valid variation if the customer doesn't write these tests but tells the developer what to do.

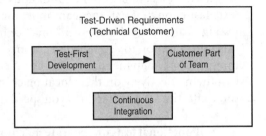

Figure 44-2   Variation on test-driven requirements when the customer is technical—things begin with the practice of Test-First Development

REFERENCES

Avrams, A., and Marinescue, F., "Domain Driven Design Quickly," www.infoq.com/minibooks/domain-driven-design-quickly.

Evans, E., *Domain-Driven Design: Tackling Complexity in the Heart of Software*, Upper Saddle River: Addison-Wesley Professional, 2003.

Ron Jeffries uses Running Tested Features as an important metric for tracking project progress. These are the functional tests used with continuous integration.

Jeffries, R., "Running Tested Features." www.xprogramming.com/xpmag/jatRtsMetric.htm.

Joshua Kerievsky describes a practice almost identical to Test-Driven Requirements, which he has named Story-Driven Development.

Kerievsky, J. "Don't Just Break Software, Make Software." www.industriallogic.com/papers/storytest.pdf.

Mugridge, R., and Cunningham, W., *Fit for Developing Software: Framework for Integrated Tests,* Upper Saddle River, New Jersey: Pearson Education, 2005.

Part 4

CASE STUDIES

The following two chapters describe the details of two different organizations' journies in adopting Agile practices. They both started their adoption efforts in early 2007 and continue to do so as of this writing—April 2008. These chapters give you a different perspective of what we've been discussing. Your Agile adoption effort will certainly be different because you are in a different environment; at the same time, I think you'll find much that is similar in these stories. Enjoy.

Chapter 45

BabyCenter

It's all too easy to get caught up in the energy of trying out new Agile practices like Pair Programming, Iterative Development, and Test-Driven Requirements and lose sight of the original motivating factors behind instituting those practices in the first place.[1]

There may be this vague notion that anything new has got to be better than what we have always (often painfully) done around here; therefore, the mere fact that you are trying something new is often good enough to justify the investment in time and effort of adopting a new practice. Yet, at the same time, so many practices now fall under the Agile umbrella that you may find yourself trying to figure out how you can possibly adopt everything at once. Maybe that one practice you ignore could be the one that makes the biggest difference.

One popular way of dealing with this madness is by picking one particular methodology or set of practices and internalizing them (or at least promoting them) to the point that your software development organization becomes an XP shop, a Scrum shop, or a UP shop. For every team member, plus half the marketing team and a few of the more enlightened senior managers, purchase a copy of your Agile Methodology Adoption book of choice, agree on a few minor details such as the time and place for your new daily stand-ups and which continuous integration tool to use, and you are well on your way to becoming a full-blown Agile development shop.

While this is a common and useful approach, its unfocused and tends to result in behavioral change simply for the sake of change. There is, however, a more targeted approach to Agile practice adoption that does not promote one particular named methodology over another but rather helps you pick and choose those practices that will best help you achieve your organizational goals. The following points summarize this approach.

---

1. This chapter is based on an article by Amr Elssamadisy and John Mufarrige for *InfoQ*, http://www.infoq.com/articles/Elssamadisy-adoption-patterns.

- **Determine business value.** It is all too easy to forget who the real customers are.
- **Weigh activities and technologies in relation to business value.** Change for the sake of change tends to dilute the desired results of becoming Agile.
- **Incrementally apply sets of practices that correspond to value sought.** You don't need to adopt every popular Agile practice to see a positive change; rather, a focused, diagnostic approach will help get you where you want to go faster and easier.

BABYCENTER AGILE ADOPTION EFFORT—Q1 2007

For this chapter, we will consider the ongoing work of the BabyCenter (BC) 2.0 team. This is a development team that is working to rewrite a successful Web site that has millions of hits per day. We will share how we identified which Agile practices would be most beneficial to adopt. We started by prioritizing a comprehensive list of possible business values to highlight those specific values that the team members felt most accurately represented what they were trying to accomplish with the BC 2.0 development effort. We then talked about which Agile practices are most closely aligned to each of their top three desired business values and found that a few key practices either influenced those business values or provided the basis on which many other business values depend. Finally, we discussed which of those Agile practices the team was currently utilizing and, based on that, crafted a plan for adopting the remaining high-impact practices.

Crafting an Agile Practice Adoption Strategy

Several steps are involved in crafting an Agile practice adoption strategy. The steps include determining business values, weighing activities and technologies in light of those values, and incrementally applying sets of Agile practices that correspond to the values.

Determine Business Value   The first step, regardless of where the team is today, is to focus on the business values that the members are trying to bring to their customers. In the case of BC, this actually required a slight step back to first identify who the customers were. As with so many public Web sites whose revenue is based on advertising sales, the end user of the site is rarely the actual source of income for the company. With this understanding, we went through an exercise where we prioritized business values as understood by the whole team. The question of business value prioritization must again be asked of the customers of BC 2.0, which will include members of advertising, publishing, and management. At this point, here is a first cut at the business values in prioritized order:

1. Value to Market/ Product Utility
2. Quality to Market
3. Visibility (to Customer)

There are possibly other business values that are important to the company, such as these:

4. Reduce Cost
5. Flexibility
6. Time to Market
7. Product Lifetime

Of the three business values deemed important, by and large Product Utility is the most important to this group, meaning that their emphasis should be on delivering a useful Web site as determined by the end users. Delivering a high-quality Web site and keeping their customers informed of ongoing changes were also high on the group's list of important business values. What's even more telling about this particular organization is the list of business values that were considered lower priority. At many companies, reducing cost, delivering quickly, and building a long-life product are key goals, which understandably should influence the practices that they adopt. However, this group's focus on building a high-quality, useful site means that members will want to emphasize different aspects of their development effort—specifically those that deal with customer involvement and feedback.

Weigh Activities and Technologies in Relation to Business Values   This next recommendation seems obvious, but in truth it is something we, the software development community, have never done well: **Drive the use of process and technology by business value**. This means that if a practice or technology cannot be related to business values as prioritized by the customer or organization, it should not be used.

Here is a list of software development practices to consider for all business values:

- Test-First Development
- Test-Last Development
- Evolutionary Design (cluster)
- Up-Front Design
- Up-Front Architecture
- Up-Front Requirements
- Refactoring

- Continuous Integration
- Simple Design
- Collective Code Ownership
- Functional Tests
- Test-Driven Requirements (cluster)
- Iteration
- Stand-Up Meeting
- Retrospective
- Pair Programming
- Kickoff Meeting
- User Story
- Use Case
- Information Radiator
- Customer Part of Team
- Evocative Document
- Prioritized Backlog
- Demo

Of these practices, here are the ones the team currently practices:

- Up-Front Architecture
- Up-Front Requirements
- Continuous Integration
- Functional Testing (beginning stages)
- Iteration
- Retrospective
- Kickoff
- User Story
- Collective Code Ownership

To help us determine which practices should be introduced or emphasized, we used the Agile practice dependency maps, shown in Figures 45-1, 45-2, and 45-3 for each of the three business values we are interested in. Each of these diagrams shows the practices that affect that business value and their interdependencies.

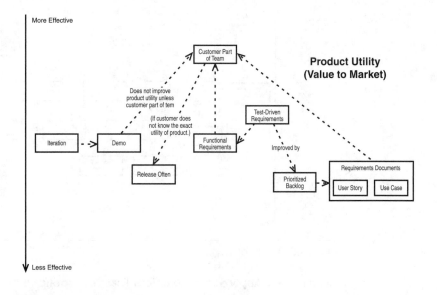

Figure 45–1 Product Utility practices

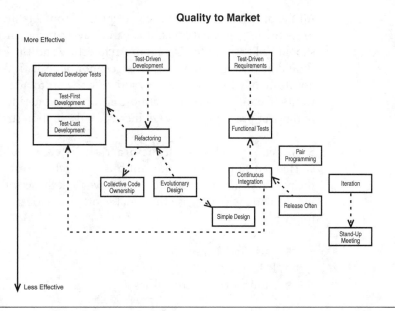

Figure 45–2 Product Quality practices

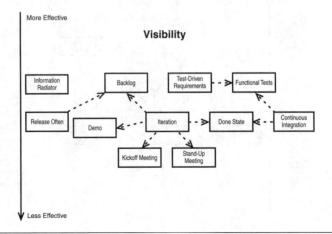

Figure 45–3   Visibility practices

Incrementally Apply Sets of Practices That Correspond to Value Sought

Based on the business value priorities, the practices in the previous diagrams should be incrementally adopted, starting with any key practices that either influence many others or have a number of practices that depend on them.

All the practices already in use (except Up-Front Architecture) directly address the high-priority business values described earlier. Those practices should be kept, and the Up-Front Architecture and Up-Front Requirements should be diminished because they cannot be realistically dropped. At this point, we have a large list of practices we want to adopt and a couple we would like to diminish. It is almost never a good idea to implement a large number of practices at once; an incremental adoption strategy is better.

So which practices, of all the practices listed, should be adopted? We started with the most important business value: Product Utility. Within the practices listed in Product Utility, we took those with the most incoming dependencies because they enable other practices. This leads us to the following:

- Customer Part of Team
- Release Often
- Automated Functional Tests

When we take a look at the next business value, Product Quality, we pull in Automated Developer Tests because many other practices depend on their presence and Pair Programming to support their adoption.

- Pair Programming
- Automated Developer Tests

From the third business value in our list, we pull a simple stand-alone practice to adopt:

- Information Radiators

When the team members have successfully adopted these practices, they will go back and pull in more practices to increase the business value they deliver. A practical adoption strategy includes an iterative approach to incorporating new practices; in other words, adopt in small steps. The BC 2.0 group will begin with these practices and learn as it goes. Members need to experience the practices for themselves and build up their own body of experience. After an adoption cycle or two, they should revisit their list of business values to see if any have changed or been noticeably addressed. In addition to their end-of-iteration retrospectives, they should periodically review the progress and feedback from their adoption efforts and use that as a steering influence for continued improvement.

Conclusions

The software development organization was more heavily focused on delivering usability and quality, which is a bit unusual in this age of almost relentless cost cutting and emphasis on time to market. Yet the development team was a fairly typical case from the standpoint of practice adoption, taking a hybrid approach of formally adopting Scrum while also incorporating individual Extreme Programming practices such as Continuous Integration and User Stories in a piecemeal fashion as opposed to taking on the entire suite of XP practices. While there is certainly nothing wrong with this configuration, we want to promote the idea that certain practice groupings can result in specific business value improvements; therefore, teams looking for the most value should pick those practices that align well with the driving forces behind their software development efforts.

BABYCENTER AGILE ADOPTION EFFORT REVISITED— Q1 2008

It is a year later. How is the BabyCenter team doing? Have they met their goals of improving product utility, quality, and visibility? Are their current top goals still the same, or has something else become important? Have the Agile practices they've adopted helped in achieving any of these goals?

As the team scrambled to meet the deployment deadline in late summer of 2007, some practices stuck with the team, some were modified, and some were dropped.

- A product owner role was created and was extremely useful in achieving product utility. It involved a significant amount of work—almost more than one person could handle.
- Pair Programming continued throughout, which helped maintain the quality of the code and ease the burden of other testing. Today the team has settled on about 50 percent Pair Programming on an as-needed basis.
- Test-driven Development using Test-first Development was maintained because the developers saw the value in significantly fewer bugs compared to other projects of the same size, which was an extremely pleasant surprise to the QA department.
- One subsystem of the project was written by a lone developer who neither paired nor practiced TDD. Although this person was an expert, the quality and maintainability of this particular piece was significantly lower than the rest of the system.
- Continuous Integration has been a vital tool to keep track of the true status of development.
- An effort to write functional tests was dropped because there was little participation by the customers, and many of the tests written were painful to maintain. Many of the tests were tightly coupled to a large database and were brittle and failed frequently when the database changed. Others were found useful and are being run today. Writing new tests has tapered off to nothing.
- An effort to write automated performance tests started but tapered off.
- Iterations were dropped during crunch time because the team felt that the time put in for iteration kickoff meetings and demos was too valuable. Developers lost visibility to the customer's priority and were working on what they thought was important. The team's momentum floundered. The team picked up iterations again after the crunch and practice them regularly today.
- The team was stressed with overtime and pressure, which affected morale.

In retrospect, the team feels that the practices they stuck with helped them, and some of the practices they dropped, such as iterations, should have been maintained even with their overhead. The team delivered BC 2.0 on time and with much less pain than before. The ultimate test of product utility is in the customer base—and BabyCenter continues to be the leader in its space. So the development effort was a success.

As of early February 2008, here's what things look like at BabyCenter. The team is still going strong. There has been some turnover, partially due to the nature of the software developer market on the west coast and partially due to the crunch at the end of development. As of today, the state of the team is as follows:

- The product owner role is still alive and well.
- TDD is still practiced, although the tests are starting to show their age because they have been treated as second-class citizens.
- Continuous Integration is still in place and running strong.
- Pair Programming caught on because it noticeably affected quality and supported other practices such as Test-Driven Development.
- Iterations were reinstated when the pressure was off and are used regularly today. The internal rhythm that iterations provided was a big plus.
- Stand-up meetings are practiced to this day as a form of synchronization.

The quality and product utility functions have greatly improved. The visibility to the customer issue has been mitigated somewhat with the product owner role, but there is still a disconnect between the customers and the development team. As the development team has improved, the bottleneck has moved to the operations department; this department has more than it can handle supporting multiple versions of multiple applications. The team is now considering the following:

- Taking another shot at functional tests and eventually test-driven requirements to continue to improve visibility, but more importantly, to add another layer of automated tests to reduce errors in deployment and consequently reduce pressure on the operations team
- Moving the done state closer to deployment to offload many of the checks the operations department has to perform before deployment

Overall, the BabyCenter team is a productive and healthy development team. It has taken a few of the Agile practices to meet its needs, is aware of its goals, and is continuously improving.

Chapter 46

COMPANY X

Company X produces office products that involve both hardware and software. The software group has traditionally been distributed all over the world. It develops and maintains programs in C/C++ that are millions of lines long, performs up-front design and architecture, and typically has a development cycle of several years, with a significant portion at the end reserved for hardening cycles. The company is having a hard time keeping up with the competition. It is slow to respond to the market and is in pain.

Over the past year, Company X has embarked upon an Agile/Lean adoption initiative from the bottom up. This chapter covers the company's story. It would be easy to dismiss this example as a failure, but it is not. It is an example of a difficult problem that will take time to address. The important thing is that Company X is moving forward and Agile/Lean practices are spreading. Also keep in mind that this is a report of Company X's progress, not recommendation of what you should do. It is, however, a realistic example of a difficult problem and a team's moving forward and adopting Agile practices.

COMPANY X AGILE ADOPTION EFFORT—Q1–Q2 2007

In January 2007, Company X had the first of four training sessions to introduce Lean and Agile concepts. Over two weeks, two different groups—a total of 30+ employees—learned the basics of many Agile and Lean theories and the practices to implement them. The attendees left with a commitment to practice what they had been taught in their day-to-day work. They understood it was going to be difficult, but they also saw the potential benefits from these practices to the quality of work they produced.

Six months after the first class—and only seven weeks after the last—I came to find mixed results. One team had already started and dropped most of the practices it had learned, a second team had started and kept practicing most of what it had learned, a third team had individuals who were determined to practice what they learned and others who were not, and a fourth team had uneven training of its members and was struggling to decide which way to go.

Context for This Report

For two weeks, I spent time with various teams and managers as part of the Lean training contracted with Craig Bigshot Consultant. The goal of these two weeks was to follow up on the class that many employees attended with coaching and mentoring directly related to their day-to-day efforts. Each of the teams (Remote Output, Core System, OS, QA, and Systems) received approximately one day of my time, and they were allowed to choose how best to use my time. I also ran several ad hoc training sessions to introduce many of the new members of the teams to Agile theory and practices.

During those two weeks, I also gained an understanding of how the different teams work together and what many of their pains and successes were. Of course, there is only so much you can soak up within a couple of weeks, so there will be some misconceptions and errors in my report. Before leaving, I debriefed the management team whose members are Sam, Simon, and Steve in person. Nonetheless, I will document my findings and recommendations here. Please feel free to contact me for clarifications or further information.

Current Business Goals

Reaching function-complete for the Himalaya project by end of year is critical. Himalaya is strategically important for Company X in the marketplace, and time to market is the primary concern for the next six months. Furthermore, quality is a Company X mandate; there is a 20-week stabilization cycle after function-complete to ensure this.

At the same time, the company has started an internal project called Atlantis. This is a drive to have the geographically distributed sites function as a single entity. Toward that goal, the common architecture initiative is aimed at building a core set of components that are shared among all the products. This will enable Company X to reduce rework, increase reuse, and eventually bring down the costs of development.

From the Trenches

Each team was different. Here is what we did and what I have observed about each team.

QA Team Both John and Adam had completed the Lean training earlier, but none of their people had had a chance to practice what they had learned. John is keen on getting his testing group involved early with the Systems and Development teams. He is willing to co-locate his people with the teams and have them start writing acceptance tests at the *beginning* of each iteration.

Adam completely supports John's direction and efforts. They both want to get the testing team involved *now*.

I did not meet with any of the testers in person. None had completed the training courses, and they were not closely working with the development teams. My impression was that testers were seen as second-class citizens at Company X, and they were not considered part of the development team. Furthermore, they were all contract employees, which sent an implicit message that testing was not important and was something done as an afterthought. Because the stabilization cycle was significant at Company X, loss of these employees before Himalaya completion would put both time to market and quality at risk.

Systems There are currently three members of the Systems team who have gone through the training: Andy, Al, and Ralph. We spent a half day performing a retrospective, which is a facilitated meeting to gather information about the effectiveness of the current work environment and determine a few realistic action items to move things forward. In summary, the Systems team is in pain, and few of its problems are under its control. They did, however, come up with three action items to focus on.

- Achieve 50 percent completion.
- Achieve 75 percent Integrates System Test completion.
- Come up with specific and achievable goal suggestions for management to help alleviate its pain and then communicate those goals to management.

These action items are indicative of the Systems teams predicament: They almost never take things to completion. Requirements are written and put on the shelf for several iterations. Andy has the full notes from that exercise.

The Systems team is at risk. It has experienced high employee turnover, recently losing a significant part of its team. The morale is low. Individual team members are not trained to the same level; therefore, some of them see Agile as a real opportunity to improve things, and others don't. Although they are one team, they work individually. Their work is highly reliant on the work of others, and that work is frequently late. Finally, they are asked to meet a 90 percent completion goal by the current compensation strategy. This is unrealistic; they are currently functioning at 40 percent and are slowly moving toward 50 percent with an increasing backlog of items that have not been completed.

Remote Output   The Remote Output team is probably the most comfortable and successful of the development teams. Marge is running the iterations well, leading the team in effective daily stand-up meetings and tracking the completion of tasks regularly via a burn-down chart. Gerry is mentoring new team members on functionality. Nick is protective of his work and is not amenable to sharing that knowledge.

I did not spend much time with the Remote Output team because they were doing well. The time I did spend, I spent with Steve, who is new to the team and did not complete the training. We had two sessions together, one of which was cut short because of scheduling issues. I was unsuccessful in teaching Steve about unit testing.

The team is functioning well and has few problems. It is scheduled to grow by three more new developers soon, which will slow down the more experienced members even more. Furthermore, it takes about six months on average for a new team member to be fully productive.

OS   The OS team was the first of all development teams at Company X to adopt Agile practices. Many compromises were made to accommodate its interfacing with other teams. It is telling that the OS team has dropped nearly all the development practices from Lean and is no longer a self-organizing team.

I spent a full day with the OS team and later facilitated a short retrospective. The team had completely dropped iterative development practices, and the team members were sporadically writing unit tests when the opportunity presented itself. Looking back, they feel that the company sees their Agile efforts as a failure. This is unfortunate because most of the problems they faced were exposed rather than caused or introduced by the practices they had adopted. The members of the team were not in agreement about how well their Agile practices had worked. Roughly, the team's impressions were as follows:

- Having a visible backlog was extremely useful.
- Pair programming was a positive experience that significantly improved code and design quality. Unfortunately, it was seen as wasted time and effort by management.
- A ScrumMaster that protected the team from interruptions let the team members focus on their work but gave a bad impression to other teams trying to work with the platform team.

- Iterative development with a constant time box was seen as yielding mixed results. The effort of breaking tasks up into one-month increments was difficult, and many tasks were not completed in time. This, in turn, made the team members feel self-conscious, and they felt that they had failed.

The remainder of the first day was spent pairing with Karl, who had recently joined the team after leaving the Remote Output team. A week later, I had the chance to spend another two hours with the team, where I facilitated a quick retrospective. The team came up with the following action items that members committed to performing.

- Communicate the work lists, mainly for ourselves, but potentially also for other teams that may be interested in knowing what were doing. We were not sure about the best format of delivery to others, but for us it was enough to have it in a document on shared space.
- Define a bit better our role as a team by making a list of the things (pieces of software, technical support, and so on) that we
  - Are in practice doing or contributing to
  - Would like to be doing

That, again, is to help us have a common understanding of what we are about but also to let others know what we do. We also talked about making a list of the things that we are perceived to do or be responsible for, but we decided that wouldnt really help us define our role in the end.

Core System (Digital Output, Scheduler, and Imaging) I spent a full day with each of the three Core System teams. The first half of each day was dedicated to a retrospective where each team examined the current way it practiced software development and the elements of Agile and work lists it was using. They were all positive experiences for both those who had attended the training and those new to these practices. The teams were able to generate insight and get to the core of many of their concerns. Each team came up with its own action plan for the next month to move it forward:

Digital Output
The Digital Output team came up with the following action items.

- Ask for additional hardware so that end-to-end testing can be performed for every feature during an iteration.
- A Scrum meeting (daily stand-up meeting) is to be run by the team, not by an external manager (as had been the practice).

- The team will choose how much work it can do and rescope during each iteration. Furthermore, team members will choose their own work instead of having it assigned to them.

Scheduler

The Scheduler team listed the following action items.

- Have a trial run of pair programming. Each team member will pair for at least one hour a day. Revisit the results in a future retrospective.
- The done state is to include working unit tests.
- Reduce noise. Have large meetings in break-out rooms.
- Organize a sprint (iteration) backlog so that work does not conflict with other teams.

Imaging

The Imaging team's list included these action items.

- Get a digital camera for the team to quickly capture whiteboard notes and conversations as evocative documents.
- Have a 2-round Scrum (daily stand-up meeting) separating tasks and time.
- Have everyone commit to a trial run of test-driven development—at least one hour a day of TDD.
- Deliver code changes to the baseline once a week instead of at the end of the iteration to catch integration problems early.
- Decompose sprint items into 1- to 2-day chunks and ensure all team members understand each task in their team's sprint. (This should be documented within SRC/CQ.) Define what completing a task means and ensure completion before changing to another task.

The Core System teams were energized and wanted to do all they could to implement the practices—especially Test-First Development. They frequently came to me at unscheduled times to discuss testing strategies and design trade-offs. As I left, many members of each team were determined to more rigorously execute Agile/Lean practices.

From my time with the teams and discussions with others, I have observed many things that are working well and others that need to be addressed to help Company X meet its goals.

What Currently Works Here is the list of things that currently work.

- Company X has incredibly talented people. It is doing its best to make things work, and teams are willing to do what's needed to get things done.
- Some teams, like the Core System teams, are seeing incremental improvements as they move toward adopting Agile practices.
- Testing is ready, willing, and able to participate in cross-functional teams *now*.

Current Problems Much of what follows is the perception of the people on the ground, so keep that in mind while reading this list. But their perception is also their reality.

- **Us Versus Them**—This is a critical problem at Company X, and it impedes all progress. This problem has several dimensions, as indicated in the following list. There is no easy answer to this, but it all begins with communication—the higher the bandwidth the better. Many of the suggested practices that follow help alleviate this pain.

  The pain points for this Us Versus Them thinking include the following:
  - Management versus Developers
  - Platform versus Project Initiatives
  - Local versus Overseas
  - Team versus Team
- **Lack of trust**—Past experiences have led to lack of trust on all sides. There is lack of trust that the development team will deliver on schedule because of historical dates that have been missed. Likewise, there is lack of trust in management because it has forced unreasonable re-estimation—which produced estimates that the development teams simply could not meet. Also there is lack of trust between teams because they blame each other for faulty code. The lack of face-to-face interactions with the entire team does not help this trust issue. Managers talk predominantly to team leads.
- **Little visibility**—Neither development nor management has good visibility into each other's progress. From a development standpoint, it does not see what is coming, and this has caused mid-iteration requirement changes. From a management standpoint, most tasks are in progress for the majority of an iteration, and managers only begin to see when something will be missed when it is already close to its deadline.

- **Mixed messages**—Is Company X serious about Agile?
  - The transformation role has zero power.
  - The work list practices are perceived as forced, and they confuse the issues of what practices to adopt.
  - There is highly unbalanced training. Many of the practices are difficult, and some of them are nonintuitive. Those members who have not been through the training are having a difficult time committing to a way of working that they don't understand or agree with.
- **Lack of alignment of reality and expectations**—The word on the street—in both software and hardware—is that there is no way the teams will make the date. Yet management continues to give the message that scope is nonnegotiable, the deadline is set, and quality is nonnegotiable. This is an impossible situation; no development team in the world can meet these constraints. Either the deadline or the scope should be variable. Either way, there should be a prioritized and visible list of the requirements for the entire Himalaya project. Without that, people feel they are on a death-march project. They are demoralized and work less efficiently—and many of them leave.

Suggested Practices for the Remainder of 2007

Given the reality on the ground within the context of the Himalaya initiative and the focus on Time to Market and Quality, here are a set of recommended practices to instill, encourage, and start *today*. Time is running out, and six months will be over before you know it.

Go Faster Practices These practices will help the team go faster immediately. Members need little or no slow down to eventually speed up time.

- **Iteration with a done state.** An iteration in Agile is one where tasks are specified and developed and acceptance tested by the end of the cycle. This is much more than just incremental development. Starting all tasks in parallel in the hopes of finishing all of them is a recipe for failure. At the end, you may have 80 percent of the requirements 80 percent completed and only 20 percent of the requirements completed. This also does not give enough time for acceptance testing if it is not yet automated. A better alternative is to work on only a few requirements at a time, finish them and allow testing to begin, and then move onto the next batch. That way, if estimates are off, you will at least have a larger percentage of the requirements completely done.

- **Early tester involvement.** Co-locate testers with the development team. Have them work with the systems engineers early to write acceptance test scripts that developers can use as they are building the software. This will enhance the quality of the requirements because testers frequently ask for clarifications from systems engineers. It will also reduce the hardening period later because many of the tests have already been created and performed.
- **Early systems engineer involvement.** Co-locate a systems engineer with the development team when possible. This requires systems engineers to incrementally produce requirements, which is not their normal working procedure. Given that most in systems engineering have not been trained, it would be useful to give them a few days of focused tutorials/workshops on Agile.

Go Slower Practices These are not necessarily bad practices—in fact, many of them are beneficial—but they are worth calling out since the primary business value is time to market.

- **New hires.** It typically takes six months for a developer to become fully productive on such a large project. Furthermore, new hires take the time of the best and most experienced of the group to mentor them. This slows down all groups, and the return will not begin to bear fruit until the end of 2007.
- **Distributed teams.** Communication, misunderstandings, and long feedback cycles because of time zone differences are contributing factors that slow things down.
- **Low-bandwidth communication.** Communication between teams and between developers and managers is predominantly document- and e-mail-based. Documents are durable, but they are easily misunderstood. It takes time and effort to transfer knowledge via documents because many rounds of explanations and clarifications must take place.
- **Common architecture.** Because the common architecture couples different projects, such as Himalaya and Sherwood, there is now the possibility of work in one project affecting another. In fact, it has already happened, and this will only increase over time. This risk must be addressed and mitigated before it becomes serious.
- **Test-driven development.** It is debatable whether tests slow down or speed up development. Tests do take time to write and time to learn to do within a code base as large as Company X's. On the other hand, an hour or two invested in writing tests has already saved significant time in testing on hardware. Tests also help mitigate the common

architecture risk and reduce the hardening time. In six months, if practiced with discipline, the tests will enable developers to work faster, and the practice will move to the Go Faster group.

Increase Quality Practices   These practices increase the quality of the product and indirectly decrease time to market.

- **Iterations.** Iterations are described in the "Go Faster Practices" section. They increase quality because defects are found early. The cost of fixing a defect is directly proportional to how early it is found.
- **Test-driven development.** TDD is described in the "Go Slower Practices" section. Testing at this level finds defects earlier than any other practice. Automated testing also keeps defects that have been already fixed from being reintroduced because they will flag faults in the nightly build.
- **Communication.** Higher bandwidth communication reduces misunderstandings, which directly affects defect rate.
- **Visibility.** Increasing visibility enables all involved to make better work scheduling and design decisions. It helps avoid rework and misunderstandings.

Moving Forward   Based on the current goals of Company X, the current problems, and the previous practices, here are my recommendations for moving forward.

- Build trust and begin to address the Us Versus Them problem by communicating goals rather than solutions. Let the Company X employees who are valued and trusted make decisions about their work. They are most qualified to do so.
- Improve and increase communication by increasing frequency and face-to-face interactions with the whole team instead of just the leads.
- Consider facilitated retrospectives that include management and the individual teams. Beware of increasing the Us Versus Them problems.
- Do all the practices listed in the "Go Faster Practices" section. They have little to no slowdown effects and will increase the speed of development today.
- Co-locate a tester and systems engineer with every development group when possible. This will move their level of communication to high-bandwidth, face-to-face interactions and will enable many of the Go Faster practices. It will also partially address the Us Versus Them problem.

- Distinguish between incremental and iterative development. Iterative is much more powerful because it forces defects to be caught early and encourages high-bandwidth communication.
- Work on the testing bottleneck. Testing is currently difficult, error-prone, and time-consuming because of the need to schedule a machine, reload the correct version of the software, and test manually. This issue can be addressed in two complementary ways:
  - Co-locate testers with the team and have them work on creating acceptance tests every iteration.
  - Relieve the experienced team members by focusing those new to the team on creating automatic system tests each iteration. They will learn the system, directly address the bottleneck, and create tests that will help in the current iteration and in the hardening period after function-complete.

- Give a clear message that Agile development is a priority. Show this by action. This means enabling the preceding practices and encouraging them by not micromanaging work and changing estimates or scope within an iteration. Distinguish and constantly encourage teams who strive to apply the practices they've learned.

Proof and Concerns The Company X team is a large, distributed team with a domain that contains software and electromechanical components. For such a complex environment, it is prudent to ask what proof there is that these practices work. Unfortunately, detailed studies do not exist.

The Agile community is still in the early majority phase of adoption. It has already passed the early adopter phase, which means there is extensive anecdotal evidence concerning its practices. One of Company X's main competitors is already adopting these practices. However, other companies from different product sectors have even larger adoptions going on. For example, Nokia has an adoption effort that includes 16,000 employees worldwide.

Also if you look to the software engineers, systems engineers, and testers who went through the training, you'll see that they overwhelmingly see the value in these practices. They just need the support of management so they are not fighting against artificial constraints. This is not just a fad. Before the Lean/Agile initiative, the developers took six-sigma training. The practices learned in that training were left in the classroom. They were never used in practice because the developers found no real value in applying six-sigma to software development. Walk around and ask how many of the practices they learned in that training are actually used. You will find the answer to be none. That is not the case with the Lean/Agile practices.

Long Term

After function-complete and six months of practicing my recommendations, it will be time to re-evaluate business goals and the on-the-ground reality of the development team. Problem areas should be addressed in priority order with respect to the business strategy. The appropriate practices to adopt or modify will be obvious.

Conclusion

As you can see, things look very difficult for Company X. It is a large and distributed organization with a code base that is more than 15 years old written in C/C++. The company's culture is historically formal, and it has always built its code by components and spent several months in hardening iterations trying to remove bugs after integration. This is further complicated by the fact that not all the larger distributed team is trained in Agile development. Finally, one of the problems for adoption in Company X is uneven training. Not all developers are trained in the technical practices, and most of the management is not.

These problems are not unusual for a large organization. The next report for Company X is in Q1 2008. All is not lost!

COMPANY X AGILE ADOPTION EFFORT—REVISITED

In December 2007, Company X had its team burn the midnight oil to meet the mandate to arrive at the mythical code complete stage. The team is now in an extended hardening phase that will last for several months and get the product ready for delivery to the end customer. So what were the results of the partial training done last year? Are there any positive outcomes, or is this an instance of a failed Agile adoption effort? What is currently happening a year later?

Current State

Company X knew that traditional methods were not working. Management wanted empirical data proving that Lean and Agile were going to work before going all-out, but that data is presently not available. Management has decided to incrementally adopt Lean and Agile methods and monitor its effectiveness closely. This is currently where things stand.

- Management started training in November of 2007. The training gave managers insight into the theory behind Lean and Agile. They are slowly getting on board with the development teams.
- A dedicated Agile Adoption Manager role for all the software development teams has been created to coordinate among the different teams. Company X is now giving a clear message that it is serious about Agile.
- Continued training for the rest of the teams is in the works now that the rush for code completion is over.
- 100 percent of teams are doing Scrum, but development is still incremental instead of iterative—that is, components are being built instead of features.
- 30 percent of the teams that have been trained in the technical practices are doing test-driven development and continually refactoring the legacy code. They have come to a working agreement with the other teams to maintain the integrity of the tests. They have been doing this for 6 months on a large and old code base, so only pockets of the system have started to show improvement. The majority of the system code is as it has always been.
- Component teams are still the norm. To move to feature teams, the rest of the developers have to be trained, and management must be willing to pay the price of co-locating the teams.
- A hardening cycle has been started as efforts to remove bugs and get to an integrated, deployable system are under way. This is a multi-month effort that is extremely time-consuming. With the previous experience with the limited rollout of Lean and Agile practices, successes have been recognized, and pain points have become clearer. The primary need now is to decrease time to market and improve quality. Scrum is already being practiced.

These are the practices that are currently being adopted to address today's most urgent business values: time to market (see Figure 46-1) and quality to market (see Figure 46-2):

- Co-Location
- Cross-Functional Teams
- End-to-End Development (that is, feature instead of component development, done state)

Time to Market

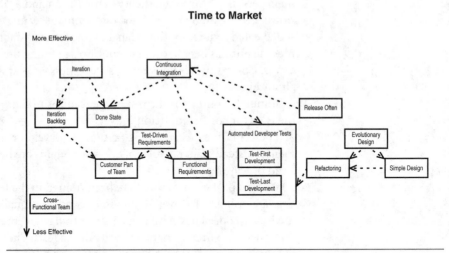

Figure 46–1   Time to Market practices

Quality to Market

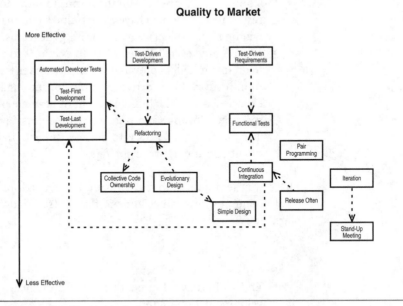

Figure 46–2   Quality to Market practices

Company X is now in the hardening cycle. The technical practices need training, and the company is moving forward with it. Team members are already practicing iterations, backlogs, and stand-up meetings. They are moving forward with done state, cross-functional teams, and co-located teams to move toward improving their needed goals.

Company X is still feeling a lot of pain. At the same time, it is slowly moving forward and digging itself out of a 15+ year-old ditch. Its current goals are still to improve time to market and quality, and it is gaining its own experiences with Lean and Agile practices. Agile and Lean are not magic bullets, but they do help immensely. Large problems require time, effort, and patience.

Why is Company X having such a hard time, and what could be done better? Company X has such large teams that it is almost impossible to get everyone on the same page—especially upper management. Upper management wants to see the empirical proof that Agile methods work, and that is not available today. Even though quality and time to market are the most important business values, not everyone is convinced that Agile practices are the way to go. Over the past 18 months, as evidenced by the recent report, partial adoption results have begun to build trust. The local results from TDD and the quality improvement have allowed a more concerted effort. I expect the next year to have more positive results as Company X's adoption effort begins to show more and more positive results.

Part 5

APPENDICES

Appendix A

PATTERN TO BUSINESS VALUE MAPPINGS

The clusters and practices in each cell in Table A-1 are ordered according to their effectiveness with respect to the given business value. Therefore, if you were to address "reduce time to market," you would consider adopting the Simple Design practice before you considered Functional Tests.

Table A–1 Practices and Clusters That Improve Business Value

Business Value	Clusters of Agile Practices	Agile Practice Patterns
Reduce time to market	Iteration, Test-Driven Development, Evolutionary Design, Test-Driven Requirements	Iteration, Continuous Integration, Release Often, Iteration Backlog, Done State, Test-First Development, Test-Last Development, Test-Driven Requirements, Simple Design, Refactoring, Customer Part of Team, Functional Requirements, Cross-Functional Team
Increase value to market	Test-Driven Requirements,	Customer Part of Team, Functional Tests, Iteration, Demo, Release Often, Prioritized Backlog, Requirements Documents
Increase quality to market	Test-Driven Development, Test-Driven Requirements, Evolutionary Design	Test-First Development, Test-Last Development, Refactoring, Functional Tests, Pair Programming, Continuous Integration, Collective Code Ownership, Iteration, Release Often, Simple Design, Stand-Up Meeting

continues

Table A-1 Practices and Clusters That Improve Business Value *(continued)*

Business Value	Clusters of Agile Practices	Agile Practice Patterns
Increase flexibility	Evolutionary Design, Iteration, Feedback, Test-Driven Development, Test-Driven Requirements	Self-Organizing Team, Backlog, Done State, Simple Design, Refactoring, Retrospective, Iteration, Demo, Automated Developer Tests, Functional Tests, Cross-Functional Team, Stand-Up Meeting, Customer Part of Team, Evocative Document, Collective Code Ownership, Continuous Integration
Increase visibility	Feedback, Test-Driven Requirements	Backlog, Functional Tests, Information Radiator, Release Often, Iteration, Done State, Continuous Integration, Demo, Kickoff Meeting, Stand-Up Meeting
Reduce cost	Evolutionary Design, Test-Driven Development, Test-Driven Requirements, Iteration	Refactoring, Simple Design, Evocative Document, Functional Tests, Automated Developer Tests, Backlog, Iteration, Done State, Retrospective, Self-Organizing Team, Cross-Functional Team, Continuous Integration
Increase product lifetime	Test-Driven Development, Evolutionary Design, Test-Driven Requirements	Refactoring, Automated Developer Tests, Functional Tests, Pair Programming, Collective Code Ownership, Simple Design, Self-Organizing Team, Cross-Functional Team, Evocative Document

Appendix B

PATTERN-TO-SMELL MAPPINGS

The clusters and practices in each cell in Table B-1 are ordered according to their effectiveness with respect to the given smell. Therefore, if you were to address "Hundreds of Bugs in Bug Tracker," you would consider adopting the Test-First Development practice before the Continuous Integration practice.

Table B-1 Practices and Clusters That Alleviate Smells

Smell	Clusters of Agile Practices	Agile Practice Patterns
Us Versus Them	Feedback	Information Radiator, Prioritized Backlog, Release Often, Demo, Iteration, Done State, Customer Part of Team, Cross-Functional Team
Customer Asks for Everything Including the Kitchen Sink	Test-Driven Requirements, Iteration	Customer Part of Team, Functional Tests, Backlog, Planning Poker, Co-Located Team, Demo, Release Often, Information Radiator, Iteration, Kickoff Meeting, Stand-Up Meeting
Direct Input from Customer Is Unrealistic	Test-Driven Requirements	Backlog, Functional Tests, Information Radiator, Iteration, Demo, Release Often, Stand-Up Meeting
Management Is Surprised	Iteration, Test-Driven Requirements	Backlog, Information Radiator, Done State, Demo, Release Often, Iteration, Kickoff Meeting, Stand-Up Meeting, Continuous Integration
Bottlenecked Resources		Pair Programming, Automated Developer Tests, Functional Tests, Self-Organizing Team, Cross-Functional Team, Stand-Up Meeting, Collective Code Ownership, Continuous Integration, Co-Located Team
Churning Projects		Backlog, Customer Part of Team, Cross-Functional Team, Co-Located Team, Information Radiator, Iteration, Release Often
Hundreds of Bugs in Bug Tracker	Test-Driven Development, Test-Driven Requirements	Automated Developer Tests, Functional Tests, Simple Design, Pair Programming, Iteration, Done State, Refactoring, Continuous Integration
Hardening Phase Needed		Automated Developer Tests, Functional Tests, Done State, Continuous Integration, Iteration, Demo, Release Often

Appendix C

GETTING THE MOST FROM AGILE PRACTICE PATTERNS

Part 1 of this book, "Thoughts about Software Development," addresses how to go about setting your goals and choosing the appropriate practices to achieve them. Once you have them, the team should answer the following questions explicitly. If the team does not answer explicitly, it will find itself answering them implicitly as it stumbles along. For the set of questions that follow, assume that the team will adopt Practice A.

- Where does Practice A fit within an adoption strategy? Does it come first? Do we introduce it a few months after getting warmed up with other practices?
- Which development practices are related to Practice A? Are there any prerequisite practices for Practice A to be effective? Is Practice A a prerequisite to other practices? Is Practice A part of a cluster of related development practices that have a value as a whole much greater than the sum of its parts?
- Should we adopt Practice A in stages or in one step? Are there any special mechanics to help adopt Practice A?
- Are there any pitfalls to be wary of when adopting Practice A? Can something go wrong? What does it look like? What does it smell like? What are the symptoms when Practice A goes wrong?
- Are there circumstances where we should *not* adopt Practice A?
- Can we adapt Practice A to other forms without changing its substance? What is its substance anyway?
- Are there any assumptions about values shared by the team that are necessary for Practice A to be effective?
- Finally, consistent with the spirit of Agility, what business value does Practice A bring to a development team?

All the preceding questions matter. They should be asked when a team decides to adopt a development practice. Some of the answers to these questions are far from obvious. However, most of these questions can be succinctly answered using this book.

READING A PATTERN EFFECTIVELY

The patterns I've written about here have a natural level of overlap. This is not by accident. Removing the overlap would affect the readability of these patterns individually.

There is also a natural redundancy within each pattern. The "Forces" section lists the problems that the pattern resolves. The "Therefore" section resolves those problems and refers to those forces in doing so. Frequently, the "But" section discusses breakdowns in the practice that lead back to the original forces. Finally, the "Adoption" section overlaps with the "Therefore" section because the two sections describe different aspects of the same practice.

You can use the patterns in this book in numerous ways. Many of them involve skipping around within a pattern itself, which is supported by redundancy. I hope you will agree with me that the redundancy, although sometimes annoying, is better than the alternative of having to flip pages to tie different parts together.

You can read a pattern in several ways. Here are some ways you can use the patterns depending on the situation:

- I am already practicing the pattern. There are no problems. I just want to see how others have used the same pattern.
  - Look up the pattern by name.
  - Read the context to see if you are using the pattern in the same environment as others have done.
  - Read the "Therefore" and "Variation" sections to match to the way you are using the practice.
- I am practicing a pattern, but it doesn't seem to be very useful. Am I incorrectly using the pattern? Or is the pattern just not useful in my environment?
  - Look up the pattern by name.
  - Read the "Context" section. If your environment doesn't match the context, maybe you should consider modifying the practice or dropping it altogether.
  - Read the "Forces" section. Are you trying to solve the same type of problems? If not, consider that the practice might be working but that you need another practice to solve the problems you have in mind.
  - Check out the "But" section. You will find how others have gone wrong and get some advice on correcting the problems to get the full benefits from the practice.

- I have problems on my team that I want to solve by adopting Agile practices.
  - Go back to Chapter 4, "Smells," on smells and try to match your problems to smells.
  - Read the practice(s) that address that smell.
  - For each practice
    - Read the context and make sure it applies to your environment.
    - Read the rest of the pattern.
    - If you decide to adopt the practice, follow the advice in the "Adoption" section.
    - Periodically check for any of the smells documented in the "But" section.
- I couldn't find the problems I want to solve in Chapter 4. Does that mean that none of the practices can help?
  - No. Read the forces of the individual patterns and see if you can find similar problems to the ones you want to address. You will probably find a match.
- We are adopting a particular practice. Are we there yet? Have we successfully used the pattern to its fullest?
  - Find the practice pattern by name.
  - Check the "Forces" section. Are any of the problems in the forces still problems on your team?
  - Check the "But" section. Are any of the smells in that section present? If so, address them.

If none of the problems occur, you have gone beyond what is documented in this book. You probably have enough experience and intuition to tailor the patterns on your own. Congratulations!

Appendix D

FURTHER READING

Each pattern has its own reference section that list books and articles that are directly related to that pattern. Many references, however, do not directly address these practices but help set Agile in a larger context. These references are not in alphabetical order but in order of priority of reading.

WORKING WITH PEOPLE

These are books that address the hard problems—the people problems. Start with yourself because that is the one person you have the best chance to truly affect. Then learn to work with others. Remember—people build software.

- Avery, C., *Teamwork Is an Individual Skill*, Berrett-Koehler Publishers, San Francisco, 2001.
- Covey, S., *The Seven Habits of Highly Effective People*, Free Press, 2004.
- Manns, M., and Rising, L., *Fearless Change*, Pearson Education, Boston, 2004.
- Tabaka, J., *Collaboration Explained: Facilitation Skills for Software Project Leaders*, Pearson Education, Upper Saddle River, New Jersey, 2006.

THEORY OF CONSTRAINTS

Theory of constraints is an effective way at looking at problems. It helps you focus on the most important things to address because you can't address everything at once.

- Goldratt, E., and Cox, J., *The Goal, Third Edition*, The North River Press, Great Barrington, Massachusetts, 2004.
- Goldratt, E., *Critical Chain*, The North River Press, Great Barrington, Massachusetts, 1997.
- Anderson, D., *Agile Management for Software Engineering: Applying the Theory of Constraints for Business Results*, Pearson Education, Upper Saddle River, New Jersey, 2004.

LEAN MANUFACTURING AND LEAN SOFTWARE

Lean theory focuses on value. Once we agree on what value is, everything else—everything—is waste. Eliminate waste where you find it, but don't forget what you learned from the previous "Theory of Constraints" topic.

- Womack, J., and Jones, D., *Lean Thinking: Banish Waste and Create Wealth in Your Corporation*, Free Press, New York, 2003.
- Poppendieck, M., and Poppendieck, T., *Implementing Lean Software Development: From Concept to Cash*, Pearson Education, Upper Saddle River, New Jersey, 2006.

OO ANALYSIS AND DESIGN

No matter what anyone says, analysis and design skills are still very important. These books have helped me and countless others learn about these two essential software development skills.

- West, D., *Object Thinking*, Redmond Washington: Microsoft Press, 2004.
- Beck, K., *Implementation Patterns*, Upper Saddle River, New Jersey: Pearson Education, 2008.
- Freeman, E., and Freeman, E., *Head First Design Patterns*, Sebastopol, California: O'Reilly Media, 2004.
- Ambler, S., *Agile Modeling*, New York: Wiley Computer Publishing, 2002.
- Evans, E., *Domain-Driven Design:* New York: *Tackling Complexity in the Heart of Software*, Upper Saddle River, New Jersey: Pearson Education, 2004.
- Fowler, M., *Analysis Patterns: Reusable Object Models*, Reading, Massachusetts: Addison-Wesley, 1998.

BIBLIOGRAPHY

Ambler, S., *Agile Modeling*, New York: Wiley Computer Publishing, 2002.

Ambler, S., and Jeffries, R., *Agile Modeling: Effective Practices for Extreme Programming and the Unified Process*, Wiley, 2002.

Anderson, D., *Agile Management for Software Engineering: Applying the Theory of Constraints for Business Results*, Upper Saddle River, New Jersey: Pearson Education, 2004.

Astels, D., *Test-Driven Development: A Practical Guide*, Upper Saddle River, New Jersey: Prentice Hall, 2003.

Avery, C., *Teamwork Is an Individual Skill*, San Francisco: Berrett-Koehler Publishers, 2001.

Beck, K., *Implementation Patterns*, Upper Saddle River, New Jersey: Pearson Education, 2008.

Beck, K., *Test-Driven Development by Example*, Boston: Addison-Wesley, 2003.

Beck, K., and Andres, C., *Extreme Programming Explained: Embrace Change (Second Edition)*, Upper Saddle River: Addison-Wesley Professional, 2004.

Belshee, A., "Promiscuous Pairing and Beginners Mind," *Agile*, 2005.

Cockburn, A., *Agile Software Development: The Cooperative Game (Second Edition)*, Boston: Addison-Wesley Professional, 2006.

Cockburn, A., *Writing Effective Use Cases*, Indianapolis: Addison-Wesley Professional, 2000.

Cohn, M., *Agile Estimating and Planning*, Boston: Prentice Hall, 2005.

Cohn, M., *User Stories Applied: For Agile Software Development*, Upper Saddle River: Addison-Wesley, 2004.

Covey, S., *The Seven Habits of Highly Effective People*, NY: Free Press, 2004.

Demarco, T., and Lister, T., *Waltzing with Bears*, NY: Dorset House Publishing Company, Inc., 2003.

Derby, E., and Larson, D., *Agile Retrospectives: Making Good Teams Great*, Raleigh, North Carolina: Pragmatic Bookshelf, 2006.

Duvall, P., Matyas, S., and Glover, A., *Continuous Integration: Improving Software Quality and Reducing Risk*. Boston: Addison-Wesley.

Elshamy, A., and Elssamadisy, A., "Applying Agile to Large Projects: New Agile Software Development Practices for Large Projects," XP 2007: 46–53.

Elshamy, A., and Elssamadisy, A., "Divide After You Conquer: An Agile Software Development Practice for Large Projects," XP 2006.

Elssamadisy, A., "Human Computer Interaction (HCI) and Agile Compatibility," www.infoq.com/news/2007/06/hci_agile, accessed November 2007.

Elssamadisy, A., "Is Pipelined Integration a Good Idea?" www.infoq.com/news/2007/09/CI_Pipeline.

Elssamadisy, A., and Schalliol, G., "Recognizing and Responding to Bad Smells in XP," *Proceedings of the 24th International Conference on Software Engineering*, 2002.

Evans, E., *Domain-Driven Design: Tackling Complexity in the Heart of Software*, Upper Saddle River, New Jersey: Pearson Education, 2004.

Feathers, M., *Working Effectively with Legacy Code*, Upper Saddle River, New Jersey: Prentice Hall, 2005.

Fowler, M., *Analysis Patterns: Reusable Object Models*, Reading, Massachusetts: Addison-Wesley, 1998.

Fowler, M., "Continuous Integration," www.martinfowler.com/articles/ continuousIntegration.html.

Fowler, M., *Refactoring: Improving the Design of Existing Code*, Boston: Addison-Wesley, 1999.

Freeman, E., and Freeman, E., *Head First Design Patterns*, Sebastopol, California: OReilly Media, 2004.

Gandhi, P., Haugen, N., Hill, M., and Watt, R., 2005, "Creating a Living Specification Document with FIT," Agile 2005 Conference.

Goldratt, E., *Critical Chain*, Great Barrington, Massachusetts: The North River Press, 1997.

Goldratt, E., and Cox, J., *The Goal, Third Edition*, Great Barrington, Massachusetts: The North River Press, 2004.

Hartmann, D., "Co-Located Teams vs. the Cubicle Farm," www.infoq.com/ news/collaborative-team-space-study.

Hartmann, D., "Designing Collaborative Spaces for Productivity," www. infoq.com/articles/agile-team-room-wishlist.

Hartmann, D., "Interview: Jim Johnson of the Standish Group," www. infoq.com/articles/Interview-Johnson-Standish-CHAOS, accessed November 2007.

Hoehn, D., "The Renaissance of Paper," *Agile Journal*, www.agilejournal.com/ articles/articles/the-renaissance-of-paper.html, 2007.

Jeffries, R., "Essential XP: Card, Conversation, Confirmation," www. xprogramming.com/xpmag/expCardConversationConfirmation.htm, accessed November 2007.

Jeffries, R., *Extreme Programming Adventures in C#*. Redmond, Washington: Microsoft Press, 2004.

Jeffries, R., "Running Tested Features," www.xprogramming.com/xpmag/jatRtsMetric.htm.

Kerievsky, J., "Don't Just Break Software, Make Software," www.industriallogic.com/papers/storytest.pdf

Kerievsky, J., *Refactoring to Patterns*, Boston: Addison-Wesley, 2004.

Kerth, N., *Project Retrospectives: A Handbook for Team Reviews*, NY: Dorset House Publishing Company, 2001.

Korzybski, A., *Science and Sanity: An Introduction to Non-Aristotelian Systems and General Semantics (Fifth Edition)*, Institute of General Semantics, 1994.

Larman, C., *Agile and Iterative Development: A Manager's Guide*, Addison-Wesley Professional, 2003.

Larman, C., *Applying UML and Patterns: An Introduction to Object-Oriented Analysis, Design, and Iterative Development (Third Edition)*, Addison-Wesley, 2004.

Manns, M. L., and Rising, L., *Fearless Change: Patterns for Introducing New Ideas*, Addison-Wesley, 2004.

Marick, B., 2002, "Bypassing the GUI," *Software Testing and Quality Engineering*, September/October, 41–47.

Martin, R., *The Responsibility Virus*, New York: Basic Books, 2002.

Martin, Robert C., *Agile Software Development: Principles, Patterns, and Practices*, Upper Saddle River, New Jersey: Prentice Hall, 2003.

Massol, V., *Junit in Action*, Greenwich, Connecticut: Manning Publications, 2004.

Mugridge, R., and Cunningham W., *Fit for Developing Software: Framework for Integrated Tests.* Upper Saddle River, New Jersey: Pearson Education, 2005.

Naur, P., "Programming as Theory Building," *Microprocessing and Microprogramming*, 15:55, 253–261, North Holland, 1985. (Also reprinted in Cockburn's *Agile Development*.)

Poppendieck, M., and Poppendieck, T., *Implementing Lean Software Development*, Addison-Wesley Professional, 2006.

Rainsberger, J. B., *Junit Recipes: Practical Methods for Programmer Testing*, Greenwich, Connecticut: Manning Publications, 2004.

Schwaber, K., and Beedle, M., *Agile Software Development with SCRUM*, Upper Saddle River: Prentice Hall, 2001.

Senge, P., *The Fifth Discipline: The Art and Practice of the Learning Organization*, NY: Currency, 2006.

Shore, J., "A Vision for Fit," www.jamesshore.com/Blog/A-Vision-For-Fit.html.

Standish Group, "CHAOS Report," 2006 (can be purchased at www.standishgroup.com/chaos_resources/index.php).

Surowiecki, J., *The Wisdom of Crowds*, NY: Anchor, 2005.

Tabaka, J., *Collaboration Explained: Facilitation Skills for Software Project Leaders*, Upper Saddle River, New Jersey: Pearson Education, 2006.

Venners, B., 2005, "Erich Gamma on Flexibility and Reuse: A Conversation with Erich Gamma, Part II," www.artima.com/lejava/articles/reuse.html.

West, D., *Object Thinking*, Redmond, Washington: Microsoft Press, 2004.

Williams, L., and Kessler, R., *Pair Programming Illuminated*, Boston: Pearson Education, 2002.

Womack, J., and Jones, D., *Lean Thinking: Banish Waste and Create Wealth in Your Corporation*, New York: Free Press, 2003.

INDEX

Note: Page numbers followed by *n* refer to footnotes

A

adoption patterns
  Agile Iteration
    adoption, 260-261
    business value, 257
    common problems, 261
    context, 258
    description, 259-260
    forces, 258-259
    overview, 257
    references, 262
    sketch, 258
    variations, 261-262
  agile practice to business value mappings, 38-43, 323
  agile practice to smell mappings, 43-48, 325
  Automated Developer Tests
    adoption, 167-170
    business value, 164
    common problems, 170-171
    context, 165
    definition, 163
    description, 166-167
    forces, 165-166
    references, 172
    sketch, 164-165
    variations, 171-172

Backlog
  adoption, 84
  business value, 81
  common problems, 85
  context, 82
  description, 83
  forces, 82-83
  iteration backlogs, 82
  overview, 81
  product backlogs, 82
  references, 86
  sketch, 81-82
  variations, 86
character roles, 58-59
Classroom Training
  adoption, 250-251
  business value, 249
  common problems, 252
  context, 250
  description, 250
  forces, 250
  overview, 249
  sketch, 249
  variations, 252-253
Coach
  adoption, 232-233
  business value, 231
  common problems, 233
  context, 232
  definition, 231
  description, 232

forces, 232
references, 234
sketch, 231
variations, 234
Collective Code Ownership pattern
adoption, 221
business value, 219
common problems, 222
context, 220
description, 221
forces, 220
overview, 219
references, 222
sketch, 219
variations, 222
Co-Located Team
adoption, 121-122
business value, 119
common problems, 122
context, 120
description, 121
forces, 120
overview, 119
references, 123
sketch, 119-120
variations, 122
Communication cluster
adoption, 266
business value, 264
common problems, 267
context, 264
description, 265-266
forces, 265
overview, 263
references, 268
sketch, 264
variations, 267
Continuous Integration
adoption, 191-194
business, 189
common problems, 194-195
context, 190
definition, 189

description, 191
forces, 190
references, 196
sketch, 189-190
variations, 195-196
Cross-Functional Team
adoption, 134
business value, 131
common problems, 134-135
context, 132
description, 133
forces, 133
overview, 131
references, 135
sketch, 132
variations, 135
Customer Part of Team
adoption, 139-140
business value, 137
common problems, 140-141
context, 138
description, 139
forces, 138
overview, 137
references, 142
sketch, 137-138
variations, 142
Cycle
adoption, 67
business value, 65
common problems, 67
context, 66
description, 66
forces, 66
overview, 65
references, 68
sketch, 65
variations, 68
definition, 55
Demo
adoption, 105
business value, 103
common problems, 105-106

context, 104
definition, 103
description, 104-105
forces, 104
references, 107
sketch, 103
variations, 106
Done State
adoption, 101
business value, 99
common problems, 101-102
context, 100
definition, 99
description, 100
forces, 100
references, 102
sketch, 99-100
variations, 102
Engage the Community
adoption, 236-238
business values, 235
common problems, 238
context, 236
description, 236
forces, 236
overview, 235
references, 238
sketches, 235
variations, 238
Evocative Document
adoption, 145-146
business value, 143
common problems, 146
context, 144
definition, 143
description, 145
forces, 144-145
references, 147
sketch, 143-144
variations, 146-147
Evolutionary Design
adoption, 273-274
business value, 269

common problems, 274-275
context, 271
description, 272-273
forces, 271-272
overview, 269
references, 275
sketch, 269-270
variations, 275
format, 55-57
Functional Tests
adoption, 210-211
architecture smells, 214-215
benefits of, 208-210
business value, 203
context, 204
definition, 203
description, 206
forces, 204-205
implementation smells, 211-213
Item Inventory, 206-208
references, 217
sketch, 203-204
variations, 215-217
Goal, 61-63
references, 64
variations, 63-64
Information Radiator
adoption, 158-159
business value, 157
common problems, 159
context, 158
definition, 157
description, 158
forces, 158
references, 160
sketch, 157
variations, 160
Iteration
adoption, 74
business value, 71
common problems, 75-76
context, 72
description, 73

forces, 72-73
overview, 71
references, 76
sketch, 72
variations, 76
Kickoff Meeting
    adoption, 79-80
    business value, 77
    context, 78
    description, 78
    forces, 78
    overview, 77
    references, 80
    sketch, 77-78
    variations, 80
overview, 37
Pair Programming
    adoption, 225-226
    business value, 223
    common problems, 226
    context, 224
    definition, 223
    description, 224-225
    forces, 224
    references, 227
    sketch, 223
    variations, 226-227
Planning Poker
    adoption, 89-90
    business value, 87
    common problems, 90-91
    context, 88
    definition, 87
    description, 88-89
    forces, 88
    references, 91
    sketch, 87-88
Reading Circle
    adoption, 241-242
    business value, 239
    common problems, 242
    context, 240

definition, 239
description, 240-241
forces, 240
references, 243
sketch, 239-240
variations, 242-243
reasons for adopting agile practices, 13
Refactoring
    adoption, 185
    business value, 183
    common problems, 186
    context, 184
    definition, 183
    description, 184-185
    forces, 184
    references, 187
    sketch, 183-184
    variations, 186-187
Release Often
    adoption, 117
    business value, 115
    common problems, 118
    context, 116
    description, 117
    forces, 117
    overview, 115
    references, 118
    sketch, 116
    variations, 118
Retrospective
    adoption, 112
    business value, 109
    common problems, 112-113
    context, 110
    definition, 109
    description, 111-112
    forces, 110-111
    references, 113
    sketch, 109-110
    variations, 113
Self-Organizing Team
    adoption, 127-128
    business value, 125

common problems, 128
context, 126
description, 127
forces, 126-127
overview, 125
references, 129
sketch, 125-126
variations, 129
Simple Design
    adoption, 200
    business value, 197
    common problems, 200-201
    context, 198
    definition, 197
    description, 199
    forces, 198
    references, 201
    sketch, 197-198
    variations, 201
Stand-Up Meeting
    adoption, 95-96
    business value, 93
    common problems, 96
    context, 93
    definition, 93
    description, 94-95
    forces, 94
    references, 98
    sketch, 93
    variations, 97
successful adoptions, 14
Test-Driven Development
    adoption, 280-281
    business value, 277
    common problems, 281-282
    context, 278
    description, 279-280
    forces, 278-279
    overview, 277
    references, 282-283
    sketch, 277-278
    variations, 282

Test-Driven Requirements
    adoption, 288
    business value, 285
    common problems, 289-290
    context, 286-287
    description, 287-288
    forces, 287
    overview, 285
    references, 290-291
    sketch, 286
    variations, 290
Test-First Development
    adoption, 180-181
    business value, 177
    common problems, 181
    context, 178
    definition, 177
    description, 179-180
    forces, 178-179
    references, 182
    sketch, 177-178
    variations, 181
Test-Last Development
    adoption, 175
    business value, 173
    common problems, 175-176
    context, 174
    definition, 173
    description, 175
    forces, 174
    references, 176
    sketch, 173-174
tips for use, 57-58
unsuccessful adoptions, 14
Use Case
    adoption, 155
    business value, 153
    common problems, 155-156
    context, 154
    definition, 153
    description, 154
    forces, 154

references, 156
sketch, 153
variations, 156
User Story
adoption, 151
business value, 149
common problems, 151-152
context, 150
definition, 149
description, 150-151
forces, 150
references, 152
sketch, 149-150
variations, 152
Workshop
adoption, 247
business value, 245
common problems, 247
context, 246
description, 246-247
force, 246
overview, 245
references, 248
sketch, 245-246
variations, 247
adoption strategies
building, 51
test-driven adoption strategies, 49-50
agile adoption patterns. *See* adoption
patterns
Agile Alliance, 237
Agile conferences, 237
Agile Estimating and Planning, 89
Agile iterations
adopting, 260-261
business value, 257
common problems, 261
context, 258
description, 259-260
forces, 258-259
overview, 257
references, 262
sample adoption scenario, 258
variations, 261-262

Agile Journal, 238
Agile Project Leadership Network (APLN),
237
agile software development
agile adoptions. *See* adoption patterns
business values. *See* business
daily cycles, 6
demos, 6
development of, 5
iterations, 6
learning
communication, 7-9
impact on time spent on projects, 3-4
importance of, 3
learning bottlenecks, 9-11
recognizing and responding to change,
5-7
management tests, 7
personal agility, 18-19
releases, 7
Responsibility Process model
adopting, 16
illustration, 15
individual responsibility, 18
overview, 15-17
and response to change, 18
responsibility of agile team members, 17
retrospectives, 6
scrum of scrums, 7
smells
business smells, 30-32
definition, 29
overview, 29
process smells, 32-35
success of, 5
TDR (test-driven requirements), 6
test-first development, 6
analysis paralysis, 85
APLN (Agile Project Leadership Network),
237
architecture smells (functional tests),
214-215
automated developer tests
adopting, 167-170

business value, 164
common problems, 170-171
context, 165
definition, 163
description, 166-167
forces, 165-166
references, 172
sample adoption scenario, 164-165
variations, 171-172

B

BabyCenter case study
  overview, 295-296
  Q1 2007, 296-301
    applying software development practices,
      300-301
    determining business value, 296-297
    selecting software development practices,
      297-298
  Q1 2008, 302-303
  results, 302-303
backlogs
  adoption, 84
  business value, 81
  common problems, 85
  context, 82
  description, 83
  forces, 82-83
  iteration backlogs, 82
  overview, 81
  product backlogs, 82
  references, 86
  sample adoption scenario, 81-82
  variations, 86
Basili, Victor, xiv
Better Software, 238
bibliography, 333-337
bottlenecks
  bottlenecked resources, 33-34, 47, 325
  learning, 9-11
bugs, 34, 47, 325
build monkeys, 160
building adoption strategies, 51
burn-down charts, 160

business smells
  customer asks for everything, 32, 45
  definition, 30
  delivering new features to customer takes,
    30
  features are not used by customer, 30-31
  quality delivered to customer is, 30
  software is to expensive to build, 31
  software not useful to customer, 31
  us versus them, 31-32, 44
business values
  agile practice to business value mappings,
    38-43, 323
  determining, 26-27, 296-297
  driving processes/technologies with,
    297-298
  increased flexibility, 24-25
  increased product lifetime, 26
  increased product utility, 24
  increased quality to market, 24
  increased visibility, 25
  mapping to patterns, 323
  as organizational goals, 26
  overview, 23
  reduced costs, 25
  reduced time to market, 23

C

cargo cults, 12
case studies
  BabyCenter
    applying software development practices,
      300-301
    determining business value, 296-297
    overview, 295-296
    Q1 2007, 296-301
    Q1 2008, 302-303
    results, 302-303
    selecting software development practices,
      297-298
  Company X
    business goals, 306
    context, 306
    current problems, 311-312

Digital Output team, 309-310
Imaging team, 310
OS team, 308-309
overview, 305
QA team, 306-307
Remote Output team, 308
results, 316-319
Scheduler team, 310
suggested practices, 312-316
Systems team, 307
what currently works, 311
change, recognizing and responding to, 5-7
character roles, 58-59
chickens, 96
churning projects, 34, 47, 324-325
Classroom Training pattern
adoption, 250-251
business value, 249
common problems, 252
context, 250
description, 250
forces, 250
overview, 249
sketch, 249
variations, 252-253
clusters
Agile Iteration
adoption, 260-261
business value, 257
common problems, 261
context, 258
description, 259-260
forces, 258-259
overview, 257
references, 262
sketch, 258
variations, 261-262
Communication
adopting, 266
business value, 264
common problems, 267
context, 264
description, 265-266
forces, 265

overview, 263
references, 268
sample adoption scenario, 264
variations, 267
Evolutionary Design
adoption, 273-274
business value, 269
common problems, 274-275
context, 271
description, 272-273
forces, 271-272
overview, 269
references, 275
sketch, 269-270
variations, 275
mapping to business value, 323
mapping to smells, 325
Test-Driven Development
adoption, 280-281
business value, 277
common problems, 281-282
context, 278
description, 279-280
forces, 278-279
overview, 277
references, 282-283
sketch, 277-278
variations, 282
Test-Driven Requirements
adoption, 288
business value, 285
common problems, 289-290
context, 286-287
description, 287-288
forces, 287
overview, 285
references, 290-291
sketch, 286
variations, 290
coaches
adoption, 232-233
business value, 231
common problems, 233
context, 232

definition, 231
description, 232
forces, 232
references, 234
sample adoption scenario, 231
variations, 234
Cohn, Mike, 89
collective code ownership
adopting, 221
business value, 219
common problems, 222
context, 220
description, 221
forces, 220
overview, 219
references, 222
sample adoption scenario, 219
variations, 222
co-located teams
adoption, 121-122
business value, 119
common problems, 122
context, 120
definition, 8
description, 121
forces, 120
overview, 119
references, 123
sketch, 119-120
variations, 122
communication, 7-9
Communication cluster pattern
adoption, 266
business value, 264
common problems, 267
context, 264
description, 265-266
forces, 265
overview, 263
references, 268
sketch, 264
variations, 267
community, engaging
adoption, 236-238
business values, 235

common problems, 238
context, 236
description, 236
forces, 236
overview, 235
references, 238
sketches, 235
variations, 238
Company X case study
business goals, 306
context, 306
current problems, 311-312
Digital Output team, 309-310
Imaging team, 310
OS team, 308-309
overview, 305
QA team, 306-307
Remote Output team, 308
results, 316-319
Scheduler team, 310
suggested practices
Go Faster practices, 312-313
Go Slower practices, 313-314
Increase Quality practices, 314
long term recommendations, 316
proofs and concerns, 315
recommendations for moving forward,
314-315
Systems team, 307
what currently works, 311
conferences, 237
constraints, 331
continuous integration
adopting, 191-194
business definition, 189
common problems, 194-195
context, 190
definition, 189
description, 191
forces, 190
references, 196
sample adoption scenario, 189-190
status, 160
variations, 195-196

Core System teams, 309-310
costs
    expense to build software, 31
    reducing, 25, 42, 324
cross-functional teams
    adopting, 134
    business value, 131
    common problems, 134-135
    context, 132
    description, 133
    forces, 133
    overview, 131
    references, 135
    sample adoption scenario, 132
    variations, 135
Customer Part of Team pattern
    adoption, 139-140
    business value, 137
    common problems, 140-141
    context, 138
    description, 139
    forces, 138
    overview, 137
    references, 142
    sketch, 137-138
    variations, 142
customers
    including on teams
        adoption, 139-140
        business value, 137
        common problems, 140-141
        context, 138
        description, 139
        forces, 138
        overview, 137
        references, 142
        sample adoption scenario, 137-138
        variations, 142
    input, 32-33
cycles
    adopting, 67
    business value, 65
    common problems, 67
    context, 66
    daily cycles, 6

definition, 65
description, 66
forces, 66
references, 68
sample adoption scenario, 65
variations, 68

D
daily cycles, 6
delivering new features, 30
demos
    adopting, 105
    business value, 103
    common problems, 105-106
    context, 104
    definition, 103
    description, 104-105
    forces, 104
    overview, 6
    references, 107
    sample adoption scenario, 103
    variations, 106
design
    evolutionary design
        adopting, 273-274
        business value, 269
        common problems, 274-275
        context, 271
        description, 272-273
        forces, 271-272
        overview, 269
        references, 275
        sample adoption scenario, 269-271
        variations, 275
    simple design
        adopting, 200
        business value, 197
        common problems, 200-201
        context, 198
        definition, 197
        description, 199
        forces, 198
        references, 201
        sample adoption scenario, 197-198
        variations, 201

Design Patterns: Elements of Reusable Object-Oriented Software, 187
determining business values, 26-27
Digital Output teams, 309-310
documents
  evocative documents
    adoption, 145-146
    business value, 143
    common problems, 146
    context, 144
    definition, 143
    description, 145
    forces, 144-145
    references, 147
    sample adoption scenario, 143-144
    variations, 146-147
  information radiators
    adopting, 158-159
    build monkeys, 160
    burn-down charts, 160
    business value, 157
    common problems, 159
    context, 158
    continuous integration, 160
    definition, 157
    description, 158
    forces, 158
    happy face/sad face, 160
    impediment charts, 160
    references, 160
    sample adoption scenario, 157
    storyboards, 160
    variations, 160
  use cases
    adopting, 155
    business value, 153
    common problems, 155-156
    context, 154
    definition, 153
    description, 154
    forces, 154
    references, 156
    sample adoption scenario, 153
    variations, 156

user stories
  adopting, 151
  business value, 149
  common problems, 151-152
  context, 150
  definition, 149
  description, 150-151
  forces, 150
  references, 152
  sample adoption scenario, 149-150
  variations, 152
Domain-Driven Design, 211
done states
  adoption, 101
  business value, 99
  common problems, 101-102
  context, 100
  definition, 99
  description, 100
  forces, 100
  references, 102
  sketch, 99-100
  variations, 102

E
engaging community (Engage the Community pattern)
  adoption, 236-238
  business values, 235
  common problems, 238
  context, 236
  description, 236
  forces, 236
  overview, 235
  references, 238
  sketches, 235
  variations, 238
estimation
  estimation paralysis, 85
  Planning Poker pattern
    adoption, 89-90
    business value, 87
    common problems, 90-91
    context, 88

definition, 87
description, 88-89
forces, 88
references, 91
sketch, 87-88
Evan, Eric, 211
evocative documents
adoption, 145-146
business value, 143
common problems, 146
context, 144
definition, 8, 143
description, 145
forces, 144-145
references, 147
sample adoption scenario, 143-144
variations, 146-147
evolutionary design
adopting, 273-274
business value, 269
common problems, 274-275
context, 271
description, 272-273
forces, 271-272
overview, 269
references, 275
sample adoption scenario, 269-270
variations, 275

F

Feathers, Michael, 171
features
delivering, 30
features not used by customer, 30-31
feedback practices
Backlog pattern
adoption, 84-85
business value, 81
common problems, 85
context, 82
description, 83
forces, 82-83
iteration backlogs, 82

overview, 81
product backlogs, 82
references, 86
sketch, 81-82
variations, 86
Co-Located Team pattern
adoption, 121-122
business value, 119
common problems, 122
context, 120
description, 121
forces, 120
overview, 119
references, 123
sketch, 119-120
variations, 122
Cross-Functional Team pattern
adoption, 134
business value, 131
common problems, 134-135
context, 132
description, 133
forces, 133
overview, 131
references, 135
sketch, 132
variations, 135
Customer Part of Team pattern
adoption, 139-140
business value, 137
common problems, 140-141
context, 138
description, 139
forces, 138
overview, 137
references, 142
sketch, 137-138
variations, 142
Demo pattern
adoption, 105
business value, 103
common problems, 105-106
context, 104

definition, 103
description, 104-105
forces, 104
references, 107
sketch, 103
variations, 106
Done State pattern
   adoption, 101
   business value, 99
   common problems, 101-102
   context, 100
   definition, 99
   description, 100
   forces, 100
   references, 102
   sketch, 99-100
   variations, 102
Evocative Document pattern
   adoption, 145-146
   business value, 143
   common problems, 146
   context, 144
   definition, 143
   description, 145
   forces, 144-145
   references, 147
   sketch, 143-144
   variations, 146-147
Information Radiator pattern
   adoption, 158-159
   business value, 157
   common problems, 159
   context, 158
   definition, 157
   description, 158
   forces, 158
   references, 160
   sketch, 157
   variations, 160
Iteration pattern
   adoption, 74
   business value, 71
   common problems, 75-76

context, 72
description, 73
forces, 72-73
overview, 71
references, 76
sketch, 72
variations, 76
Kickoff Meeting pattern
   adoption, 79-80
   business value, 77
   context, 78
   description, 78
   forces, 78
   overview, 77
   references, 80
   sketch, 77-78
   variations, 80
Planning Poker pattern
   adoption, 89-90
   business value, 87
   common problems, 90-91
   context, 88
   definition, 87
   description, 88-89
   forces, 88
   references, 91
   sketch, 87-88
Release Often pattern
   adoption, 117
   business value, 115
   common problems, 118
   context, 116
   description, 117
   forces, 117
   overview, 115
   references, 118
   sketch, 116
   variations, 118
Retrospective pattern
   adoption, 112
   business value, 109
   common problems, 112-113
   context, 110

definition, 109
description, 111-112
forces, 110-111
references, 113
sketch, 109-110
variations, 113
Self-Organizing Team pattern
adoption, 127-128
business value, 125
common problems, 128
context, 126
description, 127
forces, 126-127
overview, 125
references, 129
sketch, 125-126
variations, 129
Stand-Up Meeting pattern
adoption, 95-96
business value, 93
common problems, 96
context, 93
definition, 93
description, 94-95
forces, 94
references, 98
sketch, 93
variations, 97
Use Case pattern
adoption, 155
business value, 153
common problems, 155-156
context, 154
definition, 153
description, 154
forces, 154
references, 156
sketch, 153
variations, 156
User Story pattern
adoption, 151
business value, 149

common problems, 151-152
context, 150
definition, 149
description, 150-151
forces, 150
references, 152
sketch, 149-150
variations, 152
finding smells, 36
FIT, 206
Fit for Developing Software, 210
FITNesse, 206
flexibility
increasing, 24-25
practices, 41
Fowler, Martin, 169
functional tests
adopting, 210-211
benefits of, 208-210
business value, 203
common problems
architecture smells, 214-215
implementation smells, 211-213
references, 217
variations, 215-217
context, 204
definition, 203
description, 206
forces, 204-205
Item Inventory Management Test example,
206-208
sample adoption scenario, 203-204

G

Gamma, Erich, 187
"The Goal, Question, Metric Approach"
(paper), xiv
goals
adopting, 63
business values, 26, 61
common problems, 63
context, 62

description, 62
forces, 62
references, 64
S.M.A.R.T. goals, 62
sample adoption scenario, 61
variations, 63-64
grok, 97

H

happy face/sad face radiators, 160
hardening phase, 34-35, 48, 325
Highsmith, Jim, 5

I

Imaging teams, 310
impediment charts, 160
implementation smells (functional tests),
    211-214
incentives, pain as, 35
increasing
    flexibility, 24-25
    product lifetime, 26
    product utility, 24
    quality to market, 24, 323
    visibility, 25
individual responsibility, 18
InfoQ, 238
information radiators
    adopting, 158-159
    business value, 157
    common problems, 159
    context, 158
    definition, 8, 157
    description, 158
    forces, 158
    references, 160
    sample adoption scenario, 157
    variations, 160
input from customers, 32-33
integration, continuous, 35
    adopting, 191-194
    business definition, 189
    common problems, 194-195
    context, 190

definition, 189
description, 191
forces, 190
references, 196
sample adoption scenario, 189-190
variations, 195-196
Item Inventory Management Test example,
    206-208
iteration backlogs, 82
Iteration pattern
    adoption, 74
    business value, 71
    common problems, 75-76
    context, 72
    description, 73
    forces, 72-73
    overview, 71
    references, 76
    sketch, 72
    variations, 76
iterations
    Agile Iteration pattern
        adopting, 260-261
        business value, 257
        common problems, 261
        context, 258
        description, 259-260
        forces, 258-259
        overview, 257
        references, 262
        sample adoption scenario, 258
        variations, 261-262
    Iteration pattern
        adoption, 74
        business value, 71
        common problems, 75-76
        context, 72
        description, 73
        forces, 72-73
        overview, 71
        references, 76
        sketch, 72
        variations, 76

K

Kerievsky, Joshua, 187
kickoff meetings
    adopting, 79-80
    business value, 77
    context, 78
    description, 78
    forces, 78
    overview, 77
    references, 80
    sample adoption scenario, 77-78
    variations, 80

L

lean manufacturing, 332
learning
    communication, 7-9
    impact on time spent on projects, 3-4
    importance of, 3
    learning bottlenecks, 9-11
    recognizing and responding to change, 5-7
lifetime of products
    increasing, 26
    practices, 43

M

mailing lists, 237
management tests, 7
mappings
    patterns to business values, 323
    patterns to smells, 325
    agile practice to business values, 38-43, 323
    agile practice to smells, 43-49, 325
Martin, Robert, 5
meetings
    kickoff meetings
        adopting, 79-80
        business value, 77
        context, 78
        description, 78
        forces, 78
        overview, 77

references, 80
sample adoption scenario, 77-78
variations, 80
reading circles
    adopting, 241-242
    business value, 239
    common problems, 242
    context, 240
    definition, 239
    description, 240-241
    forces, 240
    references, 243
    sketch, 239-240
    variations, 242-243
retrospectives
    adopting, 112
    business value, 109
    common problems, 112-113
    context, 110
    definition, 109
    description, 111-112
    forces, 110-111
    references, 113
    sketch, 109-110
    variations, 113
stand-up meetings
    adopting, 95-96
    business value, 93
    common problems, 96
    definition, 93
    description, 94-95
    references, 98
    variations, 97
"Mock Roles, Not Objects" (paper), 169
models, Responsibility Process model, 18
    adopting, 16
    illustration, 15
    individual responsibility, 18
    overview, 15-17
    and response to change, 18
    responsibility of agile team members, 17

O

ObjectMother, 169
OO analysis and design, 332
organizational goals, 26
OS teams, 308-309

P

pair programming
  adopting, 225-226
  business value, 223
  common problems, 226
  context, 224
  definition, 8, 223
  description, 224-225
  forces, 224
  references, 227
  sample adoption scenario, 223
  variations, 226-227
patterns. *See* adoption patterns
personal agility, 18-19
pigs, 96
Planning Poker pattern
  adoption, 89-90
  business value, 87
  common problems, 90-91
  context, 88
  definition, 87
  description, 88-89
  forces, 88
  references, 91
  sketch, 87-88
practices. *See specific practices*
process smells
  bottlenecked resources, 33-34, 47
  churning projects, 34, 47
  definition, 32
  direct and regular customer input is
    unrealistic, 32-33, 45
  hardening phase needed at end of release
    cycle, 34-35, 48
  hundreds of bugs in bug tracker, 34, 47

integration is infrequent, 35
  lack of visibility, 33, 46
product backlogs, 82
products
  lifetime
    increasing, 26
    practices, 43
  utility
    increasing, 24
    practices, 39
projects, churning, 34, 47, 324-325

Q

QA teams, 306-307
quality
  to market, 24, 40, 323
  unacceptable, 30

R

reading patterns, 328-329
Reading Circles
  adopting, 241-242
  business value, 239
  common problems, 242
  context, 240
  definition, 239
  description, 240-241
  forces, 240
  references, 243
  sketch, 239-240
  variations, 242-243
recognizing change, 5-7
reducing
  costs, 25, 42
  time to market, 23
refactoring
  adopting, 185
  business value, 183
  common problems, 186
  context, 184
  definition, 183

description, 184-185
forces, 184
references, 187
sample adoption scenario, 183-184
variations, 186-187
Refactoring to Patterns, 187
release cycle, 34-35, 48, 325
releases, 7
releasing often
   adopting, 117
   business value, 115
   common problems, 118
   context, 116
   description, 117
   forces, 117
   overview, 115
   references, 118
   sketch, 116
   variations, 118
Remote Output teams, 308
resources
   bottlenecked resources, 33-34, 47, 325
   on lean manufacturing, 332
   on OO analysis and design, 332
   on theory of constraints, 331
   on working with people, 331
responding to change, 5-7
Responsibility Process model
   adopting, 16
   illustration, 15
   individual responsibility, 18
   overview, 15-17
   and response to change, 18
   responsibility of agile team members, 17
retrospectives
   adopting, 112
   business value, 109
   common problems, 112-113
   context, 110
   definition, 109
   description, 111-112
   forces, 110-111

overview, 6
references, 113
sketch, 109-110
variations, 113

S

S.M.A.R.T. goals, 62
Scheduler teams, 310
scrum of scrums, 7
self-organizing teams
   adopting, 127-128
   business value, 125
   common problems, 128
   context, 126
   definition, 8
   description, 127
   forces, 126-127
   overview, 125
   references, 129
   sketch, 125-126
   variations, 129
setting goals. *See* goals
simple design
   adopting, 200
   business value, 197
   common problems, 200-201
   context, 198
   definition, 197
   description, 199
   forces, 198-199
   references, 201
   sample adoption scenario, 197-198
   variations, 201
smells
   agile practice to smell mappings,
      43-48, 325
   business smells
      customer asks for everything, 32, 45
      definition, 30
      delivering new features to customer, 30
      features are not used by customer, 30-31
      quality delivered to customer is, 30

software is to expensive to build, 31
software not useful to customer, 31
us versus them, 31-32, 44
definition, 29
finding, 36
functional tests
architecture smells, 214-215
implementation smells, 211-213
references, 217
variations, 215-217
as incentives, 35
mapping to patterns, 325
overview, 29
process smells
bottlenecked resources, 33-34, 47
churning projects, 34, 47
definition, 32
direct and regular customer input is
unrealistic, 32-33, 45
hardening phase needed at end of release
cycle, 34-35, 48
hundreds of bugs in bug tracker, 34, 47
integration is infrequent, 35
lack of visibility, 33, 46
software, releasing often
adopting, 117
business value, 115
common problems, 118
context, 116
description, 117
forces, 117
overview, 115
references, 118
sketch, 116
variations, 118
stand-up meetings
adopting, 95-96
business value, 93
common problems, 96
context, 93
definition, 8, 93

description, 94-95
forces, 94
references, 98
sample adoption scenario, 93
variations, 97
states, done. *See* done state
storyboards, 160
Stranger in a Strange Land, 97n
strategies for adoption
building, 51
test-driven adoption strategies, 49-50
supporting practices
Classroom Training pattern
adoption, 250-251
business value, 249
common problems, 252
context, 250
description, 250
forces, 250
overview, 249
sketch, 249
variations, 252-253
Coach pattern
adoption, 232-233
business value, 231
common problems, 233
context, 232
definition, 231
description, 232
forces, 232
references, 234
sketch, 231
variations, 234
Engage the Community pattern
adoption, 236-238
business values, 235
common problems, 238
context, 236
description, 236
forces, 236
overview, 235

references, 238
sketches, 235
variations, 238
Reading Circle pattern
adoption, 241-242
business value, 239
common problems, 242
context, 240
definition, 239
description, 240-241
forces, 240
references, 243
sketch, 239-240
variations, 242-243
Workshop pattern
adoption, 247
business value, 245
common problems, 247
context, 246
description, 246-247
force, 246
overview, 245
references, 248
sketch, 245-246
variations, 247
Systems teams, 307

T

TDD. *See* test-driven development
TDR. *See* test-driven requirements
teams
character roles, 58-59
coaches
adoption, 232-233
business value, 231
common problems, 233
context, 232
definition, 231
description, 232
forces, 232
references, 234

sample adoption scenario, 231
variations, 234
collective code ownership
adopting, 221
business value, 219
common problems, 222
context, 220
description, 221
forces, 220
overview, 219
references, 222
sample adoption scenario, 219
variations, 222
co-located teams
adoption, 121-122
business value, 119
common problems, 122
context, 120
definition, 8
description, 121
forces, 120
overview, 119
references, 123
sketch, 119-120
variations, 122
Company X case study
Digital Output team, 309-310
Imaging team, 310
OS team, 308-309
QA team, 306-307
Remote Output team, 308
Scheduler team, 310
Systems team, 307
concurrent membership on multiple
teams, 33-34
cross-functional teams
adopting, 134
business value, 131
common problems, 134-135
context, 132
description, 133

forces, 133
overview, 131
references, 135
sample adoption scenario, 132
variations, 135
customers, including on teams
adoption, 139-140
business value, 137
common problems, 140-141
context, 138
description, 139
forces, 138
overview, 137
references, 142
sample adoption, 137-138
variations, 142
pair programming
adopting, 225-226
business value, 223
common problems, 226
context, 224
definition, 8, 223
description, 224-225
forces, 224
references, 227
sample adoption scenario, 223
variations, 226-227
personal agility, 18-19
questions to ask, 327
references and further reading, 331
responsibility, 17
self-organizing teams
adopting, 127-128
business value, 125
common problems, 128
context, 126
definition, 8
description, 127
forces, 126-127
overview, 125
references, 129
sketch, 125-126

variations, 129
technical practices
Automated Developer Tests pattern
adoption, 167-170
business, 164
common, 170-171
context, 165
definition, 163
description, 166-167
forces, 165-166
references, 172
sketch, 164-165
variations, 171-172
Collective Code Ownership pattern
adoption, 221
business value, 219
common problems, 222
context, 220
description, 221
forces, 220
overview, 219
references, 222
sketch, 219
variations, 222
Continuous Integration pattern
adoption, 191-194
business, 189
common problems, 194-195
context, 190
definition, 189
description, 191
forces, 190
references, 196
sketch, 189-190
variations, 195-196
Functional Tests pattern
adoption, 210-211
architecture smells, 214-215
benefits of, 208-210
business value, 203
context, 204
definition, 203

description, 206
forces, 204-205
implementation smells, 211-213
Item Inventory, 206-208
references, 217
sketch, 203-204
variations, 215-217
Pair Programming pattern
    adoption, 225-226
    business value, 223
    common problems, 226
    context, 224
    definition, 223
    description, 224-225
    forces, 224
    references, 227
    sketch, 223
    variations, 226-227
Refactoring pattern
    adoption, 185
    business value, 183
    common problems, 186
    context, 184
    definition, 183
    description, 184-185
    forces, 184
    references, 187
    sketch, 183-184
    variations, 186-187
Simple Design pattern
    adoption, 200
    business value, 197
    common problems, 200-201
    context, 198
    definition, 197
    description, 199
    forces, 198
    references, 201
    sketch, 197-198
    variations, 201
Test-First Development pattern
    adoption, 180-181

business value, 177
common problems, 181
context, 178
definition, 177
description, 179-180
forces, 178-179
references, 182
sketch, 177-178
variations, 181
Test-Last Development pattern
    adoption, 175
    business value, 173
    common problems, 175-176
    context, 174
    definition, 173
    description, 175
    forces, 174
    references, 176
    sketch, 173-174
test-driven adoption strategies, 49-50
test-driven development
    adoption, 280-281
    business value, 277
    common problems, 281-282
    context, 278
    description, 279-280
    forces, 278-279
    overview, 277
    references, 282-283
    sample adoption scenario, 277-278
    variations, 282
test-driven requirements, 6
    adoption, 288
    business value, 285
    common problems, 289-290
    context, 286-287
    description, 287-288
    forces, 287
    overview, 285
    references, 290-291
    sample business scenario, 286
    variations, 290

test-first development, 62
  adopting, 180-181
  business value, 177
  common problems, 181
  context, 178
  definition, 177
  description, 179-180
  forces, 178-179
  overview, 6
  references, 182
  sample adoption scenario, 177-178
  variations, 181
testing
  automated developer tests
    adopting, 167-170
    business value, 164
    common problems, 170-171
    context, 165
    definition, 163
    description, 166-167
    forces, 165-166
    references, 172
    sample adoption scenario, 164-165
    variations, 171-172
  functional tests
    adopting, 210-211
    architecture smells, 214-215
    benefits of, 208-210
    business value, 203
    context, 204
    definition, 203
    description, 206
    forces, 204-205
    implementation smells, 211-213
    Item Inventory Management Test,
      206-208
    references, 217
    sample adoption scenario, 203-204
    variations, 215-217
  management tests, 7

test-driven development
  adoption, 280-281
  business value, 277
  common problems, 281-282
  context, 278
  description, 279-280
  forces, 278-279
  overview, 277
  references, 282-283
  sample adoption scenario, 277-278
  variations, 282
test-driven requirements, 6
  adoption, 288
  business value, 285
  common problems, 289-290
  context, 286-287
  description, 287-288
  forces, 287
  overview, 285
  references, 290-291
  sample business scenario, 286
  variations, 290
test-first development
  adopting, 180-181
  business value, 177
  common problems, 181
  context, 178
  definition, 177
  description, 179-180
  forces, 178-179
  overview, 6
  references, 182
  sample adoption scenario, 177-178
  variations, 181
test-last development
  adopting, 175
  business value, 173
  common problems, 175-176
  context, 174
  definition, 173
  description, 175
  forces, 174

references, 176
  sample adoption scenario, 173-174
test-last development
  adopting, 175
  business value, 173
  common problems, 175-176
  context, 174
  definition, 173
  description, 175
  forces, 174
  references, 176
  sample adoption scenario, 173-174
theory of constraints, 331
time to market
  practices, 38
  reducing, 23, 323
training, classroom training
  adopting, 250-251
  business value, 249
  common problems, 252
  context, 250
  description, 250
  forces, 250
  overview, 249
  sample adoption scenario, 249
  variations, 252-253
Tuckman, Bruce, 3n

U

unsuccessful adoptions, 14
us versus them (business smell), 31-32, 44,
    323-325
use cases
  adopting, 155
  business value, 153
  common problems, 155-156
  context, 154
  definition, 153
  description, 154
  forces, 154
  references, 156
  sample adoption scenario, 153

variations, 156
user groups, 237
user stories
  adopting, 151
  business value, 149
  common problems, 151-152
  context, 150
  definition, 149
  description, 150-151
  forces, 150
  references, 152
  sample adoption scenario, 149-150
  variations, 152
utility of products, increasing, 24

V

value to market, increasing, 323
visibility
  increasing, 25
  lack of, 33, 46
  practices, 42

W-X-Y-Z

Working Effectively with Legacy Code, 171
workshops
  adopting, 247
  business value, 245
  common problems, 247
  context, 246
  description, 246-247
  force, 246
  overview, 245
  references, 248
  sample adoption scenario, 245-246
  variations, 247
Writing Effective Use Cases, 155

XP Days, 237

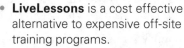

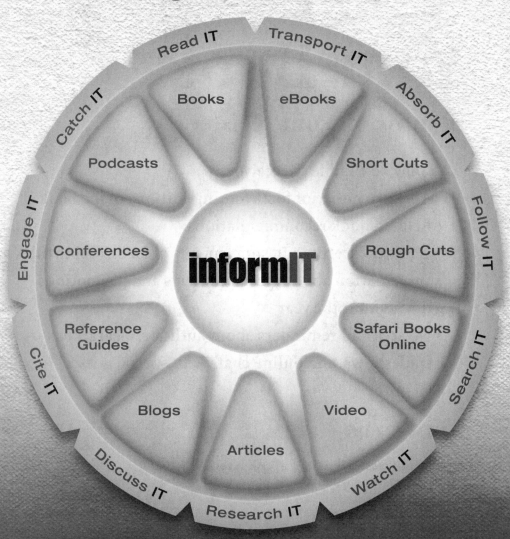

BOOKS ONLINE

ENABLED

THIS BOOK IS SAFARI ENABLED

INCLUDES FREE 45-DAY ACCESS TO THE ONLINE EDITION

The Safari® Enabled icon on the cover of your favorite technology book means the book is available through Safari Bookshelf. When you buy this book, you get free access to the online edition for 45 days.

Safari Bookshelf is an electronic reference library that lets you easily search thousands of technical books, find code samples, download chapters, and access technical information whenever and wherever you need it.

TO GAIN 45-DAY SAFARI ENABLED ACCESS TO THIS BOOK:

- Go to **informit.com/safarienabled**

- Complete the brief registration form

- Enter the coupon code found in the front of this book on the "Copyright" page

If you have difficulty registering on Safari Bookshelf or accessing the online edition, please e-mail customer-service@safaribooksonline.com.